T0205201

Physician engagement is difficult—and if you treat every physician the same, it's nearly impossible to attain. Carson Dye and his colleagues provide perspective and dispel the stereotyped approach that creates barriers to physician engagement. This book is an essential guide for every health system leader. It provides both insight and wisdom in helping to solve the physician engagement enigma.

Akram Boutros, MD, FACHE
President and CEO
The MetroHealth System

I am a big fan of thought leaders who spend time in the trenches, so I am a big fan of Carson Dye and his work. He not only writes about physician leadership but also recruits, teaches, and mentors physician leaders. This book provides practical advice, not theory. It makes the point that improvements in the physician engagement space cannot happen without significant growth from both the engagers and the engagees.

Nathan S. Kaufman
Managing Director
Kaufman Strategic Advisors

The COVID-19 global pandemic has stretched virtually every country's healthcare capabilities to the brink—and the United States is no exception. Carson Dye and his fellow authors have picked a prophetic moment to look at physician engagement from multiple perspectives and make provocative observations. Their insights allow us to see that physicians remain the tent's center post in times of crisis but need many other supports for that tent to stay up in a storm. *Enhancing Physician Engagement* captures the many elements of physician engagement in a comprehensive and understandable manner and is valuable reading for anyone who wishes to understand our complex healthcare system.

Jacque J. Sokolov, MD
Chairman and CEO
SSB Solutions

PRAISE FOR
ENHANCED PHYSICIAN ENGAGEMENT

In healthcare, we have all long known that physician engagement is paramount to the overall success of our organizations. Unfortunately, it has remained elusive for some—until now. Thankfully, the authors of this book have outlined a road map to help organizations on the journey to attain this goal. Their ability to simplify and demystify the process is uncanny.

Michael O. Ugwueke, DHA, FACHE
President/CEO
Methodist Le Bonheur Healthcare

With this book, Carson Dye and his team of contributing authors shine a bright light on the issue of physician engagement, an important area of focus. Through their insights and sometimes opposing points of view, they clearly show that a physician engagement strategy is the path to future success and sustainability for health systems.

Davin G. Turner, DO, FACHE
Chief Medical Officer and President
Mosaic Life Care Medical Center
Mosaic Life Care

Never before has it been more important for physicians to be engaged in confronting the extraordinary challenges facing healthcare. Emerging from COVID-19, healthcare organizations are urgently taking steps to better support, equip, engage, and mobilize physician leaders at all levels to solve complex problems and transform healthcare for the better. *Enhanced Physician Engagement* is a rich and valuable resource for those doing this important and difficult work.

Matt Cornner
Managing Director—Executive Development Solutions
Advisory Board

Enhanced Physician Engagement

CARSON F. DYE, EDITOR

Enhanced Physician Engagement

VOLUME 2

Tools and Tactics for Success

ACHE Management Series

Library of Congress Cataloging-in-Publication Data
Names: Dye, Carson F., editor.
Title: Enhanced physician engagement / Carson F. Dye, editor.
Other titles: Management series (Ann Arbor, Mich.)
Description: Chicago, IL : Health Administration Press, [2022] | Series: HAP/ACHE
    management series | Includes bibliographical references and index. | Contents: v. 1.
    What it is, why you need it, and where to begin—v. 2. Tools and tactics for success. |
    Summary: "This book examines physician engagement as a strategic and tactical priority.
    Recognized physician leaders share personal views on what successful physician engagement is,
    approaches to developing strategy, and practical methods for addressing issues such as burnout,
    the burden of electronic health records, and accountability"—Provided by publisher.
Identifiers: LCCN 2021013743 (print) | LCCN 2021013744 (ebook) | ISBN 9781640552678
    (v. 1 ; paperback : alk. paper) | ISBN 9781640552722 (v. 2 ; paperback : alk. paper) |
    ISBN 9781640552647 (v. 1 ; epub) | ISBN 9781640552654 (v. 1 ; mobi) |
    ISBN 9781640552692 (v. 2 ; epub) | ISBN 9781640552708 (v. 2 ; mobi)
Subjects: MESH: Hospital-Physician Relations | Hospital Administration | Leadership
Classification: LCC RA971 (print) | LCC RA971 (ebook) | NLM WX 160 | DDC
    362.11068—dc23
LC record available at https://lccn.loc.gov/2021013743
LC ebook record available at https://lccn.loc.gov/2021013744

The paper used in this publication meets the minimum requirements of American National Standard for Information Sciences—Permanence of Paper for Printed Library Materials, ANSI Z39.48-1984.♾™

Acquisitions editor: Jennette McClain; Manuscript editor: Patricia Boyd; Project manager: Andrew Baumann; Cover design: James Slate; Layout: Integra

Found an error or a typo? We want to know! Please e-mail it to hapbooks@ache.org, mentioning the book's title and putting "Book Error" in the subject line.

For photocopying and copyright information, please contact Copyright Clearance Center at www.copyright.com or at (978) 750-8400.

Health Administration Press
A division of the Foundation of the American
    College of Healthcare Executives
300 S. Riverside Plaza, Suite 1900
Chicago, IL 60606-6698
(312) 424-2800

To my family, for whose support I am so grateful—C.F.D.

Contents

Foreword

THERE HAS NEVER BEEN a more volatile time in healthcare. Rising costs, increasing numbers of the uninsured and underinsured, and heightened competition across the spectrum were all in play even before the catastrophic effects of COVID-19 demanded radical transformation. Traditional players on the provider side, such as health systems, hospitals, and physician groups, have become increasingly competitive over the past decade with partnerships, mergers, and affiliations on the rise in an attempt to gain market share. At the same time, payers are flexing their muscles as they strive to control as many lives as possible and drive down payments to providers. Additionally, the entrance into healthcare of nontraditional groups and megacorporations with enormous resources has the industry on edge. As Amazon, Google, Walmart, and others strategize their most impactful and profitable methodologies for gaining a foothold, providers and payers will struggle to maintain a competitive edge. Finally, the COVID-19 pandemic has vastly accelerated the obvious need for a more nimble, responsive, consumer-friendly, and digitally sophisticated landscape.

As health systems try to navigate these turbulent waters, an engaged physician workforce is an absolute must. In many ways, it has become more challenging than ever to develop meaningful and productive relationships with physicians. Physicians frequently have competing priorities and are being pulled in many directions—often away from the health systems they are most closely associated with—resulting in disruptions not only to hospitals and clinics but also to how care is provided. Engagement is the key to creating an environment where physicians can thrive and truly drive excellence in quality and service, yet the challenging landscape threatens to erode both physician autonomy and health system alignment.

This book is essential reading for all clinical and administrative leaders who seek to enhance and align physician engagement in their organization. Carson Dye, the editor and author of several chapters, is a nationally renowned expert in this field. He has great depth and breadth of experience in his work with physicians, physician leadership development, and physician engagement. Further, he is frequently tapped by leading healthcare organizations for guidance on this journey. His book *Developing Physician Leaders for Effective Clinical Integration* won the James A. Hamilton Book of the Year Award of the American College of Healthcare Executives.

The chapters assembled in this book create a logical roadmap for engaging physicians and offer myriad tools for accomplishing that. Specifically, readers will learn how to set the stage for physician engagement in their organization and then identify which physicians can help lead the way and encourage their colleagues. Once these physician leaders are identified, the path to leadership development is explored. One chapter explains how these leaders can manage disruptive physicians and how true engagement ameliorates negative behaviors. There is salient information about the devastating impacts of burnout and how an engaged physician corps can serve as an antidote to that highly prevalent problem. Closely tied to physician burnout is the impact of the electronic health record (EHR) and its ever-increasing documentation demands, and the chapter dedicated to this topic provides important tips on leveraging the EHR to maximize physician engagement and limit the downsides. The often complex relationships of chief medical officers, physician leaders, and hospital leaders, and the relationship between physicians and boards, is thoroughly examined. Ultimately, the best way to capture physicians' attention and engage them is through a shared focus on quality. As with any initiative or goal, we need to define metrics to determine our progress.

In summary, the richness and depth of this book provide the necessary tools to achieve meaningful physician engagement. With it, Carson Dye has crafted an essential resource for all healthcare leaders.

Elizabeth Ransom, MD, FACS
Executive Vice President and Chief Physician Executive
Baptist Health
Jacksonville, Florida

Preface

"How can I get our physicians to become more engaged?"

"Well, just pay them, and they'll be engaged."

"We do, and they aren't."

"Well, pay them more."

"We can't."

"Oh, that's bad. Maybe you should just get them more involved."

"We tried that, and it's just the same few who get involved. The others say they're too busy."

As the preceding scenario of a typical conversation between healthcare leaders goes, physician engagement has long challenged healthcare organizations. There may currently be no more important topic than the need for greater physician engagement. The healthcare world has been turned upside down with COVID-19, and the challenges to cost, quality, and consumer value press hard on industry leaders. With physicians controlling or at least driving the bulk of cost and quality, it is imperative that they be heavily involved as major changes occur over the next decade.

Consider exhibit P.1. Healthcare leaders throughout the industry see physicians as a key element for all these measures of performance. As go physicians, so goes the organization. That is not to say that other healthcare workers are not important; in fact they are. But it is physicians who form the core of our healthcare system and process. Lee and Cosgrove (2014) say it well: "Fixing health care will require a radical transformation, moving from a system organized around

Exhibit P.1 Physician Engagement Is the Linchpin in All Aspects of Healthcare

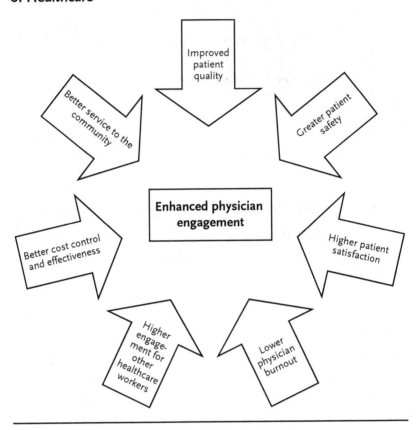

Improved patient quality

Better service to the community

Greater patient safety

Enhanced physician engagement

Better cost control and effectiveness

Higher patient satisfaction

Higher engagement for other healthcare workers

Lower physician burnout

individual physicians to a team-based approach focused on patients. Doctors, of course, must be central players in the transformation: Any ambitious strategy that they do not embrace is doomed." Physician engagement is the linchpin to success in all aspects of healthcare. A key question to ask is, If I agree with that premise, what should I do? Where should I start?

The topic of engagement is a somewhat confusing one. While there is very little evidence-based information about employee engagement, there is even less about physician engagement. Some observers would say that these are one and the same, but they are probably not.

Physicians enter the workforce after far more education and training than do most other employees, and they are held more accountable than are other employees. Although most physicians today are employed by some larger corporate entity, they do not function the same way that typical employees do. And most healthcare leaders recognize that physicians are typically independent—in both their thinking and their action. To consider physicians the same way we consider most other employees in an organization is not only foolish but also an approach that will usually backfire. Additionally, the legal expectations of physicians are far broader than those of all other employees.

Physician engagement comes in many shapes and sizes—just like physicians. Early in their careers, physicians are likely to feel engaged by incentives different from those of physicians nearing retirement. Office-based physicians may have needs and interests different from proceduralists or hospitalists who work mostly in an acute-care setting. Some physicians show interest in becoming more involved in the management and leadership aspects of their healthcare organizations, whereas others have none. And though understanding the motivational aspects of physician engagement is certainly important, many healthcare leaders simply want specific tactics. This book examines all these differences and presents a variety of approaches and tactics healthcare leaders can use to enhance physician engagement.

MULTIPLE VOICES OF PHYSICIANS

The clear intent of this book is to present the multiple voices of many kinds of physicians. Although I am not a physician, I have made a great effort to enlist the support, viewpoints, and counsel of experienced and knowledgeable physicians. I enjoyed a great deal of interaction with each individual chapter author. The process was not as simple as "Send me your chapter, and I will include it." Instead, there was extensive collaboration between and among the various contributors and me. Ultimately, this collaboration led to a more robust presentation of different ideas and viewpoints. While there are no major conflicts in the book, the points of view and approaches to the issue differ. Physician engagement is a complex topic; after reading the various viewpoints, the reader should have a broader and deeper understanding of the subject.

Readers may not find the exact answers to all their questions, but most angles are covered in some manner in the book. Often, the small kernel of a basic idea can take root and help propel substantive strategic initiatives that will pay great dividends. This book should help address such questions as these:

- How can burnout affect physician engagement, and what steps might we take organizationally to reduce physician burnout?
- How can we best assess physicians for leadership positions to ensure that their engagement is part of the process?
- Knowing that the electronic health record (EHR) has caused great consternation among physicians, how can we get them more engaged in this useful technology?
- How do the various ways of organizing leadership, such as through dyads and triads, affect physician engagement?
- How should we go about developing a physician leadership development program?
- How can we manage some physician behavior problems so that they do not diminish physician engagement?

Readers may also consider the book's companion volume, *Enhanced Physician Engagement*, Volume 1, *What It is, Why You Need It, and Where to Begin*. Volume 1 provides an in-depth discussion of the various theories and precepts surrounding physician engagement, including motivational and leadership aspects. The foundational support in volume 1 will help readers skillfully deploy the strategies and tactics found in volume 2.

Carson F. Dye

REFERENCE

Lee, T. H., and T. Cosgrove. 2014. "Engaging Doctors in the Health Care Revolution." *Harvard Business Review* 92 (6): 104–38.

Acknowledgments

WORKING IN A LARGE academic medical center, one of the best children's hospitals in the world, and two outstanding Catholic hospitals, combined with more than 20 years of consulting and executive search work, has given me a rich and diverse set of experiences. My career has encompassed a myriad of adventures in all types of healthcare organizations, working with many talented leaders—including many physicians and physician leaders. Over the years, I have conducted numerous physician leadership searches and have had the chance to get to know countless physician leaders in great depth. I have facilitated several affinity groups of physician leaders and have met with them twice yearly to listen to their challenges, solutions, and innovative ideas. Acknowledging everyone here would not be possible because of the many pages that would be required. However, several individuals deserve special recognition.

Exposure to highly effective leaders over the years has taught me much—and I am thinking especially of Sister Mary George Boklage, Dr. John Byrnes, Michael Covert, Dr. Kathleen Forbes, Mark Hannahan, Dr. Scott Ransom, and Dr. Lonnie Wright. Others who have demonstrated highly effective leadership include Dr. Imran Andrabi, Dr. John Baniewicz, Dr. Gary Chmielewski, Dr. Michael Choo, Dr. Bob Coates, Dr. Dave Drinkwater, Dr. David James, Dr. Dave Kapaska, Dr. Walter Kerschl, Dr. Mark Laney, Dr. Steve Markovich, Dr. Terry McWilliams, Gene Miyamoto, Dr. Marci Moore-Connelley, the late Dr. Mark Peters, Dr. Ed Pike, Bill Sanger, Randy Schimmoeller, Dr. David Shulkin, Dr. Herb Schumm,

Dr. Sergio Segarra, Kam Sigafoos, Dr. Doug Spotts, Dr. Rodney Stout, Dr. David Tam, Dr. Davin Turner, Dr. Tom Whalen, and Dr. Raúl Zambrano.

Special thanks goes to my friend and coauthor, Dr. Jacque Sokolov, who always has unique and cogent insights into physician leadership and engagement. Our work together on the book *Developing Physician Leaders for Successful Clinical Integration*, published by Health Administration Press in 2013, was insightful and opened many doors for me in my work.

Why am I so focused on *physician* engagement? There are multiple reasons, but a couple stand out. From my very first day at Clermont Mercy Hospital, Sister Mary George Boklage instilled in me a respect for physicians, a deep understanding of what they do and how they fit into the healthcare world. She also helped me gain leadership credibility among physicians early in my career. Even though I was the hospital's chief human resources officer, she expected me to be actively involved in all types of physician matters, and that was instructive. Most important, physicians were never greedy people or mere RVU producers to Sister Mary George. She definitely never saw them as cats to herd. She saw them as partners, collaborators, allies, and coworkers in patient care.

My following years at Cincinnati Children's Hospital and The Ohio State University Wexner Medical Center took me into the core of medical education. Not only was I fortunate to have a front-row seat, but I also often found myself "inside the ring." My experiences in these two great institutions gave me incredible street cred with physicians. I found myself providing informal counsel in all sorts of physician matters to chairs, division chiefs, and other physician leaders. It was also instructive to see and appreciate how these physician-led organizations excelled.

At the close of my hospital career at St. Vincent Mercy Medical Center, I was exposed to expert physicians and several consummate physician leaders. As I began my consulting career, I found myself getting more and more involved in various physician leadership matters. Circling back to the question posed earlier—why am I so focused on *physician* engagement?—I think the answer is clear: I have worked in organizations where physicians were highly engaged and passionate about their craft. I have seen the positives that occur in quality, cost management, organizational pride, and esprit de corps when organizations have strong physician engagement.

My consulting and executive search career continues to keep me deeply involved in physician leadership and physician engagement. Over the course of many searches for chief medical officers, chief quality officers, chief medical information officers, and other types of physician leader positions, I have learned firsthand how highly effective physician leaders drive robust physician engagement. And helping to establish many physician leadership academies over the years has given me invaluable access to cadres of highly engaged physicians in all types of healthcare organizations.

My coauthors in this journey bring great expertise, and I am so appreciative of their time and input. They helped to create the ultimate how-to guide. All of them are great physician leaders and share my passion for physician engagement. Thanks to them, I am confident that readers will find fresh, innovative approaches and solutions to the physician engagement challenge in this book. They include Dr. John Byrnes, system chief medical officer for Adventist Health; Dr. Kevin M. Casey, chief clinical officer at Mercy Health–Toledo; Dr. Mary Dillhoff, surgical oncologist at Wexner Medical Center at The Ohio State University; Dr. Daniel Eiferman, associate professor in the Department of Surgery at Wexner Medical Center at The Ohio State University; Dr. Lily Jung Henson, FACHE, CEO of Piedmont Henry Hospital; Dr. Walter C. Kerschl, chief medical officer at Camden Clark Medical Center of West Virginia University Medicine and recently appointed senior director and chief medical officer at Cerner; Dr. Terry R. McWilliams, director and chief clinical consultant at HSG Advisors; Dr. Katherine A. Meese, assistant professor in the Department of Health Services Administration at the University of Alabama at Birmingham (UAB) and director of wellness research at UAB Medicine; Dr. Kevin Post, chief medical officer of Avera Medical Group; Dr. Scott B. Ransom, FACHE, partner at

Oliver Wyman; Dr. Bhagwan Satiani, FACHE(R), professor emeritus in the Department of Surgery at Wexner Medical Center at The Ohio State University; and Dr. Margot Savoy, chair and associate professor in the Department of Family and Community Medicine at the Lewis Katz School of Medicine at Temple University.

Several others have helped so much and merit recognition. The staff at Health Administration Press (HAP) are at the top of that list. We are so fortunate to have this publisher in our field. They stay on top of our issues and concerns and are rigorous in their endeavors. They offer wonderful and innovative textbooks for those who are advancing in their educational preparation. Michael Cunningham leads HAP and has some great teammates including Andrew Baumann, Jennette McClain, and Nancy Vitucci, among others. Jennette was a steady presence as I tried to recruit and direct multiple authors. Prior to this book, I always wrote solo or was paired with a single coauthor. Having multiple authors with different viewpoints and different styles was challenging, and Jennette assisted me tremendously. Finally, I have saved mention of Editor Patty Boyd to the end—and she deserves the capital *E*. She did more than just edit; she partnered, she added great thoughts, and she made sure the book has both melody and harmony (multiple authors = multiple singers).

I close with mention and recognition of those nearest to me. Over many years, my wife Joaquina has been a helpful friend and companion, and always a kind critic. Her support has allowed me to excel in many ways. The rest of my family is just as special: daughters Carly, Emily, Liesl, and Blakely; sons-in-law Jeremy, Phil, and Nick; grandsons Carson, Benjamin, and Andrew; and granddaughter Celine have all tolerated my frequent absences as I traveled for work and spent lots of time at the computer. This book would not have been possible without their support.

Carson F. Dye

Introduction

Carson F. Dye

People sometimes ask me why physician engagement is challenging for so many health care organizations. It's a funny question because physicians are engaged. They're engaged in doing their job, trying to do the best they can for their patients, with many demands on their time, attention, and energy. Just because the physicians in your organization are not engaged in the project you're putting in front of them, it doesn't mean they don't care about improvement. There is probably something else they care about deeply. And identifying what they care about is the key to physician engagement.
—Carol Peden, MB ChB, MD, "A New Way to Engage Physicians," 2018

PHYSICIAN ENGAGEMENT IS NOT UNIDIMENSIONAL; many factors drive it. And in the preceding epigraph, Peden (2018) clearly alludes to these many factors. Her summary is worth repeating: "Identifying what they [physicians] care about is the key to physician involvement." Perreira and colleagues (2019) also describe the many causes and effects of engagement: "The antecedents of 'physician engagement' include accountability, communication, incentives, interpersonal relations, and opportunity. The results include improved outcomes such as data quality, efficiency, innovation, job satisfaction, patient satisfaction, and performance. Defining physician engagement enables physicians and health care administrators to better appreciate and more accurately measure engagement and understand how to better engage physicians." It is incumbent on healthcare leaders to study and understand physician engagement and to develop plans and tactics that measure it and enhance it. (For an in-depth look at the defining concepts surrounding physician engagement, see the companion volume of this book: *Enhanced Physician Engagement*, Volume I, *What It Is, Why You Need It, and Where to Begin*.)

Having a robust and well-developed physician engagement plan is as important as is having a strategic plan. It should not be left to the chief medical officer (CMO), nor should it be a matter that is thought about on occasion. As Chokshi and Swensen (2019) observe, "Health care organizations should have a well-communicated and well-understood formal strategy for clinician engagement."

The fundamentals of this book can be expressed in a few sentences:

- Know what physician engagement is.
- Know that it has many dimensions.
- Know that it is complex.
- Know that improving it can bring many dividends.
- Have a plan of action to address physician engagement that is both strategic and tactical.
- Most important, include many physicians in the development of the plan.

No matter how well your plans are conceived, the physicians themselves have to buy into your strategy. As the Healthcare Financial Management Association concluded in a study of physician engagement, "the success of any physician strategy will depend on its effectiveness in engaging the physicians themselves" (HFMA 2014).

As I invited various other authors to join me in the development of this book, I shared a number of my viewpoints with them. While these were not intended as directives for their chapter content, the ideas were to serve as the foundational precepts for the book. In the next few paragraphs, I summarize these precepts.

Physician engagement has taken on a contemporary importance. Of course, physician engagement has always been vital in the healthcare field. But frankly, COVID-19 has added a sense of criticality and significance that requires us as healthcare leaders to view the topic with a fresh and stronger focus. The changes that will occur in healthcare over the next several years will be historic. Much like the advent of Medicare, the introduction of DRGs (diagnosis-related groups), the Balanced Budget Act of 1997, and the US Institute of Medication's publication of *To Err Is Human* (Kohn, Corrigan, and Donaldson 2000), the changes in our field in the next few years will have great impact. No longer can physician engagement be relegated to the fifth or sixth page of an organization's strategic plans. Physicians—and not just those who function as administrative leaders—must be actively involved in many ways to shape this change. Their active participation in healthcare change requires significant engagement. It is simply a critical initiative.

There are two sides to the physician engagement coin. Physician engagement can be viewed from the perspective of individual clinical care but also from the angle of the dynamics of the larger organization in which those individual patient encounters occur. In some organizations, unfortunately, physician engagement has been defined from the perspective of the annual physician engagement survey. The typical physician, the full-time clinician, is already highly engaged. However, that engagement relates to the care of the patient, the interactions in the clinical setting, and the information gathering that then drives the clinical reasoning done with each individual patient. An informal conversation with practically every physician about clinical care will reveal high levels of engagement. Yet organizational leaders want physicians to view engagement from *their* perspective, which involves the more macro view that converges organizational vision, strategy, and larger-scale operations into the delivery of patient care. But clearly, physician engagement must be far more than "marching in lockstep," following orders given from on high by organizational leaders.

Physician engagement is multifaceted. While it is admirable that organizations do conduct formal physician engagement surveys and attempt to address issues that are identified therein, physician engagement is much more than the sum of the answers on these surveys. Engagement is a complex subject and involves both tangible and intangible elements. Interestingly, there is little academic evidence for a single definition of physician engagement. Perreira and colleagues (2019) state it well: "The term 'physician engagement' is used quite frequently, yet it remains poorly defined and measured."

Healthcare leaders would do well to dive deeply into the topic and learn its many dimensions. This book's examples underscore this advice and suggest that there are many ways to engage physicians. Moreover, there are many types of physicians; they cannot simply be lumped together as one sort of personality. Engagement approaches that work well with some physicians have no effect on other physicians. Younger physicians have different motivations than do older physicians; specialists have different needs than generalists have. One size does not fit all.

Multiple efforts are required. Because of these differences among physicians—and organizations—institutions need a variety of plans and initiatives to drive enhanced physician engagement. This book recognizes that healthcare leaders will need a bigger toolbox and more tools to aid their efforts to boost physician engagement. Some of the chapters herein may have little application to some healthcare leaders, while other chapters may provide the spark of an idea that could be quite beneficial to an organization.

All clinical providers are considered. While this book mainly addresses the issues that affect *physician* engagement, we recognize that advanced practice providers (APPs) also provide clinical care in many areas. We also understand that all healthcare workers face challenges in trying to be engaged and that they have come through some of the most challenging times in memory. All of us who helped develop this book recognize and appreciate everyone who serves and helps in healthcare. Our focus on physicians is not intended as a slight in any way. But because of the unique nature of physicians and because physicians drive practically all the clinical decisions in healthcare, this book is targeted at them.

Full-time clinicians can be engaged in broader strategic matters. While we have suggested that full-time clinicians are usually deeply engaged in their individual patient activities, healthcare leadership can also get them involved in and excited about organizational strategies. For too long, organizations have viewed physicians from the lenses of their physician leaders—the chief medical officer (CMO), medical executive committee members, or the medical directors in various departments. Many organizations relegate the job of improving physician engagement solely to these physician leaders. That is a shortsighted approach. Organizations that view their full-time clinicians as *organizational partners and collaborators* will see great value in broadening their approaches. And the organizations that have recently developed physician leadership programs have learned how incredibly engaged their full-time clinicians can be—even when these clinicians may have absolutely no leadership roles. Providing education and exposure to the various issues of healthcare finance, public policy, and organizational management can often help physicians who feel overwhelmed with the changes in the field. And as new expectations emerge for all physicians to help shape future changes in how care is delivered, the physicians who have a broader understanding of healthcare will be better equipped to provide meaningful input on those changes. And that dichotomy between administration and clinical physicians that exists in many organizations—the them-versus-us attitude—can be minimized or even eliminated.

It is *not* about herding cats. Whether it is called herding cats or some other more benevolent description, the idea of managing, directing, controlling, or manipulating physicians has no place whatsoever in developing physician engagement. Jacque Sokolov and I argued strongly in our 2013 book, *Developing Physician Leaders for Effective Clinical Integration*, that phrases like "herding cats" should be avoided because we simply did not accept or believe it. We wrote, "Phrases such as this create a negative environment, fail to be constructive, and cause a distorted representation of reality." Physician engagement encompasses a recognition of physicians as true partners and not animals to be trained and herded. Organizations who have strong physician engagement do not take this approach; instead, they collaborate, they work together in partnership, and they develop common goals together.

OVERVIEW OF CHAPTERS

The book opens with a wide-ranging discussion of engagement by Margot Savoy, MD. Chapter 1, "Preparing Physicians to Be Engaged," is foundational to a broad understanding of engagement and sets up the rest of the book to delve into more specific approaches. An increasing topic of concern, physician burnout, is closely related to physician engagement. It does seem somewhat logical that if physicians were highly engaged, they would likely be less burned out. Chapter 2, "Physician Engagement as an Antidote to Burnout," written by Kevin M. Casey, DO, tackles this matter directly.

Chapter 3, "The Electronic Health Record," hits directly at an issue that many claim has caused high burnout and low engagement—the introduction of the electronic health record (EHR). Author Walter C. Kerschl, MD, provides expert insight into the issue and makes several excellent suggestions to avoid potential problems.

Many healthcare leaders place the responsibility for physician engagement at the feet of their chief medical officers (CMOs). In chapter 4, "Making the Most of the Chief Medical Officer," Terry R. McWilliams, MD, describes the dilemmas that CMOs often face in the conflict between the clinical and the administrative sides of healthcare. He discusses how CMOs can help smooth this conflict. Certainly a key way to enhance physician engagement is to get more physicians involved in leadership. In chapter 5, "Dyads, Triads and Quads, Oh My!" Dr. McWilliams provides insight into how the use of the dyad model and its various derivations can provide additional opportunities for physicians to learn leadership and to be involved in leadership. In chapter 6, "Assessing Physicians for Leadership," Kevin M. Casey, MD, gives ample thoughts on how more physicians can become involved in leadership roles. He offers suggestions for how to enlist them and develop them as leaders.

As mundane as it might sound, highly effective healthcare leaders realize that supply-chain issues can be both a headache for their organizations but also an great opportunity for increasing the engagement of some physicians. In chapter 7, "Supply-Chain Issues," Scott B. Ransom, DO, drills down on how to enlist physicians in managing the supply chain. Dr. Ransom also discusses how their involvement will give them a more expansive view of the healthcare organization.

Chapter 8, "The Roles of Boards of Trustees," by Bhagwan Satiani, MD, and Mary Dillhoff, MD, provides a contemporary look at the role that physicians can and should play on boards. In chapter 9, "Quality: A Cornerstone of Physician Engagement," author John Byrnes, MD, presents support for why quality and patient safety may be one of the most effective ways to get many physicians involved and highly engaged. A less positive but nevertheless important topic is covered by Lily Jung Henson, MD. In chapter 10, "Disruptive Physician Behavior," Dr. Henson shows how this significant issue can have a deleterious impact on physician engagement across any organization. She describes the possible causes and ways to prevent this problem or address it.

Following up on chapter 6's introduction to physician leadership, chapter 11, "Physician Leadership Development," gives specific suggestions for and descriptions of physician leadership development programs. Authors Dr. Satiani and Dr. Eiferman also give resources for healthcare leaders looking to set up such curricula.

Since the start of the COVID-19 pandemic, the entire issue of telehealth has come front and center. Chapter 12, "Telehealth," by Kevin Post, DO, examines the many issues of telemedicine and how it affects physician engagement and patient, community, and population health. In chapter 13, "Engagement Ideas from the Front

Lines," I present and summarize the survey results from many healthcare leaders I asked to share their best ideas for how they grow physician engagement. In chapter 14, "Measuring Physician Engagement," Katherine A. Meese, MD, and I assert that if physician engagement is indeed necessary for high-quality patient care and the flourishing of healthcare systems, then healthcare leaders need to measure this essential factor. We answer three fundamental questions about measurement: why measure, how to do it, and who and what to measure.

In the conclusion, I summarize all the contributors' chapters in a few brief paragraphs. It is hoped that readers will finish this book with a stronger understanding of how to advance and sustain physician engagement in their organizations.

This book also has a companion volume, *Enhanced Physician Engagement*, Volume 1, *What It Is, Why You Need It, and Where to Begin*, which explores the primary concepts and theories surrounding physician engagement and leadership. Readers may want to review this volume first if they have not done so already.

REFERENCES

Chokshi, D. A., and S. Swensen. 2019. "Leadership Survey: Why Clinicians Are Not Engaged, and What Leaders Must Do About It." NEJM Catalyst. Published August 8. https://catalyst.nejm.org/doi/full/10.1056/CAT.19.0630.

Dye, C. F., and J. J. Sokolov. 2013. *Developing Physician Leaders for Successful Clinical Integration*. Chicago: Health Administration Press.

Healthcare Financial Management Association (HMFA). 2014. "HFMA's Value Project: Phase 3 Strategies for Physician Engagement and Alignment." Published November. www.hfma.org/content/dam/hfma/Documents/PDFs/Strategies%20for%20Physician%20Engagement%20and%20Alignment.pdf.

Kohn, L. T., J. M. Corrigan, and M. S. Donaldson (eds.), for US Institute of Medicine. 2000. *To Err Is Human: Building a Safer Health System*. Washington, DC: National Academies Press.

Peden, C. 2018. "A New Way to Engage Physicians." Institute for Healthcare Improvement. Published April 25. www.ihi.org/communities/blogs/a-new-way-to-engage-physicians.

Perreira, T. A., L. Perrier, M. Prokopy, L. Neves-Mera, and D. D. Persaud. 2019. "Physician Engagement: A Concept Analysis." *Journal of Healthcare Leadership* 11: 101–13.

Preparing Physicians to Be Engaged

Margot Savoy

A Scenario with a Challenge

It has been two months since you announced your newest program—Journey to Excellent Experiences. It was a masterpiece of data and evidence-based approaches to improve the patient satisfaction scores across the institution. You heard the feedback from your organization's Achieving Access initiative launched three months ago and made key changes to the rollout. You held a town hall at 7 p.m. to tell the physicians about the new program and to give them a chance to share feedback. You created a curriculum that explains the need for better patient satisfaction and gave practical tips for improving the patient experience. You developed a dashboard that pushes out data weekly so that the physicians can see their progress. Now, you let out a deep sigh as you click on your dashboard and see that only a handful have actually logged into the course and even fewer have completed it. Frustrated, you begin to wonder if you can ever figure out how to herd these cats.

READERS, PLACE YOURSELF in the preceding scenario. What would you do? At chapter's end are some answers.

DEFINING ENGAGEMENT

Employee engagement is a management concept introduced in the 1990s and growing into widespread use in the 2000s (Kahn 1990). William Kahn, professor of organizational behavior and the "father of employee engagement," defines it as "the harnessing of organization members' selves to their work roles; in engagement, people employ and express themselves physically, cognitively, and emotionally during role performances"(Kahn 1990). He believed that when three primary psychological needs are met, employees become engaged. Employees need personal feelings of meaningfulness (one is valued and appreciated), psychological safety (one can do and work without fear of negative consequences), and availability (one has the physical and mental resources without distractions to engage at work) (Kahn 1990). Later industry leaders coined alternative terms such as *employee satisfaction* and *employee experience*. The consistent theme remains an attempt to identify the key measures linking the traditional concepts of job satisfaction, employee retention, and organizational commitment.

It did not take long for the healthcare industry to begin exploring the value of engaging physicians and staff in hospitals and other health systems as a driver of profitability and improved retention. Kruse (2015) shows the links between employee engagement and profit in what he calls the "Engagement Health System Profit Chain" (exhibit 1.1).

Initial efforts to better engage healthcare employees have been directed at nurses; studies show that clinical outcomes as measured by such key metrics as mortality rate correlated with nurse engagement (Blizzard 2005). As physicians' roles in hospitals and other health systems have changed over the years because of increased physician employee agreements and shared-payment models such

Exhibit 1.1 The Connection Between Employee Engagement and Profit in a Healthcare System

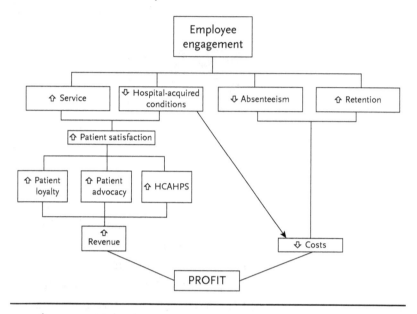

Note: ↑ = increased; ↓ = decreased; HCAHPS = Hospital Consumer Assessment of Healthcare Providers and Systems Survey.

Source: Adapted from Kruse (2015).

as accountable care organizations, interest in ensuring an engaged physician community has intensified as well.

WHAT IS PHYSICIAN ENGAGEMENT?

Despite the number of hours that leaders have spent discussing, learning about, and writing about physician engagement, there is still no universally accepted definition. According to a literature review by Perreira and colleagues (2019), physician engagement is a "regular participation of physicians in (1) deciding how their work is done, (2) making suggestions for improvement, (3) goal setting, (4) planning, and (5) monitoring of their performance in activities

Exhibit 1.2 Key Input Drivers and Outcomes of Physician Engagement

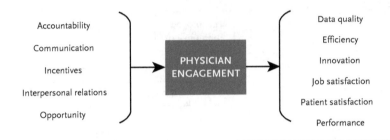

Source: Adapted from Perreira et al. (2019).

targeted at the micro (patient), meso (organization), and/or macro (health system) levels." They went on to describe the five key inputs and six outcomes of physician engagement (exhibit 1.2).

If engaging physicians can be boiled down to five key drivers, why do so many systems appear to struggle at achieving meaningful and sustainable physician engagement programs? Common barriers include misalignment of intention, failure to achieve true involvement, and underestimating the level of commitment needed.

Misaligned Intentions: Differing Points of View

Physicians and administrators often find themselves in somewhat opposite roles in the healthcare system (exhibit 1.3). Administrators tend to view themselves primarily as businesspeople with skills and talents geared toward optimizing the operations and finances of the organization. Physicians view themselves as independent patient advocates who are best positioned to identify optimal care. These different perspectives create a natural source of tension as the overall market forces affecting medicine put pressure on health systems and practices to produce more at lower costs while pushing for enhanced quality.

Exhibit 1.3 Typical Characteristics of Physicians and Administrators

Physicians	Administrators
Science-oriented	Business-oriented
One-on-one interactions	Group interactions
Value autonomy	Value collaboration
Focus on patients	Focus on organization
Identify with profession	Identify with organization
Independent	Collaborative
Solo thinkers	Group thinkers

Source: Dye and Sokolov (2013).

Encouraging Involvement

Initially, systems look to engage physicians by including them in system-level decisions. When the inclusion is handled well, physician leaders gain insight into the rationale of decisions. Having a seat at the table empowers these physicians to own and champion initiatives and other projects. But involvement and input are not the same thing (exhibit 1.4). Unfortunately, many leaders mistake providing seats at the table for input as a surrogate for true involvement.

Commitment to Engagement

Healthcare organizations must continuously aim to engage physicians; the process requires commitment and dedicated resources. If leadership adds engagement to its system-level goals without giving this goal thoughtful attention, engagement is not likely to improve and could even be diminished. Similarly, bringing in outside consultants for a limited exploration of the culture of engagement will fail to yield sustainable progress alone. True commitment

Exhibit 1.4 Differences Between Involvement and Input

Involvement	Input
Physicians are always at decision-making meetings.	Physicians are sometimes invited.
Physicians are viewed as partners.	Physicians are viewed as tokens.
Executive leadership sees physicians as aligned.	Executive leadership seeks alignment from physicians.
Physician involvement is ongoing.	Physician input is sporadic.
Physicians remain in the process.	Physicians are occasional players.
Seeing physicians at the table is common.	Seeing physicians at the table is rare.

Source: Dye and Sokolov (2013).

requires an investment in data capture and assessment; identifying a team responsible for pinpointing opportunities; developing, implementing, and evaluating interventions; and making ongoing improvements.

Most experts recommend that physician engagement (and that of other healthcare employees) be measured annually and that results and plans for improvement be presented transparently. Major companies such as Gallup and Press Ganey offer surveys with additional services such as dashboards and consulting support. Some health systems will choose to develop and deliver their own internal tools.

Most engagement surveys ask a wide range of questions about the workplace environment, experience with key leadership, and individual personal development and experience. Key areas identified by Gallup in surveying physicians include the following:

- *Growth:* feeling that you are advancing and learning new things

- *Recognition:* feeling appreciated
- *Trust:* trusting that the organization has a bright future

One key insight consistent across surveys is that much like employee engagement, physician engagement is closely tied to the manager. Compensation, celebrations, and individual recognition programs are unlikely to improve overall engagement if physicians do not feel supported and appreciated by their managers. If senior leaders fail to prepare managers and physician leaders with the knowledge and skills to tactfully share the results with their teams, foster growth and discussion, and elicit specific improvement ideas from the front line, the overall engagement process will struggle to succeed.

PRACTICAL APPROACHES TO ENGAGE PHYSICIANS

Knowing what needs to be put in place to begin the journey to a culture of engagement and then implementing the steps to achieve goals can be challenging. Fortunately, the literature contains many case reports of successful engagement journeys. For example, Enloe Medical Center in Chico, California, improved its overall physician engagement from the 44th percentile in 2009 to the 85th percentile in 2017 using a variety of techniques as shown in exhibit 1.5 (Nelson 2019).

Creating a Culture of Accountability

High-performing teams require mutual trust and commitment. If physicians are to be deeply engaged in an organization, both administrative and physician leaders need to feel a sense of mutual responsibility. In business models, this prerequisite is called *creating a culture of accountability*. To ensure a valuable, shared learning experience as organizations strive to improve performance and

Exhibit 1.5 Example of Actions for Physician Engagement

Administration Domain	Physician Group Culture Domain	Physician Leadership Domain
Seek physician input.	Create flexible schedules.	Hold annual off-site leadership retreats with medical directors, department chairs, and administrators.
Appreciate physician time.	Hold group social functions.	
Prioritize recruiting.	Promote journal clubs.	Prioritize physician leadership of quality initiatives.
Use locum tenens physicians when needed.	Value physician participation on hospital committees.	Hold regular medical director meetings with administration.
Provide a comfortable physician lounge.	Lead quality initiatives.	Create monthly medical staff officer meetings with the CEO and chief medical officer (CMO).
Host physician receptions.	Use technology, such as HIPAA-compliant texting, to connect with and support group members.	Recognize and celebrate excellence in medical staff.
		Create department meetings that value participation by all.

Source: Adapted from Nelson (2019).

raise their professional standards, the leaders must be transparent about their goals, their actual results, and their own responsibilities. One model, developed by culture management consultant Partners In Leadership and titled The Results Pyramid, reminds leaders that focusing exclusively on actions and results misses key foundational drivers of success (exhibit 1.6). In this model, leaders are encouraged to create experiences that enable physicians

Exhibit 1.6 The Results Pyramid

Source: Partners In Leadership (2019). Used with permission.

to examine their beliefs about their interactions and to make the desired change. This step helps physicians identify actions they can take to get the results everyone is hoping to achieve (Partners In Leadership 2019).

Set Expectations

Leaders must always set clear expectations. They cannot assume that each member of a team knows what is expected or which quality and performance measures are highest in priority (James 2019). By communicating the overall mission and vision of the organization, how this work supports that goal, and how each team member supports the work, leaders help get everyone on the same page. Some health systems consider using team charters or professional codes of conduct that are created by the organization to engage the frontline physicians in the discussions and to allow their input to help drive ownership of the final product.

Monitor and Report Progress

Improving physician engagement is a performance- and quality-improvement project. Like other initiatives, this project must identify key metrics, measure performance, and share the results. To reduce confusion, leaders need to include the full team when they identify the performance metrics and the sources of data being used to measure success. Shared agreements about critical definitions for professional behaviors or standards will make it easier for peer observation and assessment. In addition to helping the team see areas in need of ongoing improvements, leaders will be able to identify and celebrate areas of success. Feedback about progress encourages ongoing conversations, identifies roadblocks, and further engages teams as they work together to identify needed resources and support (James 2019). Leaders who check in with frontline team members will develop relationships and trust if they establish ongoing opportunities for communication.

Encourage Conversations About Accountability

Leaders can encourage people to share accountability with their peers by identifying how to have difficult conversations in a respectful way. In doing so, they will improve the chances that these interactions will occur. Setting the expectation that all team members are empowered to hold accountability conversations opens the door to bidirectional feedback that can identify and address concerns early. When a team member faces no consequences for poor performance, repeated failures to meet obligations, or unprofessional behavior, trust is quickly eroded and other team members will no longer feel obligated to commit to the established agreements. Although the person performing poorly may find the behavior easy, those who must give this person feedback may find doing so difficult. Leaders and peers may feel uncomfortable giving critical or negative feedback. Teaching specific feedback and conversation techniques can be valuable personal and leadership development for team members. Exhibit 1.7 gives examples of techniques and resources that leaders can use to encourage accountability among team members.

Exhibit 1.7 Examples of Feedback Techniques and Models

Cup-of-Coffee Conversation Example	
Technique	**Example**
Your aim is not to pass a verdict, but rather to raise awareness of the issue and to gain a better understanding from the other person's perspective.	**Manager:** "I was surprised to hear you have been late to the OR every day the past week."
Be curious, and don't assume you have the whole picture already. Start with, "I was surprised to hear . . ." or "Perhaps you can help me understand this better . . ."	**Employee:** "My childcare has fallen through because of COVID-19, and I've been trying to get my daughter to school and still make it to my 7 a.m. start time. It has been really difficult, but I didn't want to just take the whole day off."
After listening, you can then share your feedback in the appropriate context and remind the person how the individual actions play into the bigger picture.	**Manager:** "That sounds stressful. When you start late, it has a ripple effect on the other teams using the OR that day. Could we look at the schedule and figure a temporary rescheduling of your early cases until the childcare is covered?"

DESC Discussion	
Technique	**Example**
Describe: Use "I" statements to clearly describe the behavior you observed. Using "you" can come across as aggressive. Focus on just one recent action, and try to use nonjudgmental language. **Express:** Objectively describe the impact the action had on you, team members, and the business, including how it made you feel.	"I have noticed that you have been taking more than two weeks to finish your office notes. Twice, the physicians covering your patients were unclear on what the plan was, because the note was not completed in the chart. This was frustrating because they felt that they could not deliver optimal patient care. How can we help you finish your notes in a more timely way?"

(continued)

(continued from previous page)

Technique	Example
Specify: Clearly specify what you would like the person to do differently next time. You can do this through a directive ("What I would like to see happen in this situation next time is . . .") or a participative question ("How can we avoid this in the future?"). Request agreement from the individual.	
Consequences: Make it clear what the consequences of this behavior change will be. Ensure that the person knows the positive impact this change will have for both of you. If necessary, explain the negative consequences of not making these changes.	

McKinsey's Model	
Technique	**Example**
Part A is the action, event, or behavior you would like someone to change Part B is the impact of that behavior. Part C is a suggestion for what the person could do differently the next time.	"I notice you are late to clinic. It causes patients to be upset, and when you run late, the staff has to work overtime. I'd like you to arrive ten minutes before the session begins, so that you can start on time."

Stanford Method	
Technique	**Example**
Use a combination of these phrases in your feedback: "I like," "I wish," and "What if . . . ?"	"I like that you spend time with patients, getting to know them better. I wish you could do that without running an hour late during your clinic. What if we

(continued)

(continued from previous page)

Technique	Example
	thought about ways to streamline your visits so that you continue to have time to chat with patients?"

SKS Method	
Technique	**Example**
Use these three ideas in your feedback: • Stop • Keep • Start	"You are coming to the OR late, and I need that to stop. When you arrive, you are great at organizing the team and getting the cases done efficiently. Can we start moving your cases to the second slot so that you can be on time and still get your cases done?"

SBI Model	
Technique	**Example**
Situation: Describe the situation with specifics. **Behavior:** Describe the behavior observed; do not try to guess at motives or causes of the behavior. **Impact:** Describe the impact the observed behavior had.	"You have clinical sessions on Monday and Tuesday afternoons that are running more than an hour late. This is causing the staff to have to work overtime hours that they do not want to work, and patients are complaining."

BEEF Model	
Technique	**Example**
Describe the situation, using these aspects in order: • Behavior • Example • Effect • Future	"Your OR sessions are starting one hour late. For example, on Tuesday your first case was scheduled at 7 a.m. and you did not arrive until 8 a.m. The lateness caused the OR schedule for the rest of the day to be delayed. In the future, we need to start OR sessions on time."

(continued)

(continued from previous page)

AID Model	
Technique	**Example**
Describe the situation using three ideas: • Action • Impact • Development or desired behavior	"Your office notes are not done within 48 hours as we have agreed on. This means your colleagues are unable to see your plans when covering your patients. We need you to finish your office notes within 48 hours."

BIFF Model	
Technique	**Example**
Describe the situation using these four approaches: • Behavior • Impact • Future • Feelings	"Your office notes are not done within 48 hours as we agreed on. This lateness means your colleagues are unable to see your plans when covering your patients. In the future, we need you to finish your office notes within 48 hours. Do you feel this is something you can do?"

Pendleton Model	
Technique	**Example**
Check that the employee wants and is ready for feedback. Let the employee give comments or background about the behavior or situation that has been observed.	**Manager:** "I need to give you some feedback about your OR start times. Do you have time to talk now?" **Employee:** "Yes."
The employee identifies what went well.	**Manager:** "How have your OR sessions been going recently?"
The manager identifies what went well.	**Employee:** "A bit stressful, to be honest. I catch up by the end of the day, but I have been starting

(continued)

(continued from previous page)

Technique	Example
The employee states what could be improved.	late because I have to get my kid to school and the before-school daycare is closed because of COVID-19."
The manager states what could be improved.	
	Manager: "So, things going well include that the team is working well together and functioning efficiently during the day?"
The employee and manager agree on an action plan for improvement.	
	Employee: "Yes!"
	Manager: "And one area that could improve is the late start to the first session?"
	Employee: "Yeah."
	Manager: "Do you have any thoughts about the late starts?"
	Employee: "I don't know when the daycare will be open again, but I also don't want to take off, since we need to catch up on cases. Maybe I could move my first case to later in the day?"
	Manager: "That sounds like it might work. Let's look at the OR schedule together."

STAR Model	
Technique	**Example**
Situation/task: Describe a particular situation or task the employee was involved in; be as specific as possible.	"We are over on our budget for staff overtime hours this past month. Dr. X has been starting late each day and finishing more

(continued)

Chapter 1: Preparing Physicians to Be Engaged   25

(continued from previous page)

Technique	Example
Action: Write down the action the employee took, including details of what was said and done. This action could be positive or negative. Don't just use a generic phrase, but describe how the person accomplished the action.	than an hour late. Dr. X's sessions are causing overtime that the practice cannot afford. We need to find a way to arrive and finish the session on time."
Result: Identify the result of the action so that the employee understands what the person did wrong or right.	

Interpersonal Relationships

Relationship building can sometimes be overlooked in the workplace because it seems so basic, and yet it is foundational to a culture of engagement. The NEJM Catalyst Insights Council comprises a qualified group of US executives, clinical leaders, and clinicians at organizations directly involved in healthcare delivery. In this group, 90 percent of the group members chose interpersonal skills as the top attribute a leader needs to lead physicians, and 82 percent of them chose the same skills as the top attribute needed to successfully run a healthcare organization. Administrative skills, clinical training, and negotiation skills each received 69 percent or less (Zeis 2017).

Building and fostering relationships requires some intentional development and planning. To strengthen interpersonal relationships, leaders will want to be approachable, build trust, express gratitude, build alliances, and practice other interpersonal skills. Some examples of strategies to improve in those areas are listed in exhibit 1.8. One successful strategy for developing good interpersonal relationships is the use of leadership teams, a topic discussed in the next section.

Exhibit 1.8 Strategies for Strengthening Interpersonal Relationships

- Be approachable.
- Actively listen.
- Respect people: Refrain from talking down to them, avoid sarcasm, watch out for nastiness.
- Start conversations, and ask about the other person.
- Initiate repeated interactions and connections.
- Be mindful of cultural norms.
- Follow open-door policies.
- Avoid sweeping judgments.
- Have in place conflict management plans.
- Express gratitude.
- Build alliances.
- Don't blindside people—avoid ambushing your coworkers.
- Encourage team-building activities, such as ice breakers and other ways to learn how other think, communicate, and solve problems.

- Strive for optimism.
- Be flexible, adaptable.
- Build trust.
- Keep commitments and deadlines.
- Share credit for work and contributions of ideas.
- Respect others' time, and streamline business meetings.
- Be authentic; take responsibility for actions and decisions.
- Support teamwork.
- Plan occasional non-work-related social activities.
- Recognize people's birthdays, anniversaries, important life events, and so forth.
- Support other people, and help them find their greatness.
- Be inclusive; involve others in your discussion, projects, and activities.
- Share information about shared interests.

Source: Adapted from Baldwin, Dimunation, and Alexander (2011); Zismer and Brueggemann (2010).

Leadership Teams

Traditionally, healthcare organizations use an operations leadership model based on a team of supervisors, managers, and directors working together under the leadership of a single vice president who coordinates and implements organizational initiatives (Baldwin, Dimunation, and Alexander 2011; Zismer and Brueggemann 2010). This hierarchy model diminishes physician engagement. Aside from the CMO, most physicians would be excluded from positions of legitimate authority and influence because they would lack a formal leadership role (Baldwin, Dimunation, and Alexander 2011).

Dyad and triad teams are a leadership partnership model that pairs leaders with different skills to oversee patient care, operational decisions, and clinical improvements for an organization unit (Zismer and Brueggemann 2010). There are various designs. Typically, an administrative leader and a clinical leader form a two-person team, or dyad. Each expert brings complementary skills and experience, ultimately forming a dynamic leadership team that shares accountability for outcomes. The triad model adds a nurse leader to the equation.

The dyad or triad model has several advantages, including these:

- It supports a shared vision.
- The model increases interactions between clinical and administrative leaders.
- It reduces leadership burnout.
- It allows access to a fuller spectrum of leadership skills than that afforded by one leader alone.
- The model maximizes the key skills and knowledge at the top of each leader's license or strengths.

Healthcare organizations are increasingly using these shared physician-and-administrator models of leadership. Just more than 70 percent of NEJM Catalyst Insights Council members say they use the dyad leadership model, and 85 percent think the approach is extremely effective, very effective, or effective, with 50 percent reporting extremely or very effective (Zeis 2017). The Medical Group Management Association surveyed 303 healthcare leaders, and 77 percent reported using a physician and administrator (dyad) leadership team model (Comstock 2019).

One example of successful implementation comes from Mayo Clinic. In 2015, the clinic reorganized the leadership structure of the emergency departments under a physician–administrator dyad. The pair worked together to develop regional steering committees, each committee led by a triad of a physician, a nurse, and an administrator. Mayo Clinic identified this change in leadership structure as a key driver in its successful transformation and key to gaining momentum for its journey toward system improvement. Buell (2017) discusses other organizations that have successfully implemented dyad models.

Dyads do have some potential pitfalls. First, selection of the leaders is critical. Their success will greatly depend on their ability to work together. Organizations should choose leaders who believe in shared leadership and who are system-level thinkers interested in problem solving. They should be well respected among their peers and be strong communicators. Second, the leaders must communicate with one another early in the relationship to set expectations and coordinate the work efforts. Having two leaders duplicating work or unclear about their own responsibilities would be ineffective and potentially harmful. The roles need to be transparent and shared with the whole team so that everyone knows whom to consult in different situations. In addition to the common goals and outcomes, leaders should consider identifying complementary key metrics and aspects each individual leader can own. Finally, the leaders in the dyad should have decision-making authority in their own domain of accountability (Baldwin, Dimunation, and Alexander 2011; Zismer and Brueggemann 2010).

Leadership Rounds

With a strategy called *leadership rounds*, system-level leaders intentionally make time to regularly visit each unit in the organization. Sometimes combined with other meetings such as daily team huddles, these opportunities for contact between the leadership and frontline staff are frequently beneficial. Although these visits could be simply social, most leaders will find that creating a purposeful interaction can be a value-added connection that drives interpersonal relationships, improves communication, and builds trust. In one helpful model developed by a healthcare staffing company and labeled RELATE, the leaders are not only meeting with the clinical team but joining them on patient rounds and interacting with them as well (see exhibit 1.9).

Exhibit 1.9 A Model for Purpose-Driven Leadership Rounds

Reassure	Use this step to alleviate or reduce patients' fears about being admitted to the hospital or staff's fear about delivering care. Being present and empathetic during rounds can reduce these concerns. Be sure to introduce yourself and share your role and how long you have been with the organization.
Explain	Explain what rounding is and, without using any technical or medical jargon, explain its purpose. Employees should understand that rounding is a bidirectional opportunity for feedback, with the goal being to improve care delivery.
Listen	Encourage clinicians and staff to express concerns, ask questions, and be mindful of not judging anything that is said. Be aware that reading body language and other nonverbal expressions is an essential part of "listening."
Answer	Validate any questions that are asked, and clearly restate information. Use paraphrasing or teach-back activities so that staff and clinicians understand what is being explained or asked.
Take action	After gathering feedback, address any concerns that come up, and start to build a well-informed action plan. Manage staff and clinician expectations while taking proactive steps to exceed them.
Express appreciation	At the end of the interaction, thank employees, explain how the discussion will be followed up, and reiterate how nice it was to get to know the participants and understand their concerns.

Source: Adapted from HealthStream (2017).

Communication

Effective communication is critical in healthcare. Communication between healthcare leaders and between leaders and the frontline clinicians sets the tone of the organization and drives the overall ability of a group to deliver safe, high-quality, and patient-centered care across the continuum. Leaders must create an environment of open communication by modeling appropriate behavior, setting expectations, and investing in support systems in the structure of the organization. Managers and other leaders at all levels of the organization should promote patient-centered communication as integral to safe, high-quality care (Merlino 2017).

Effective communication is a skill that can be taught. Even good communicators can benefit from additional training, feedback, and practice. Training should not be limited to senior leadership. Enhancing the communication skills of all team members will increase efficiency, improve outcomes, and support team building.

Exhibit 1.10 shares highlights of best practices to consider for some common communication technology modalities, but these alone are probably not enough to improve the communication in your organizations. Having access to a variety of modalities and identifying which are preferable for your organization will be an individual decision. Most physician engagement work would benefit from a mix of modalities, with no one modality being optimal for all situations. For example, for a major new policy, it may be useful to deliver paper copies, send an e-mail, and follow up with a meeting (virtual or in person) to review the key details, while a small update could be sent out as a part of a standing e-mail newsletter or Yammer message. Knowing your physician audience and their preferences for access and communication will also help guide your choices.

Learning to communicate better will be a key development investment in better physician engagement. Communication training approaches can vary with the needs of an organization or a team, but some practical considerations include learning to adapt to another

Exhibit 1.10 Some Considerations for Communication Technology Modalities

Memos	
Pros	**Cons**
• Work well for physicians who prefer paper or who have limited access to internet	• May be lost or discarded without being seen • May receive limited attention because of large volumes of paper-based patient communications

E-mail	
Pros	**Cons**
• Is easy to send • Can create newsletters with multimedia • Imposes little or no cost	• May be screened out as spam, because of increased fraudulent e-mail • Many e-mails from multiple sources mean a single message can be overlooked easily

Texting	
Pros	**Cons**
• Allows short messages to go directly to physicians • Is accessible to most physicians through their smartphones • Is good for quick reminders	• Can share only limited information (which can be expanded with links to other sites, but links require physician action) • Can cost physicians not on an unlimited texting plan

Social Media	
Pros	**Cons**
• Offer a wide variety of options	• Typically require a separate account and log-in

(continued)

(continued from previous page)

Pros	Cons
• Can be public (e.g., Facebook, Twitter, Instagram) or private (e.g., Yammer or Slack) • Can allow for conversation chains across groups	• Are potentially limited to physicians interested in social media • Can expose organization to potentially problematic external feedback when external accounts are used

Podcasts	
Pros	**Cons**
• Allow leaders to get deeper background to important issues and engage key physicians • Offer a discussion and learning tool for new concepts • Are easy for some frontline physicians to hear (familiar and common way to access continuing medical education and news)	• Require an additional modality to create and access • Require significant preparation by podcaster • Can be costly to produce and store depending on available resources

Video Messages	
Pros	**Cons**
• Can be combined with other modalities • Allow everyone to see the leader, allowing for an improved sense of recognition • Can share emotion along with message	• Require an additional modality to access • Can require time-consuming and costly filming, editing, and production, depending on the resources available • Can be blocked by e-mail servers

(continued)

(continued from previous page)

In-Person Meetings	
Pros	**Cons**
• When planned well, promote group discussion and interpersonal interaction • Encourage transparency of discussion and decisions • Present opportunities for workshops and team-building and other activities	• Can be time-consuming • Are difficult to schedule, because of large groups and busy work schedules • Can be costly if refreshments are provided

Virtual Meetings	
Pros	**Cons**
• Allow for group discussion and interaction but with an additional barrier, given the video interface • Increase access for physicians unable to travel to the meeting location • Make discussion and decisions more transparent • Can encourage participation from traditionally silent members who will type comments but not speak in a large group • Can use polling and other interactive platform tools	• Require internet access • Can make one-on-one conversations difficult • Can leave participants distracted or not as engaged since they are not physically present

person's styles, learning to tell stories, and taking advantage of standardized communication tools.

Adapting to People's Communication Styles
Although personality testing may have fallen out of fashion, each member of a team has some preferences for how to communicate.

Exhibit 1.11 Four Basic Communication Types

Thinkers	Prefer numbers, graphs, and expert opinions. • Make quick, rational decisions. • Want to know "what if?" • Will bring you a computer printout of all their home-glucose readings (with trends).
Planners	Prefer organized information. • Need time to process, analyze, and reflect. • Want to know "what?" • Will take information home to think about it, and will follow up to share decisions later.
Dreamers	• Prefer big picture ideas. • Respond to creative examples and metaphors. • Want to know "how?" • Will take your one or two options for management and brainstorm ten more options.
Feelers	Prefer stories and people-based explanations. • Feel concern about impacts. • Want to know "why?" • Will tell you about their grandchildren and their last vacation before talking about any medical concerns.

Source: Savoy and Yunyongying (2013).

Helping leaders and team members identify their preferences can help leaders communicate more effectively and in ways that feel more individualized to the physician (Savoy and Yunyongying 2013). Exhibit 1.11, reprinted from Savoy and Yunyongying (2013), describes the preferences of different types of communicators.

The Power of Storytelling

Regardless of the communication style, learning to tell an effective story will help leaders convey complex messages simply and evoke the emotion needed to rally a team to action. Storytelling allows leaders to communicate the values and beliefs of the organization and team using a method that makes the listener feel and think beyond the data or slides. Because stories attach emotions to the data, the memories become stickier, giving a leader who can create and share good stories a powerful leadership advantage (O'Hara

Exhibit 1.12 Types of Business Stories

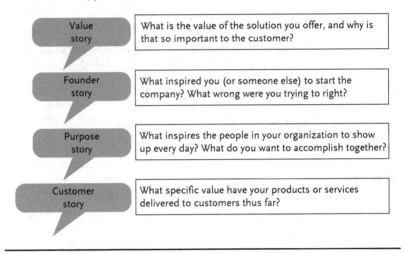

Value story	What is the value of the solution you offer, and why is that so important to the customer?
Founder story	What inspired you (or someone else) to start the company? What wrong were you trying to right?
Purpose story	What inspires the people in your organization to show up every day? What do you want to accomplish together?
Customer story	What specific value have your products or services delivered to customers thus far?

Source: Adapted from Hall (2019).

2014). Fortunately, all leaders can hone their storytelling skills. As Kindra Hall (2019) explains in *Stories That Stick*, there are four types of business stories (exhibit 1.12), but leaders may need to use a combination, depending on their situation.

Becoming a storytelling leader does not have to be overly complicated. The process consists of three steps highlighted in exhibit 1.13 (Hall 2019; O'Hara 2014). The most effective stories

Exhibit 1.13 Tips for Creating a Memorable Story

Find	• Start with a clear message.
	• Mine your own (or the team's) experiences.
Craft	• Highlight a struggle.
	• Keep it simple.
	• Don't make yourself the hero.
Tell	• Practice makes perfect.

Source: Adapted from Hall (2019) and O'Hara (2014).

have a clear message or point and are relatable to the audience. Using examples from the team or your own personal experience will add a level of authenticity that cannot be matched. Give enough detail to help the listener understand the context and characters, but keep it simple. Having the main protagonist of the story hit a challenge that needs to be overcome and resolving the challenge (or prepping the team to discuss how to resolve the challenge) draws the group in and holds their attention. Avoid the temptation to make yourself the hero of your own story. While you can highlight the team, any statements about how great you are will probably be seen as self-aggrandizing and will backfire. Finally, remember that the more you practice and encourage the team to share stories, the better the group will become. Consider using leadership rounds as an opportunity not only to gather stories but also to share meaningful stories that help the team members see their contributions in action (HealthStream 2017).

Standardizing Communication Through SBAR

In addition to making it easier for your team to hear you by adapting to their preferred communication styles and telling stories that illustrate your key messages, using standardized team tools such as the SBAR (situation, background, assessment, and recommendation) protocol described in the next section or team huddles can also improve communication with the team.

Communication tools are most commonly studies in patient-care settings where one team or clinician needs to hand off or otherwise convey critical information to another team or clinician. The gold standard of patient handoff communication tools was originally developed by the US Navy to hand off information during shift changes on submarines. In a healthcare setting, the SBAR protocol was first introduced at Kaiser Permanente in 2003 as a framework for structuring conversations between doctors and nurses about situations requiring immediate attention (exhibit 1.14). The SBAR tool organizes information so that both parties know what to expect (Shahid and Thomas 2018).

Exhibit 1.14 Use of SBAR Protocol Across Healthcare Situations

Protocol Tool	Primary Question	Clinical Situation	Administrative Situation
Situation	Why are you calling or having this meeting?	I am calling because Mr. Jones in Room 3 is having chest pain.	We are meeting because we have had three patients complain today that they cannot get a timely appointment.
Background	What is the context or background?	He is the 65-year-old whom we admitted earlier for chest pain.	We have been working on improving access by adding additional appointment slots, but these were filled with hospital discharges.
Assessment	What did you assess?	I saw him, and he is diaphoretic and is clutching his chest. He has bradycardia, and his last troponin is elevated.	I reviewed the schedule, and there are open slots in the telemedicine schedules.
Recommendation	What do you recommend?	I think he is having an acute myocardial infarction. He needs an EKG, and cardiology needs to see him immediately.	I recommend we update our appointment script to offer patients telemedicine slots if we cannot see them in person in the time they prefer.

Team Huddles

Huddles are short meetings, typically ten minutes or less, held at the beginning of a clinical session or day to confirm that the team is starting out on the same page (Scoville et al. 2016). They are often used to actively manage quality and safety concerns, identify and brainstorm solutions for anticipated difficulties, and share key communication issues. These short meetings may also be an excellent place for leaders to hear and share stories about the practice—stories that can motivate the team. Some settings will hold a brief all-team huddle, in which the clinicians and staff working that day review practice or unitwide announcements. These huddles are then followed by smaller "teamlet" huddles (between, for example, the physician and a medical assistant) to review the specific checklists for the day. To run an effective huddle, most teams follow a standard agenda usually organized by a communication checklist or another tool. For maximum efficiency, the team members must typically do some preparation work before the huddle begins.

Incentives

The term *physician incentives* often conjures up the idea of paying physicians extra compensation for improved performance. While financial compensation is part of the concept of physician incentives, the World Health Organization defines incentives as "all the rewards and punishments that providers face as a consequence of the organizations in which they work, the institutions under which they operate and the specific interventions they provide" (WHO 2008).

While all incentives may include value, they do not have to be financial to be effective (exhibit 1.15). In addition to such financial incentives as wages, working conditions, and performance-linked payment, other incentives include career and professional development, workload management, flexible working arrangements, positive working environments, and access to benefits and support (WHO 2008). As noted in an earlier example in this chapter, a variety of financial and nonfinancial incentives helped drive Enloe Medical Center's success. Specifically, the center used physician

Exhibit 1.15 Types of Physician Incentives

Financial

Terms and conditions of employment:

- Salary or wages
- Pension
- Insurance (e.g., health)
- Allowances (e.g., housing, clothing, child care, transportation, parking)
- Paid leave

Performance payments:

- Achievement of performance targets
- Length of service
- Location or type of work (e.g., remote locations)

Other financial support:

- Fellowships
- Loans: approval, discounting

Nonfinancial

Positive work environment:

- Work autonomy and clarity of roles and responsibilities
- Sufficient resources
- Recognition of work and achievement
- Supportive management and peer structures
- Manageable workload and effective workload management
- Effective management of occupational health and safety, including a safe and clean workplace
- Effective employee representation and communication
- Enforced equal opportunity policy
- Maternity and paternity leave
- Sustainable employment

Flexibility in employment arrangements:

- Flexible work hours
- Planned career breaks

(continued)

Nonfinancial
Support for career and professional development: • Effective supervision • Coaching and mentoring structures • Access to, and support for, training and education • Sabbatical and study leave
Access to services such as the following: • Health   • Housing • Child care and schools   • Transportation • Recreational facilities
Intrinsic rewards: • Job satisfaction   • Respect of colleagues and community • Personal achievement • Commitment to shared values   • Team membership, sense of belonging

Source: Adapted from WHO (2008).

leadership development and solutions to barriers that the physician community was experiencing to deliver care as key incentives to drive engagement (Nelson 2019).

Create Opportunities for Professional Development

Senior leadership that actively creates opportunities for professional development will improve physician engagement. First, a leader needs to communicate and develop trust with physicians over time to be able to identify the skills that they should strengthen for their professional development. That initial investment demonstrates for physicians that the manager or other leader has a vested interest in their individual growth and sees them as a part of the overall future of the organization. Common concepts taught in leadership development include how to sharpen communication skills, deliver feedback, identify opportunities, and lead change. These skills directly support the other practice techniques the senior leader has put in place. Whom the organization chooses to develop, and how well these professionals will progress, will have a significant impact on the healthcare organization's outcomes. For this reason, leaders must carefully consider what type of professional development would benefit the organization. Hopkins and colleagues (2018) reviewed some models of physician leadership programs that are based on education models. The following are some questions to consider as you determine what leadership programming is needed:

- What leadership roles are you looking for the physicians to fill? (Are you looking to develop specific succession planning such as department chairs, service-line leaders, or more general skill building?)
- Among your medical staff, have you identified any common talent gaps for which universal training would be valuable? (If everyone would benefit from basic quality improvement, you may do wide-range training for everyone on the basics and then identify champions for additional professional development as needed.)
- Does your leadership team reflect the diversity of your organization and the community it serves? (Would any types of training encourage certain leaders to develop in a safe space?)
- Do you want to invest in building an internal leadership training program, send leaders out for training, bring in an external consultant, or implement a combination of these approaches? (Do you have local experts who can deliver the development programming you need?)
- How will you engage the physician leaders once they have been trained to use their new skills to support the health system?
- What metrics will you use to define the success of your leadership development program? (Will it be the completion of a training program, the outcomes of a project, the attainment of formal leadership roles, or something else?)

A Scenario with a Solution

Your Journey to Excellent Experiences program described at the beginning of this chapter may have been developed to apply data- and evidence-based approaches to improve the patient satisfaction scores across the institution. But you now realize that you have been gathering input from your physicians rather than engaging and including them. You open up a new document and begin to jot down some notes, including the name of a well-respected physician who can work with you as you move forward. You think about ways you can create more avenues for improving communication. For example, you could start leadership rounds to observe and hear more about what is going on at the front line. You will continue gathering data but will talk to the team about which metrics make the most sense to get to the goals and what barriers they see as preventing you from getting to the goal. Finally, you explore what incentives could be applied to help make the Journey to Excellent Experiences program a better success. It may not be an overnight fix, but you smile remembering the wise adage "If you want to go fast, go alone. If you want to go far, go together." This time, you are going together.

CONCLUSION

Physician engagement is a type of employee engagement that seeks to improve outcomes and profitability by ensuring that physicians feel appreciated, can work safely without fear of negative consequences, and believe they have the physical and mental resources to engage in their work without distractions. Organizations and senior leaders have to be willing to commit to physician engagement as an ongoing quality and performance improvement initiative that includes such resources as talent, time, and dollars.

Partnering administrative and physician leadership in dyad or triad teams can accelerate physician engagement by supporting each leader with the complementary skills from the other member or members of the team. Practical approaches to improving physician engagement often employ a culture of accountability, strengthen communications, identify proper incentives, and create opportunities for professional development.

REFERENCES

Baldwin K. S., N. Dimunation, and J. Alexander. 2011. "Health Care Leadership and the Dyad Model." *Physician Executive* 37 (4): 66–70.

Blizzard, R. 2005. "Nurse Engagement Key to Reducing Medical Errors." Gallup. Published December 27. https://news.gallup.com/poll/20629/nurse-engagement-key-reducing-medical-errors.aspx.

Buell, J. 2017. "The Dyad Leadership Model: Four Case Studies." *Healthcare Executive* 32 (5): 33–40.

Comstock, N. 2019. "Better Together: Most Healthcare Leaders Report Using a Dyad Leadership Model." Medical Group Management Association. Published October 31. www.mgma.com/data/data-stories/better-together-most-healthcare-leaders-report-us.

Dye, C. F., and J. J. Sokolov. 2013. *Developing Physician Leaders for Successful Clinical Integration*. Chicago: Health Administration Press.

Hall, K. 2019. *Stories That Stick: How Storytelling Can Captivate Customers, Influence Audiences, and Transform Your Business*. Nashville, TN: HarperCollins Leadership.

HealthStream. 2017. "Healthcare Leader Rounding with a Purpose: Collecting and Sharing Information." Published September 19. www.healthstream.com/resources/blog/blog/2017/09/19/healthcare-leader-rounding-with-a-purpose-collecting-and-sharing-information.

Hopkins, J., M. Fassiotto, M. C. Ku, D. Mammo, and H. Valantine. 2018. "Designing a Physician Leadership Development Program Based on Effective Models of Physician Education." *Health Care Management Review* 43 (4): 293–302.

James, T. A. 2019. "How Leaders Create a Culture of Accountability in Health Care." *Lean Forward* (Harvard Medical School blog). Published August 15. https://leanforward.hms.harvard.edu/2019/08/15/how-leaders-create-a-culture-of-accountability-in-health-care.

Kahn, W. A. 1990. "Psychological Conditions of Personal Engagement and Disengagement at Work." *Academy of Management Journal* 33 (4): 692–724.

Kruse, K. 2015. "The ROI of Employee Engagement in Hospitals." *Forbes.* Published February 26. www.forbes.com/sites/kevinkruse/2015/02/26/the-roi-of-employee-engagement-in-hospitals/.

Merlino, J. 2017. "Communication: A Critical Healthcare Competency." *Patient Safety & Quality Healthcare.* Published November 6. www.psqh.com/analysis/communication-critical-healthcare-competency.

Nelson, M. 2019. "Physician Engagement: Insights from the Front Lines." *Physician Executive Journal.* Published April 1. www.physician-leaders.org/news/engagement-insights-from-the-front-lines.

O'Hara, C. 2014. "How to Tell a Great Story." *Harvard Business Review.* Published July 30. https://hbr.org/2014/07/how-to-tell-a-great-story.

Partners In Leadership. 2019. "The Power of the Results Pyramid: Achieving Sustainable Culture Change." Published October 7. www.partnersinleadership.com/insights-publications/the-power-of-the-results-pyramid-achieving-sustainable-culture-change.

Perreira, T. A., L. Perrier, M. Prokopy, L. Neves-Mera, and D. D. Persaud. 2019. "Physician Engagement: A Concept Analysis." *Journal of Healthcare Leadership* 11: 101–13.

Savoy, M. L., and P. Yunyongying. 2013. "Getting Through to Your Patients." *Family Practice Management* 20 (6): 36.

Scoville, R., K. Little, K. Rakover, K. Luther, and K. Mate. 2016. "Sustaining Improvement." White paper. Cambridge, MA: Institute for Healthcare Improvement.

Shahid, S., and S. Thomas. 2018. "Situation, Background, Assessment, Recommendation (SBAR) Communication Tool for Handoff in Health Care: A Narrative Review." *Safety in Health.* Published July 28. https://safetyinhealth.biomedcentral.com/articles/10.1186/s40886-018-0073-1.

World Health Organization (WHO). 2008. "Guidelines: Incentives for Health Professionals." Accessed September 27, 2020. www.who.int/workforcealliance/documents/Incentives_Guidelines%20EN.pdf.

Zeis, J. 2017. "NEJM Catalyst Insights Report: Physician–Administrator Shared Leadership Models Are 85% Effective in Health Care Organizations." Cision PRWeb. Published August 17. www.prweb.com/releases/2017/08/prweb14611651.htm.

Zismer, D. K., and J. Brueggemann. 2010. "Examining the 'Dyad' as a Management Model in Integrated Health Systems." *Physician Executive* 36 (1): 14–19.

CHAPTER 2

Physician Engagement as an Antidote to Burnout

Kevin M. Casey

Engagement is the positive antithesis of burnout and is characterized by vigor, dedication, and absorption in work.
—Tait D. Shanafelt and John H. Noseworthy, "Executive Leadership and Physician Well-Being," 2017

Physician burnout is costing the U.S. about $4.6 billion annually when you conservatively estimate the costs related to physician turnover and reduced clinical hours.
—Tanya Albert Henry, "Burnout's Mounting Price Tag," 2019

An online survey of doctors finds an overall physician burnout rate of 42%, which is down from 46% five years ago.
—Sara Berg, "Physician Burnout," 2020

Physician burnout was an epidemic BEFORE the Covid-19 pandemic.
—Lipi Roy, "Doctor, Heal Thyself," 2020

BURNOUT HAS BECOME a widespread topic of discussion and debate in medical circles. While definitions might vary and the amount of reported burnout might not exactly align across studies, many physicians are experiencing some emotional, physical, and mental exhaustion that is hurting their ability to care for patients and function well in a healthcare system. Montgomery (2014) says that burnout should be viewed as "an inevitable outcome of systems . . . fostered all through the career of physicians."

Healthcare leaders who ignore burnout or believe that nothing can be done about it risk the lives of patients and physicians. Moreover, the cost impact is significant. A study done by Han and colleagues (2019) showed that "at an organizational level, the annual cost attributable to burnout in the base-case model was estimated at $7,600 per physician, varying from $3,700 to $11,000 per physician." Couple these costs with the predicted physician shortage through the 2020s, and leaders must do what they can to recruit new physicians to their institutions while retaining those who are already engaged.

Is burnout the opposite of engagement? Some say yes, while others say no. Perhaps the best examination of the question is provided by Maslach, Jackson, and Leiter (2018), who suggest, "Burnout is a psychological syndrome emerging as a prolonged response to chronic interpersonal stressors on the job. The three key dimensions of this response are an overwhelming exhaustion, feelings of cynicism and detachment from the job, and a sense of ineffectiveness and lack of accomplishment. The significance of this three-dimensional model is that it clearly places the individual stress experience within a social context and involves the person's conception of both self and others." The relationships between these three dimensions of burnout are shown in exhibit 2.1.

On the other hand, Maslach, Jackson, and Leiter (2018) also suggest an alternative viewpoint: "However, a different approach has defined work engagement as a persistent, positive affective-motivational state of fulfillment that is characterized by the three components of vigor, dedication, and absorption. In this view, work engagement is an independent and distinct concept, which is not the opposite of burnout."

Exhibit 2.1 Maslach and Leiter Burnout Definition

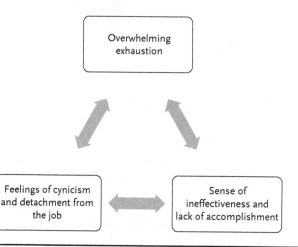

Source: Maslach, Jackson, and Leiter (2016).

IMPACT ON THE HEALTHCARE INSTITUTION

Whether or not it is the opposite of engagement, burnout is undesirable in healthcare organizations. Physicians experiencing burnout can weaken healthcare institutions in many ways. Patel and colleagues (2018) report that "burnout has adverse outcomes on physician well-being, patient care, and the health care system. Doctors who keep working despite experiencing signs of burnout are more likely to have decreased work productivity, exhaustion, and poor quality of care when compared to their earlier careers. Additionally, it can also increase the economic burden of training and recruiting new staff members when efficient physicians quit due to inability to handle stress."

Additionally, physicians experiencing burnout are more likely to retire earlier, change jobs, or exhibit behaviors that will lead to their loss of employment or admitting privileges. The effects burnout has on professional and personal relationships are almost universally negative as well. However, not all physicians are equally aware of how burnout might be affecting them. Whether physicians recognize it or not, burnout is adversely affecting the providers, the patients, and the healthcare institutions.

Burnout Is Workplace Related

According to the World Health Organization (WHO) International Classification of Diseases, "Burn-out refers specifically to phenomena in the occupational context and should not be applied to describe experiences in other areas of life" (WHO 2019). Since the WHO says that burnout is related to the workplace and not to other areas of a physician's life, leaders in healthcare organizations can take measures to help mitigate and possibly eliminate burnout in the workplace—areas that can be directly influenced and controlled by leaders in healthcare. While the idea that burnout is related to the workplace and not to outside circumstance may not be readily accepted by all readers, anyone in healthcare leadership needs to take heed of what is evidently a significant healthcare problem.

SPOTTING BURNOUT

The WHO (2019) also suggests that burnout has three components:

1. Feelings of energy depletion (emotional exhaustion)
2. Increased mental distance from one's job, feelings of negativism or cynicism related to one's job (impersonal responses, cynicism)
3. Reduced professional efficacy (diminished feeling of satisfaction from the job)

Sensing burnout in physicians early is a key tactic for healthcare leaders. Note how each of the three components just identified are what can be called *leading indicators*. By the time all three of them are present, the physician is deeply experiencing burnout, and performance is already significantly affected. An astute leader in healthcare should look for the presence of such leading indicators and, when these signs are identified, should intervene appropriately to prevent the physician from progressing along the continuum toward burnout. Waiting until the physician is demonstrating anhedonia, a depressed mood, or suicidal ideation is a preventable mistake. By the time a physician shows any of those three signs, it is probably much too late for successful intervention while the physician continues to practice medicine. Exhibit 2.2 compares some of the more common leading and lagging indicators of burnout.

What Physicians Say About Burnout

Physicians often report on the consistent contributors to burnout. Many articles have pointed to increasing amounts of bureaucracy, decreasing respect, less autonomy, additional tasks not directly

Exhibit 2.2 Leading and Lagging Indicators of Burnout

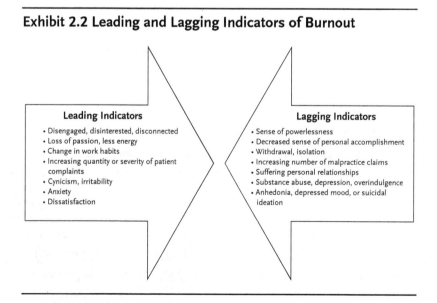

Leading Indicators

- Disengaged, disinterested, disconnected
- Loss of passion, less energy
- Change in work habits
- Increasing quantity or severity of patient complaints
- Cynicism, irritability
- Anxiety
- Dissatisfaction

Lagging Indicators

- Sense of powerlessness
- Decreased sense of personal accomplishment
- Withdrawal, isolation
- Increasing number of malpractice claims
- Suffering personal relationships
- Substance abuse, depression, overindulgence
- Anhedonia, depressed mood, or suicidal ideation

related to the care of patients, and longer working hours with the pressure of family and social responsibilities as drivers of burnout.

Moreover, contrary to what many people may believe, burnout is not about money. Kane (2020) discusses the results in Medscape's 2020 National Physician Burnout & Suicide Report: "Half the doctors said they would give up at least $20,000 in annual income in order to reduce their work hours; some even greater than $75,000 per year. These doctors included millennials, who are among the lowest earners." A more accurate statement about money is that it is a factor for some, but it is not the sole, nor usually the most important, factor contributing to physician burnout. Healthcare leaders who assume that increased pay is a primary satisfier for physicians are ignoring the bigger picture. In fact, in Medscape's 2021 National Physician Burnout and Suicide Report, Kane (2021) reports that the top three causes of burnout are "too many bureaucratic tasks, spending too many hours at work, and lack of respect from administrators/employers, colleagues, or staff."

Relating Burnout to Motivation

Pink (2009) contends that three factors increase a person's performance, satisfaction, and, therefore, engagement in the workplace:

1. **Autonomy:** the desire to be self-directed; increases commitment (engagement) instead of mere compliance
2. **Mastery:** the desire to improve in skills and knowledge
3. **Purpose:** the desire to do something meaningful and important; a focus on profits without purpose leads to disengaged workers

Interestingly, the effects of these three factors on engagement are almost the opposite of those described by people experiencing burnout. Loerbroks and colleagues (2017) say that work engagement

Exhibit 2.3 Pink's Motivational Factors Applied to Burnout Causes

Autonomy	Mastery	Purpose
• Too many bureaucratic tasks (e.g., charting, paperwork) • Too many working hours • Longer working days; pressure of family and social responsibilities	• Too many bureaucratic tasks • Lack of respect • Tasks not directly related to patient care	• Lack of respect • Tasks not directly related to patient care • Organizational focus mainly on finance

"may be conceptualized as the beneficial counterpart of burnout." In stronger terms, *physician engagement is the antidote to burnout.* Pink's three factors are closely related to what physicians identify as the causes of burnout. In fact, as exhibit 2.3 indicates, the causes can all be traced to a problem with at least one of the three factors.

Some of the causes of burnout listed in exhibit 2.3 can be controlled; some cannot. Given the high cost and wide-ranging negative effects of burnout, healthcare organizations must make serious attempts to address the factors that can be influenced or controlled through structural, process, or interpersonal changes.

How Physicians Deal with Burnout

The 2021 Medscape National Physician Burnout & Suicide Report (Kane 2021) lists some interesting ways that physicians self-report coping with burnout. The methods include exercise, talking with family or close friends, isolating oneself from others, sleeping, eating junk food, playing or listening to music, drinking alcohol, or binge eating. Obviously, these coping mechanisms range from healthy to possibly destructive.

Institutions can help physicians find better ways of dealing with burnout through formal or informal physician wellness programs. When physicians are left to "cure" themselves, however, many of their behaviors may be counterproductive. Moreover, when approached with ideas for avoiding burnout, many physicians feel that the organization is suggesting that *they* are the burnout problem, and they resent these measures. Healthcare leaders should suggest burnout-coping mechanisms with their staff members only if the members bring up the topic themselves.

Tips for Leaders

The lenses through which healthcare administrators and physicians look are vastly different. Administrators appreciate and understand healthcare through specific metrics (e.g., productivity, relative value units, ancillary use, staffing, quality ratings, complaints), while physicians tend to look at a more global picture of quality of care, with work–life balance as a factor.

Work–life balance is an important consideration in burnout prevention. The Maslach Burnout Inventory (Maslach, Jackson, and Leiter 2018) has long been recognized as one of the best measures of assessing an individual's personal perception of burnout. The inventory asks questions addressing three primary dimensions—emotional exhaustion, depersonalization, and personal accomplishment. A fourth area, work–life balance, is also included as a significant consideration in an individual's level of burnout.

How things are measured and reported in healthcare only adds to the differences in perspective. Administrators look at most metrics from a negative vantage point (how many errors, how many complaints, lack of productivity), while physicians (like most other people) are more aware of their positives (e.g., the number of patients who say thank-you, the number of patients cared for without errors, the number of referrals received). As these examples show, administrators and physicians can often use conflicting metrics. These different metrics of physician performance often make physicians feel unappreciated by the administration and may even contribute to an adversarial relationship. Because of this potential for conflict, the right physician executive can be very valuable to the administrative team. The ability to see things from both the administrator's and the physician's points of view, and to share this understanding with credibility, can help diminish the amount of confusion and distrust between the two groups. Confusion and distrust significantly chip away at physician engagement.

For healthcare administrators wanting to mitigate physician burnout, the task can appear overwhelming. They need a framework to help manage this complexity. Administrative teams have five systemic areas of focus under their control: (1) work structures and processes, (2) input, (3) appreciation, (4) social connection, and (5) growth and development.

Healthcare leaders wisely identify which areas are more prevalent in regard to burnout in their environment. After identifying these areas, they should consider which solutions provide the best returns to the greatest number of areas, and for as many physicians as possible, and then address these factors immediately.

Work Structures and Processes

Highly reliable work structures and processes contribute much to improving quality, efficiency, and the experiences physicians have as they work. Physicians greatly value these three elements—quality, efficiency, and experience—all of which contribute to high levels of engagement.

Quality, in particular, is a vitally important area of focus for both healthcare administrators and physicians. These two groups should find it easy to cooperate to improve the quality of outcomes. Unfortunately, administrators often blame the "low-quality physician," and physicians often point toward system or facility gaps to excuse less-than-desirable quality. While there are few low-performing physicians, the system or facility gaps are real and much more prevalent. If these problems are addressed appropriately, then the quality of outcomes can improve for all providers. The solution begins when healthcare institutions recognize that they must meet their obligations to their providers. Adequate staffing with minimal turnover allows physicians to know what to expect, to work with a consistent team, and to minimize unnecessary decisions.

Appropriate tools and resources for providers are also paramount. How many times have the wrong preference cards been pulled for a surgeon? How many supply-chain errors occur in the facility weekly? For an administrator to look at each of these as a onetime mistake and not as process problems encourages the persistence of these errors. Every time providers lack the appropriate tools or resources, the deficiency should be investigated from a process-error perspective and addressed as such. Each time an error occurs, it is another proverbial straw on the camel's back and will ultimately lead to disengagement.

Efficiency is another area that challenges physicians. Healthcare system are obligated to help physicians meet their efficiency goals. In a time when physicians are being asked to see more patients in a given period, administrators need to provide these professionals with the tools to do so. Fortunately, many of the same factors that affect quality also affect efficiency. Healthcare administrators must make a concerted effort to address these items.

The use of scribes, technicians who accompany a physician on patient visits and enter the patient's information in the electronic health record (EHR), can be a great benefit to both physicians and healthcare institutions. Scribes afford improved efficiency for the physician, who, relieved of the burden of entering information in the EHR, can see more patients on a given day. Because many providers spend fewer hours in the evenings and weekends charting in an EHR when working with a scribe, they enjoy a more reasonable work–life balance and are therefore less likely to feel burnout.

Finally, the quality of charting and, therefore, reimbursement have demonstrated improvement with the use of a scribe. Gidwani and colleagues (2017) found that "scribes produced significant improvements in overall physician satisfaction, satisfaction with chart quality and accuracy, and charting efficiency without detracting from patient satisfaction. Scribes appear to be a promising strategy to improve health care efficiency and reduce physician burnout." And Mishra and colleagues (2018) indicated that "medical scribes were associated with decreased physician EHR documentation burden, improved work efficiency, and improved visit interactions. Our results support the use of medical scribes as one strategy for improving physician workflow and visit quality in primary care."

Physicians who went to medical school because they wanted to care for patients feel understandably disengaged when they have to spend more than 50 percent of their time at work inputting data into a computer. The consistency of office staff, nurse practitioners, physician assistants, operating theater staff, room layouts, and supplies allows a provider to be more efficient.

Input

For physicians, input is just as important as, or maybe more important than, it is to the general population. Physicians have been trained to be the captain of the ship, with a command-and-control approach to authority. But the teaching and expectations of medical students and residents has not kept up with the cultural changes associated with the shift from independent to employed physicians. At the turn of the new century, few medical school graduates wanted to be employed by a health system; by 2020, an overwhelming majority are employed in this way.

But these new graduates have different expectations. Physicians who once had an independent practice and are now part of a health-care system or multispecialty group are learning new ways to function and to deal with diminished control of their practices. Before they were employed in a healthcare system, a majority of physicians saw a direct correlation between the choices they made and the outcomes they experienced. Studying hard in college and partying less helped them achieve better grades and acceptance to medical school. Working hard in medical school led to their acceptance into a residency and possibly a fellowship. For those who used to practice independently, staffing and overhead costs, as well as scheduling of patients, were under their control. Their choices were directly correlated with financial results, the environment of the workplace, and work–life balance.

Unfortunately, many health systems and facilities now make decisions that directly affect physicians' practice without seeking their input. These organizations neither ask for the physicians' opinions nor communicate the what and why of already-made decisions. This lack of consideration contributes to an often-adversarial relationship between a physician and the administration.

Rounds with Physicians

Healthcare leaders need to regularly conduct rounds with physicians and ask them about what is going well, what presents opportunities for improvement, and any other feedback. When changes are being contemplated, healthcare organizations must ask the affected physicians for their opinions not only to improve engagement and mitigate burnout but also to recognize that physicians sometimes might have a different perspective that could lead to a better decision. Leaders in service lines or offices where changes are expected to continue over time need to ask the physicians to serve on the committees making the decisions. As a guiding principle, physicians should be involved in decisions that affect them. *Involved*, however, does not mean to be in control. Unlike what many administrators might think, physicians are willing to hear the word *no* as long as they believe that their thoughts and opinions have been heard. One of the most damaging things for physician engagement and the relationship with administration is the *slow no*. With a slow no, the provider is not given an answer, in the misguided hope that the concern will go away. The slow no highlights the lack of autonomy a physician is experiencing. This approach has no true benefit and should be avoided at all costs.

Compacts

A physician compact is a written agreement between healthcare leaders and a single physician or several physicians, or between physicians. Because these agreements help the parties clearly define work processes, input, and expectations, they could play a role in preventing burnout. The compact sets forth what each party can expect of the other. Dye and Sokolov (2013) explain that "the process of developing a compact should be a joint exercise and involve representatives of both parties." One of the better-known compacts, the Virginia Mason Medical Center's physician compact, often serves as a guide for other institutions wishing to develop compacts (Virginia Mason Medical Center 2004). For a deeper look at physician compacts, see Kornacki's (2015) excellent book on the subject. Given the increasing complexities that can cause burnout and decrease engagement, the compact concept is well worth consideration.

Appreciation

Demonstrating appreciation is an incredibly effective way to help mitigate burnout and increase engagement and is completely within a leader's control. Leaders' failure to appreciate true clinical work leaves many of them believing that physicians only care about money. Of course, physicians are interested in their compensation. The healthcare industry has set up financial reimbursement as the standard by which physicians can most objectively compare themselves with others to gauge whether they are valued as much as, or more than, others. But reimbursement is definitely not the best mechanism to show appreciation to physicians. Nor is it financially sustainable over the long term for most healthcare entities. There are many more effective and sustainable ways to show appreciation.

Leaders should consider weekly handwritten thank-you notes. Such notes, sent to the home address, where family members might also see them, are one of the most effective means of showing appreciation for anyone, physicians included. Formal recognition programs and processes for physicians who have excelled in any one of many dimensions allow for them to be appreciated in front of peers. And while many places have begun publishing positive patient comments, this tactic reflects the patient's and not the system's or facility leadership's gratitude. Appreciation from the leadership is crucial for increasing alignment and engagement with the healthcare team.

Social Connection

One of the most striking changes in healthcare in the twenty-first century is the loss of the hospital as the central location where physicians would run into each other, socialize, and support one another. With the growth of hospitalist models, many primary care physicians rarely set foot in a hospital at all. Cultural changes have meant that many physicians are no longer being defined by their profession, but like most others, they experience the tension of a career, spouse, family, and other outside pressures. With these changes in the social work setting, a physician's ability to interact with other physicians in a centralized location, such as the medical staff lounge or a hospital hallway, has dramatically declined.

But the dearth of these interactions has not minimized the need for them. As is true with most professions, regular interactions with those who share common experiences and stressors are of real benefit. This benefit is recognized across many dimensions, including the emotional well-being of the physicians, their connection to and engagement with the healthcare system, and quality and safety performance. Regular interactions make a medical staff or group more cohesive, and it is not unusual for a culture to change from "That emergency department doc doesn't know what's going on" to "Dr. X is reasonable, and I am sure this request is for a good reason." Healthcare leaders would wisely spend the time and expense to arrange for social events, meals, and phone calls between physicians as well as between physicians and healthcare leaders to build alignment and comradery.

Growth and Development

While many in the general population see physicians as being at or near the top of a social hierarchy, many physicians themselves feel stagnant as they continue their practice of medicine. Although a physician's feeling of "stuck" may seem counterintuitive to many outside the field, everyone needs to continue to grow, improve, and feel a sense of accomplishment and satisfaction. This need was explained by Pink (2009) as the desire for mastery. To meet this desire on the part of physicians, healthcare organizations can create processes or collaborate with groups that help physicians grow and develop. The organizations can offer opportunities for knowledge development in a specialty, in leadership abilities, or in other professional areas. A healthcare institution that offers growth opportunities for its physicians ultimately improves their engagement.

Burnout Versus Moral Injury

In some instances, physicians and others refer to "moral injury" as something synonymous with burnout. While both moral injury and burnout diminish engagement, they are not the same and must be distinguished. Burnout, as this chapter has demonstrated, can be viewed as an absence of autonomy, mastery, or purpose, and the associated work–life imbalance. Moral injury results when actions taken are in direct conflict with one's understood personal values. For physicians, moral injury often comes from feeling the need to serve competing interests. For example, consider the following vignette.

A primary care physician sees a patient in her office. At the end of the visit, she needs to chart the interaction and order laboratory work. While all this action seems routine, it is more complex and nuanced than many appreciate. The physician has four considerable stakeholders to consider in regard to the charting and ordering of the tests:

- The patient
- The employer of the physician or the healthcare entity
- The insurer
- The physician's own values

In ordering the labs, the physician is encouraged to use the laboratory and other ancillary facilities associated with the healthcare entity, and she is reminded frequently of this desire by the employer. However, the convenience, cost, and responsiveness of the associated ancillary laboratory are inferior to those of a lab closer to, and preferred by, the patient.

Conflict arises when the physician feels pressure to make a choice that is inconsistent with her personal values. In the physician's decision of which facility to recommend, the tension between patient preference, perceived quality, and stated employer preference is real. The physician might be able to be mentally justify any decision one time. But feeling forced to make that choice frequently over the span of many visits may lead to moral injury. The pressure of the decision may lead the physician to resent her employer, the patient, or both. The physician most likely would look for another venue in which she might practice without this conflict.

As this vignette shows, healthcare leaders must listen to physicians' moral quandaries. In this example, if the physician were asked why she did not use the network preferred services for her patient, the administrator should listen to and, when possible, address the physician's concerns. It is very difficult to rebuild a relationship with a physician after resentment has taken seed. Resentment is one of the strongest indicators of disengagement.

CONCLUSION

Physician burnout has been the subject of much discussion and intervention attempts for years. Much of the attention has been placed on the prevalence and recovery of the burned-out physician. A more effective strategy would be to address the causes of burnout as much as possible before a physician experiences it. Fortunately, many of the contributors to burnout are under the influence or control of the healthcare leader. An intentional, organized approach to collaborating with physicians to address these factors can pay tremendous benefits to the healthcare entity. Leaders should recognize that autonomy, mastery, and purpose increase physician engagement, improve healthcare along multiple dimensions, and are the antidotes to burnout.

REFERENCES

Berg, S. 2020. "Physician Burnout: Which Medical Specialties Feel the Most Stress." American Medical Association. Published January 21. www.ama-assn.org/practice-management/ physician-health/physician-burnout-which-medical-specialties-feel-most-stress.

Dye, C. F., and J. J. Sokolov. 2013. *Developing Physician Leaders for Successful Clinical Integration*. Chicago: Health Administration Press.

Gidwani, R., C. Nguyen, A. Kofoed, C. Carragee, T. Rydel, I. Nelligan, A. Sattler, M. Mahoney, and S. Lin. 2017. "Impact of

Scribes on Physician Satisfaction, Patient Satisfaction, and Charting Efficiency: A Randomized Controlled Trial." *Annals of Family Medicine* 15 (5): 427–33.

Han, S., T. D. Shanafelt, C. A. Sinsky, K. M. Awad, L. N. Dyrbye, L. C. Fiscus, M. Trockel, and J. Goh. 2019. "Estimating the Attributable Cost of Physician Burnout in the United States." *Annals of Internal Medicine* 170 (11): 784–90.

Henry, T. A. 2019. "Burnout's Mounting Price Tag: What It's Costing Your Organization." American Medical Association. Published July 5. www.ama-assn.org/practice-management/physician-health/burnout-s-mounting-price-tag-what-it-s-costing-your.

Kane, L. 2021. "Medscape National Physician Burnout & Suicide Report 2021: The Generational Divide." *Medscape*. Published January 22. www.medscape.com/slideshow/2021-lifestyle-burnout-6013456.

———. 2020. "Medscape National Physician Burnout & Suicide Report 2020: The Generational Divide." *Medscape*. Published January 15. www.medscape.com/slideshow/2020-lifestyle-burnout-6012460.

Kornacki, M. J. 2015. *A New Compact: Aligning Physician–Organization Expectations to Transform Patient Care.* Chicago: Health Administration Press.

Loerbroks, A., J. Glaser, P. Vu-Eickmann, and P. Angerer. 2017. "Physician Burnout, Work Engagement and the Quality of Patient Care." *Occupational Medicine* 67 (5): 356–62.

Maslach, C., S. E. Jackson, and M. P. Leiter. 2018. *Maslach Burnout Inventory: Manual.* Menlo Park, CA: Mind Garden.

Mishra, P., J. C. Kiang, and R. W. Grant. 2018. "Association of Medical Scribes in Primary Care with Physician Workflow and Patient Experience." *JAMA Internal Medicine* 178 (11): 1467–72.

Montgomery, A. 2014. "The Inevitability of Physician Burnout: Implications for Interventions." *Burnout Research* 1 (1): 50–56.

Patel, R. S., R. Bachu, A. Adikey, M. Malik, and M. Shah. 2018. "Factors Related to Physician Burnout and Its Consequences: A Review." *Behavioral Sciences* (Basel) 8 (11): 98.

Pink, D. H. 2009. *Drive: The Surprising Truth About What Motivates Us.* New York: Riverhead Books.

Roy, L. 2020. "Doctor, Heal Thyself: Physician Burnout in the Wake of Covid-19." *Forbes.* Published May 17. www.forbes.com/sites/lipiroy/2020/05/17/doctor-heal-thyself-physician-burnout-in-the-wake-of-covid-19/.

Shanafelt, T. D., and J. H. Noseworthy. 2017. "Executive Leadership and Physician Well-Being: Nine Organizational Strategies to Promote Engagement and Reduce Burnout." *Mayo Clinic Proceedings* 92 (1): 129–46.

Virginia Mason Medical Center. 2004. "Virginia Mason Medical Center Physician Compact." Accessed January 26, 2021. http://content.hcpro.com/pdf/content/289972.pdf.

World Health Organization (WHO). 2019. "Burn-Out an 'Occupational Phenomenon': International Classification of Diseases." Published May 28. www.who.int/mental_health/evidence/burn-out/en.

CHAPTER 3

The Electronic Health Record

Walter C. Kerschl

There are only two ways to influence human behavior:
you can manipulate it or you can inspire it.
—Simon Sinek, *Start with Why*, 2011

SIMON SINEK (2011) speaks to always starting with the *why* to communicate the importance of everything we do. This chapter is no different—it begins with the vision of the electronic health record (EHR) and why physician engagement is so important for its success.

In considering the EHR, we must examine why these electronic systems were first created. Even though healthcare systems aimed to improve quality and patient care by giving physicians a holistic view of each patient's record, the EHR has generally fallen short of achieving that aspiration. Initially the EHR was intended to be a way to code, bill, and collect efficiently. The record was often incomplete and took countless clicks and much data input to create even a fraction of a patient's complete medical record. Data was not interfaced between disparate systems. If any interface existed, perhaps only labs and radiology from the same healthcare organization would flow into the record. Outside records or data still existed only on paper and at best were either laboriously entered as discrete data into the record or, more likely, just scanned into the record, only to be buried in the electronic chart. This lack of an interface and the mixture of input methods created a hard-to-navigate record, with important pieces of information out of sight for physicians. Ultimately, this system left support staff, nurses, and physicians spending more time with the records and less time with patients.

There is a bright side. Over the years, organizations have made gradual progress in creating a holistic record with more interoperability. Such systems reduce the cognitive load for physicians, freeing them up to focus on what matters. With the Health Information Technology for Economic and Clinical Health Act of 2009 and meaningful-use incentives, healthcare organizations were encouraged to implement and adopt an EHR. The assumption was that care would improve with the holistic view of a patient's health record; but initially, little interoperability existed. Despite the solid vision, the incentives for physicians' adoption of the EHR did not align with its purpose.

As healthcare organizations make meaningful change and increasingly focus on physician engagement, they must clarify the purpose of the EHR and share this purpose with physicians—an effort that will further engage them. Halcom (2017) writes about five ways that the EHR improves the quality of patient care:

1. Coordination of care
2. Improved diagnosis
3. Lower cost
4. Improved patient experience
5. Fewer errors

Most healthcare leaders would agree that if the EHR is designed, implemented, taught, and supported correctly (and, of course, has all the capabilities needed), most of the five preceding outcomes can be achieved at some level. The clear link that is desperately and consistently needed is broad engagement and buy-in from physicians from the start. Engagement will in turn contribute to success, ultimately improve the care delivered to patients, and create less burnout among all who use these systems. As the future of the EHR and other technologies that promise to further improve care and help untether clinicians from the keyboard are examined, work with machine learning and other types of artificial intelligence, interoperability, and portability of the health record all hold additional promise.

MOVING PAST THE WHY

In light of the importance of the EHR, leadership's struggles to implement it, and the progress achieved so far, a pivotal factor in the EHR's effectiveness is how to better engage the physician end user. As with other healthcare efforts, physician engagement is clearly tied to the EHR's success in achieving the best patient care and experience possible. How does the EHR achieve this goal? Does the EHR vendor drive these changes? Does the government support the quest for the best possible care through the use of an electronic tool designed to keep all pertinent information readily available? Or does the end user become empowered to drive these changes? Most would agree it is a combination of all these efforts. But undeniably, without physician engagement, the endeavor will not succeed.

THE WHAT

An important consideration of EHRs is how physicians view this technology. A 2018 Harris poll indicated that 49 percent of primary care physicians consider EHRs a storage tool, not a clinical one, and about half say that EHRs detract from their clinical effectiveness (Stanford Medicine 2018). The poll also indicated that seven out of ten physicians disagree with the statement that "my EHR has strengthened my patient relationship." On the other hand, the report also says that "two-thirds of PCPs (66%) report that they are satisfied with their current EHR system," but they also believe that substantial improvements are needed. With these conflicting statistics, how will physician engagement be strengthened? Can the engagement of the end users and the way change is managed be the critical factors with these technology initiatives?

To start, let us examine why initiatives fail in the first place, regardless of what they are. Jorgensen, Bruehl, and Franke (2014) describe a study done by IBM surveying individuals whose job it was to manage change successfully. The employees in this survey were responsible for the success of various projects. Despite their presumed expertise, only 48 percent of projects finished on time and within budget and met the quality goals laid out initially. What caused the failures more than half the time? The results clearly showed the most effect on success was what was called the soft factors:

- Top management sponsorship
- A shared vision
- Corporate culture that motivates and promotes change
- Honest and timely communication
- Ownership of change by middle management
- Employee involvement
- Change agents

Jorgensen, Bruehl, and Franke (2014) also write that "driving successful change starts from the top and includes the entire organization—top management sponsorship, middle management empowerment and an overall corporate culture that promotes change at every level of the organization." Other factors like the skill sets of the project team, efficient training programs, and regular status reports (project management) were important but not to the extent of the soft factors. Healthcare leaders should take careful note that if these factors are not recognized, failure is more likely.

Soft Factors Involve Adaptive Change

What does the importance of soft factors mean for physicians and their engagement in health information technology (IT) projects and beyond? The soft factors just mentioned are what most would call *adaptive challenges*, rather than technical ones. Heifetz and Linsky (2002) explain this contrast: "Technical problems, while often challenging, can be solved applying existing know-how and the organization's current problem-solving processes. Adaptive problems resist these kinds of solutions because they require individuals throughout the organization to alter their ways; as the people themselves are the problem, the solution lies with them."

Why must healthcare leaders understand the difference between these two kinds of challenges? Technical problems are easy to identify and can lead to quick solutions. Most people understand the need for change and are receptive to the solution. Adaptive problems are just the opposite. They often are difficult to identify, require changes within ourselves, and often are resisted because we all *want change*, but no one *wants to change.*

Clinical decisions illustrate the differences between technical and adaptive change. For a patient with elevated blood pressure, for example, a physician can quickly prescribe medications to treat the blood pressure and can ignore the underlying causes. This technical solution is easy, quick, and understandable. However, blood pressure issues should be treated like adaptive challenges. Clinicians should first address lifestyle changes, which are more effective in the long term to help patients maintain a healthier lifestyle and thus succeed in their blood pressure control in the future with or without medication. If lifestyle changes are the goal, physicians should always start with the adaptive change. To change one's behavior, though, is harder and takes a while to create results, and patients often resist the change. Ultimately, if they are engaged in their care and invested in their own health, they are more likely to improve and live healthier lives.

The preceding example demonstrates clearly why the technical and the adaptive approaches are so intertwined. Technical solutions aim to quickly address the "hardware" of a problem and fix it (a physician prescribes medication). Adaptive solutions look at the big picture and try long-term, behavioral solutions (a physician encourages exercise). Because a combination of the technical and the adaptive (medication and exercise) works best, physicians must be engaged to encourage patients in the more difficult changes like an exercise regimen, which is harder to execute than is merely popping a pill. See exhibit 3.1 to understand the differences between these two types of change.

If healthcare leaders focus on the soft factors listed earlier, clear communication of the why and the shared vision will help increase

Exhibit 3.1 Technical Problems Versus Adaptive Challenges

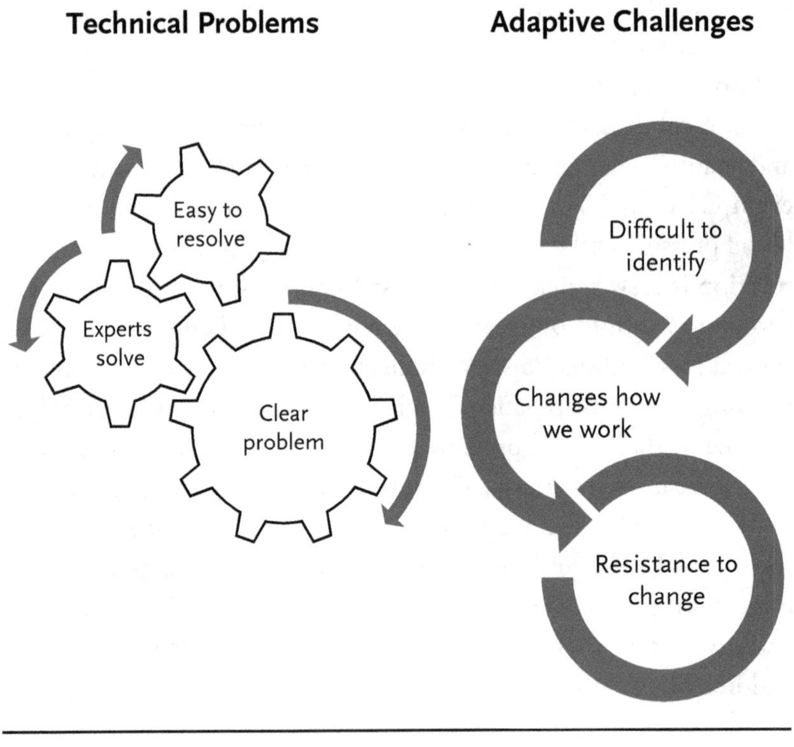

Technical Problems

Adaptive Challenges

engagement in, and commitment to, the organization's initiatives. All senior leaders and their management teams should be able to communicate this shared vision and engage physicians in their quest to deliver the very best healthcare to their patients. If leaders understand this and can ensure that all parties have the same goals, the level of engagement and partnership will increase exponentially.

Miller, Johnson, and Grau (1994) focused on how people experience a change. Their study included how it affected people's tasks, their relationships, and, finally, their identity. The researchers found that "employees receiving 'quality' information about the change in having a high need for achievement viewed the change favorably. Contrary to expectations, employees' anxiety about the change did not influence their attitude about change." Proponents of change must therefore be acutely aware of organizational culture and must make every attempt to improve the culture.

Herein lies the problem that has been perpetuated over the years and that partly explains why EHRs have not been adopted fully and have not provided the value most physicians seek. An organization should start with the why of EHRs and share its vision with physicians. Leadership should help them see that they can have better tools to care for their patients and, by using these tools, create more complete medical records. Additionally, with better systems, physicians no longer need to act like data entry clerks, a job that distracts them from patient care. Physicians also need systems that are easy to use, intuitive to navigate, and efficient in producing notes and orders such as prescriptions and patient education.

Physician engagement must be considered in the design and implementation of a change that works. If changes are run like IT projects and not clinical ones, they often are designed, built, and implemented from a technical perspective and thereby miss the true intent. The end users do not feel connected or empowered; they have no skin in the game. Obviously, they will not embrace, let alone adopt and use, a system they did not help design. Lack of end user engagement is the adaptive challenge of many technical solutions.

THE IKEA EFFECT

This is a great time to discuss the IKEA effect. Norton, Mochon, and Ariely (2012) describe the effect this way: "Labor alone can be sufficient to induce greater liking for the fruits of one's labor: even constructing a standardized bureau, an arduous, solitary task, can lead people to overvalue their (often poorly constructed) creations." Carter (2012) agrees: "The act of building something, putting your own blood and sweat (and if we're being honest, plenty of frustrated swearing) into a physical object, seems to imbue it with additional value above and beyond its inherent quality."

So, if people feel much more connected to objects they just spent hours assembling, consider how physicians would feel if they were closely involved from the get-go in choosing and designing the EHR system. Consider their feelings of inclusiveness if they interacted with the vendor on creating better workflow and working through design and build issues. Think about their buy-in if they helped train, coach, and implement *their* system. How would this inclusion affect their willingness to be engaged at all levels of a project? If the system is designed with physician input, would it be adopted fully? Would this inclusiveness help achieve the why of improving the care of patients, lowering costs and maximizing the experience of both patients and end users? If all these potential achievements sound like the quadruple aim (i.e., the standard triple aim of improving population health, patient experience of care, and lowering cost, with the addition of care for the providers constituting the fourth aim), they are indeed the quadruple aim. This aim is the ultimate why of the EHR.

THE HOW

As discussed, healthcare administrators need to lead with an understanding of the soft factors and to apply adaptive techniques to change initiatives. Also as discussed, the IKEA effect helps get people engaged. The question remains: How do physicians become engaged

Exhibit 3.2 The Power of Partnership and Shared Vision

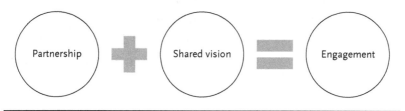

in EHR projects when their primary focus is patient care? Leaders should consider two other factors—partnering and a shared vision. Exhibit 3.2 suggests that these two factors, when combined, create engagement.

First, note that partnership is not alignment. Alignment often carries an undesirable connotation. The word *alignment* conveys to physicians the negative suggestion that they must march to the orders of the organization. With a true partnership, each party understands the value the other brings to the shared vision. And this vision should be improving patient care through enhanced quality, a better experience for the patient, and increased patient loyalty. When those elements of the vision are achieved, physicians feel empowered as a crucial and meaningful part of the organizational team. They feel a part of something important.

The other component of engagement, a true shared vision, must bring together both physicians, who are dedicated to the care of patients, and administrators, who, interestingly, are also dedicated to the same thing, in a partnership. Thus, each group respects the other and that group's expertise. This mutual vision is often misunderstood by many physicians, who believe that the administration is only focused on generating revenue. "No margin, no mission" is a common expression in this field: If a healthcare institution cannot make a profit, then it cannot support its mission. The shared vision may even need to be changed, depending on the audience, although it means the same thing: better patient experiences and care, which lead to loyalty to your organization.

The combination of a strong sense of partnership and a shared vision provides the formula for the power of engagement. When the medical staff's engagement is strong throughout the organization, physicians suddenly want to participate in the design and optimization of the EHR and use the system because they are now invested, connected, and committed to its success.

How the Informatics Department Can Help Physicians with the EHR

To achieve this level of engagement with changes in EHR processes, organizations must help physicians change how they interact with leadership, particularly with members of the organization's informatics department. Past experiences have left many physicians disengaged with the organization's decisions about IT; they believe that nothing will change, despite their input. If healthcare leaders want different results, they must work to understand why physicians are hesitant to trust the leaders in the informatics department. Connors and Smith (2011) describe the problem: "Too often, leaders attempt to change the way people act without changing the way they think (i.e., their beliefs). As a result, they get compliance, but not commitment; involvement, but not investment; and progress, but not lasting performance." In time, helping physicians develop different beliefs will then affect their actions and thereby provide different, improved results. Without understanding this concept, leaders will continue to maintain a culture that will lead to disengagement at all levels and will prevent the successful implementation of the EHR and other health IT. The following actions could help leaders avoid pitfalls in engaging physicians in an updated EHR initiative:

- Have a true shared vision that is developed by a cross-venue team.
- Make sure that an executive who is passionate about the work sponsors the project and is accountable.

- Develop a guiding coalition that engages and enables the healthcare organization by communicating the vision and empowering action.
- Allow for quick wins, which are especially valuable because they show that a person's feedback can make changes happen quickly. When physicians' input produces quick wins, people place more value on this input.
- Develop an ever-increasing champion base of physicians across all specialties. This base will support the desired changes and the adoption of the system.

Each of these actions adds to the positive experiences of physicians, who will be more likely to eventually support a desired change in EHR processes. But these actions are not without their hurdles, as truly changing culture is neither an easy nor a fast process. Some of the hurdles to engagement that should be addressed head-on include these:

- **Bad history:** The memories of past negative change experiences can loom large in the minds of physicians. Healthcare leaders should acknowledge these past difficulties and not let them become the elephant in the room. Physicians are sensitive to leaders who do not respect their input and feedback.
- **Slow or hard-to-notice improvements:** One of the quickest ways to discourage engagement efforts is to fail to show physicians how a project is progressing and thereby giving the impression of slow or no progress. Physicians usually operate in a clinical environment where progress moves quickly.
- **Vendors that appear not to listen:** Anders (2019) describes a common problem with the development of EHR systems: "Unfortunately, EHR vendors, as well as health system leaders, rarely seek direct input from

physicians to understand what doctors want and need in their EHRs." This lack of consideration, though, is changing as more vendors seek input from the end users, especially physicians. The problem that arises is resourcing from the vendor side. Vendors are often fighting with competing requests for their intellectual property such as for population health, consumerism, and artificial intelligence and machine learning ventures. All these competing demands put a strain on the speed to development in new functionality and new workflows, which again can be perceived as being slow to respond or not listening.

- **Lack of communication from IT or leadership:** As in any new business process, communication is critical. Physicians' past lack of engagement with EHRs partly stems from their sense that IT and the organization's leadership are a black hole: Physicians may bring up a concern or share an idea, but they then feel that no one ever communicates back with them. Or physicians might be waiting for the "golden upgrade" but again receive no communication about what is being done; nor is there a channel for them to give input or to receive information about how changes will affect their clinical practices.

- **Lack of true sharing or understanding of a vision:** If your vision is not created as a team undertaking, in which you invite physicians to the table and listen to them intently, it will not be your guiding light, and you are unlikely to get the engagement you need.

Physicians' engagement with the EHR depends on several areas designed to achieve better workflow, provide more efficiency, and allow physicians to spend less time in record keeping and more time with patients. The following examples are features of an EHR system that can engage physicians:

- **Customized workflow:** Customization means that the EHR meets the needs of each specialist and individual physician. It allows these professionals to practice the way they see best, not the way the vendor sees as optimal.
- **Maximum allowable participation by staff members:** Support staff should be prepping charts and participating in all the steps allowed by their license and the compliance officer, to make the EHR optimal for physicians and other end users.
- **Streamlining:** Repetitive tasks need to be streamlined and done by others when appropriate or automated as much as possible.
- **Interoperability:** Clinicians must stop being data entry specialists. The system's interoperability must be put to best use.

BUILDING SATISFACTION WITH THE EHR

The KLAS Arch Collaborative has done extensive research and surveys on the use of the EHR. In their "Arch Collaborative Guidebook 2019," Davis and Bice (2019) indicate the top three items that predict satisfaction with the EHR: (1) strong mastery by the user, (2) the ability of the EHR to meet the unique needs of the user, and (3) shared ownership of the technology.

John Lee, the former chief medical information officer at Edward-Elmhurst Health, writes, "The Arch Collaborative has taken anecdotal stories of physician dissatisfaction and given them objectivity. Instead of reflexively listening to the loudest complainer, we now have data to guide us in our efforts to make our systems work for our physicians rather than the other way around" (Lee 2020).

Strong User Mastery

Training is often undervalued both before, during, and after the EHR system is installed and goes live. The implementation of the system is not a one-and-done process, but after the system goes live, folks often feel that they are finished. They pat themselves on the back and thank everyone for a job well done. Of course, it is acceptable to thank participants for reaching this milestone, but the process has only just begun. The organization must arrange for physicians and other clinical staff to be continuously educated and trained on the use of the EHR. This training must be a priority for the initiative's present and future success. Some vendors require training. They set out parameters that the organizations must follow if they are to go live with the products. Although organizational leaders may disagree with this authoritarian approach by vendors, the point is well taken and is borne out by the Arch Collaborative results. Davis and Bice (2019) write that "perhaps more important than the requirements set by the vendors, are the ongoing EHR education expectations established by the health system for their end users. Maintaining up to date knowledge, with just a couple of hours of ongoing EHR education per year, is critical for both satisfaction and efficiency with the EHR."

The Ability to Meet User Needs

A workload that is spiraling out of control is obviously detrimental to a physician's well-being. One way to help physicians avoid this danger is by teaching them to personalize the EHR to meet their unique needs. Personalization is truly something physicians have long wanted in the EHR. While it is customary and appropriate to standardize order sets and certain pieces of the technology, the ability to create the workflow as physicians want it, in light of what they consider optimal for their own best practices, ultimately leads to better engagement overall. Again, Davis and Bice (2019) suggest that "the best part is that personalizing the EHR very rarely requires a code change. In many cases, it only takes a few minutes of instruction to show physicians that there is a different and better way of going about their day in the EHR."

Shared Ownership

As already discussed, culture is a key factor for success of any organization. If it is not intentionally understood, changed when needed, and improved as needed, organizations will face almost certain negative results. Culture should also be changed through a mutual partnership and action. Successful use of the EHR depends on a variety of groups: the end users, the health systems leadership, and the vendor. Ultimately, if the end users feel that they lack a voice or a way to influence the EHR, then it is hard to enact change. Davis and Bice (2019) present it in this manner: "The bottom line with culture is to be sure that culture is addressed. While it may be a tiresome cliché, the old saying that 'culture will eat strategy for lunch' is certainly applicable here."

PHYSICIAN WELL-BEING

The final consideration in engaging physicians in the EHR is their well-being. Leadership must consider physician well-being if they want a healthy organizational culture and a healthy medical staff. It is no secret, however, that more physicians are experiencing significant burnout. Their well-being affects not only every part of the healthcare sector but also their families, friends, and colleagues.

Shanafelt and Noseworthy (2016) explain the challenge: "Electronic health records hold great promise for enhancing coordination of care and improving quality of care. In their current form and implementation, however, they have had a number of unintended negative consequences including reducing efficiency, increasing clerical burden, and increasing the risk of burnout for physicians."

How does physician well-being or burnout relate to the EHR? Does the use of EHRs contribute to burnout? Are they the major contributors? Some might say yes, but this would be an overstatement. Many studies show that burnout has many causes. One thing is certain: EHRs should enhance physicians' well-being and the practice of medicine; any shortcomings in the technology can and should be dealt with through continuous optimization. To optimize this technology, leaders must actively seek out, listen to, and act on physician feedback. In this way, organizations can and must do better, as valuing physician feedback is a way to support and to improve care across the community.

EHR technology has seen many enhancements, and more are coming, with the move to the cloud and the investments in artificial intelligence and machine learning. Vendors are seeing that interoperability must be universal and that data blocking is no longer tolerated (it never should have been). What key principles should healthcare leaders follow to maintain everyone's well-being?

- Keep up-to-date with insurance and medical coding. Staying on top of changes is a sure way to help drive the value these systems bring. As needed enhancements are developed from the feedback of end users, these improvements will not be realized if organizations are using old code.
- Keep training alive. It is a continuous process that does not stop when the system goes live.
- Teach physicians about ways to personalize their system so that it works for their workflow style. For example, they could learn about the abilities of an EHR to allow physicians to create their own note templates, dot phrases (text expanders), or macros for repetitive documentation or tasks.

- Take advantage of the tools of artificial intelligence and machine learning, although they are in the early stages of development in the EHR, to reduce the cognitive burden.

Shanafelt and Noseworthy (2016) recommend finding ways to incorporate these tools in a manner that does not increase the clerical burden for physicians or reduce their efficiency. As they explain, "burnout has been shown to erode quality of care, increase risk of medical errors, and lead physicians to reduce clinical work hours, suggesting that the net effect of these electronic tools on quality of care for the U.S. health care system is less clear."

Engaged physicians translate into more satisfied patients and better outcomes. And optimized EHRs, partly because of involved, engaged physicians, certainly help to drive these better outcomes. Now more than ever, physicians must be engaged at the highest level in their organizations' leadership and informatics. They must participate in change—and good change, no less. If physicians are not using the systems as intended, then society will not realize the original reason behind the use of health IT. Organizations have to seek out physician input, listen carefully to it, and show quick wins to change the perceptions and experiences of the physicians. If these professionals feel and experience positive change, more will become champions and help drive the future initiatives forward in all aspects of the organization's imperatives.

CONCLUSION

Leadership must always remember the why for engagement with the EHR, the drive behind IT, and what the future holds. They must also understand and apply the keys to physician satisfaction and the principles of managing change and pay attention to physician well-being. Leaders should keep in mind the ultimate purpose of healthcare organizations: providing the best patient experiences possible with the highest level of quality. With engaged physicians at all levels of healthcare, especially in the informatics arena, medicine will be transformed, and healthcare will also achieve the quadruple aim.

REFERENCES

Anders, J. 2019. "Industry Voices: If Doctors Had Their Way, What Would They Really Want in Their EHRs?" *Fierce Healthcare*. Published October 25. www.fiercehealthcare.com/practices/industry-voices-if-doctors-had-their-way-what-would-they-really-want-their-ehrs.

Carter, T. J. 2012. "The IKEA Effect: Why We Cherish Things We Build." *Psychology Today*. Published September 13. www.psychologytoday.com/us/blog/make-your-mind/201209/the-ikea-effect-why-we-cherish-things-we-build.

Connors, R., and T. Smith. 2011. *Change the Culture, Change the Game: The Breakthrough Strategy for Energizing Your Organization and Creating Accountability for Results*. New York: Portfolio Penguin.

Davis, T., and C. Bice. 2019. "Arch Collaborative Guidebook 2019." KLAS Research. Published July 25. https://klasresearch.com/archcollaborative/report/arch-collaborative-guidebook-2019/293.

Halcom, J. B. 2017. "5 Ways EHR Software Improves Quality Patient Care." *Becker's Health IT*. Published March 9. www.beckershospitalreview.com/healthcare-information-technology/5-ways-ehr-software-improves-quality-patient-care.html.

Heifetz, R. A., and M. Linsky. 2002. *Leadership on the Line: Staying Alive Through the Dangers of Leading*. Boston: Harvard Business School Press.

Jorgensen, H.-H., O. Bruehl, and N. Franke. 2014. "Making Change Work . . . While the Work Keeps Changing: How Change Architects Lead and Manage Organizational Change." IBM Global Business Services. Published August. www.ibm.com/downloads/cas/WA3NR3NM.

Lee, J. 2020. "What Is the Arch Collaborative?" *Research and Insights* (KLAS Research blog). Accessed February 15, 2021. https://klasresearch.com/arch-collaborative.

Miller, V. D., J. R. Johnson, and J. Grau. 1994. "Antecedents to Willingness to Participate in a Planned Organizational Change." *Journal of Applied Communication Research* 22 (1): 59–80.

Norton, M. I., D. Mochon, and D. Ariely. 2012. "The IKEA Effect: When Labor Leads to Love." *Journal of Consumer Psychology* 22 (3): 453–60.

Shanafelt, T. D., and J. H. Noseworthy. 2016. "Executive Leadership and Physician Well-Being: Nine Organizational Strategies to Promote Engagement and Reduce Burnout." *Mayo Clinic Proceedings* 2 (1): 129–46.

Sinek, S. 2011. *Start with Why: How Great Leaders Inspire Everyone to Take Action*. Harlow, England: Penguin Books.

Stanford Medicine. 2018. "How Doctors Feel About Electronic Health Records: National Physician Poll by the Harris Poll." Accessed January 22, 2021. https://med.stanford.edu/content/dam/sm/ehr/documents/EHR-Poll-Presentation.pdf.

CHAPTER 4

Making the Most of the Chief Medical Officer

Terry R. McWilliams

Without a CMO, hospitals are poorly equipped to address the inherent conflicts between autonomous physicians and hospital goals.
—Martha Sonnenberg, "Changing Roles and Skill Sets for Chief Medical Officers," 2018

IT SHOULD BE a given: Physician engagement is key to organizational success in enhancing high-quality, value-based care delivery; expense management; and reimbursement. And effective physician leadership is one primary step to physician engagement. For a variety of reasons, the chief medical officer (CMO) position has become emblematic of physician leadership for organizations.

Many organizations have added CMO positions to their formal management structures over the past couple of decades. Moreover, many physicians have contemplated CMO career paths and have undertaken efforts to prepare for those roles. Yet in spite of the burgeoning presence of CMOs, those in this position often struggle with dilemmas related to their roles and responsibilities. Getting the CMO formula right is important and can significantly enhance physician engagement.

DOES THE ORGANIZATION NEED A CMO?

Organizations can struggle with the concept of adding a CMO position, for several reasons. First, the business case and return on investment for such a position can be uncertain. In most cases, the CMO is the second-highest-paid leader in the C-suite. In weighing the cost–benefit ratio of adding an actual, tangible expense against a relatively intangible value-added benefit, the organization needs to have a strong belief in the proposition and a leap of faith that the position will ultimately pay for itself. Sonnenberg (2018) suggests that "the CMO is, ultimately, like the orchestra conductor: Without that role, we may have many expert performers, and a beautifully written score, but we do not have the symphonic music that delights the listener. The CMO's role is no longer a luxury, but a necessity for the successful functioning of today's hospitals and health care organizations."

Old Battles Between the Administration and Physicians

Making that leap of faith can be a challenge for organizational leaders who carry the scars from prior physician–administration battles. Moreover, the historic us-versus-them mindset that was entrenched in interactions between medical staff and administration might well continue into the future. Stereotypes exist for a reason, and C-suite members may not be able to shake memories of interactions in which entitled physicians made unrealistic demands and threatened to take their business elsewhere unless the demands were met—playing one organization against another. And in many areas of the country, so-called splitters (physicians who maintain admitting privileges in more than one organization) still exist. Although the expansion of physician employment may limit a physician's ability to manipulate an employer with threats to move to a competing group, the organization still needs to retain and avoid alienating employed physicians. This need is juxtaposed with the desire to advance the employed physician network without alienating critical independent practices. Some organizations may view the CMO as the role responsible for achieving those balances.

Whom Does the CMO Represent?

For many CEOs, the idea of including physicians in the health system's formal leadership structure may feel like having the fox guard the henhouse. These CEOs will have a tough time looking beyond their misgivings to see the benefits of having physician leadership at the table during all debates, discussions, and operational and strategic planning sessions to create a more robust decision, initiative, or other end product. Additionally, with physicians involved, the final product of these leadership decisions may be more practically implemented and executed— and have physician ownership, which is much preferred over the need to obtain physician buy-in for administration-developed initiatives. Not only is the CMO a built-in champion for key decisions and their development processes, but medical staff are more likely to accept the decision, and do it more readily, when a CMO was involved from the start. Health executives can further solidify the medical staff's acceptance by including other physician leaders or leadership groups in the discussion and development process.

The representation and advocacy roles are critical aspects of not only the CMO but also any other physician leader position. These features also have a direct impact on any effort to enhance physician engagement. Some observers—both physicians and nonphysicians—maintain that the role of the CMO is to serve as a sort of chief union steward, someone who always sides with physicians, no matter the issue. Many physicians lament the CMOs who they believe are simply acting as suits and who are perceived to follow top-down, autocratic leadership. Organizations would be well served to fully vet the CMO and other physician leader functions to ensure clarity on the roles and responsibilities.

CMO Versus Other C-Suite Leaders

Others in the C-suite may have their own biases and battle scars. The chief nursing officer (CNO) may have not only scars from previous battles with physicians, but even open wounds—or at least carryover perceptions of prior physician–nurse hierarchies. These biases can cause tremendous reluctance to directly engage a physician in the formal leadership structure and functions. An inability to overcome past experiences is indeed unfortunate, as synergistic physician–nurse leadership or management dyads can be highly effective. Chief financial officers (CFOs) may have trouble overcoming the perception (or reality) that physicians neither understand nor care about finances, including profits and losses, or that they are unconcerned with the details. Many CFOs are surprised to find that the new generation of CMOs are better prepared and are eager to learn more about what they have not mastered.

CMOs of the Past: The Coast into Retirement

Some organizations struggle with past perceptions that CMOs were typically physicians who were nearing the end of their careers and wanted to keep busy and be involved without spending inordinate hours in direct patient care. Yet many of these types of CMOs did not devote sufficient effort to make a full transition to true leadership, and their contributions were negligible. Moreover, the rest of the C-suite executives rarely viewed them as authentic senior leaders. Most organizations have blown this model out of the water. They pursue physicians who have dedicated effort to become well versed in administrative areas and who seek a career as a physician executive in medical administration.

Organization Size for CMO Position

Some organizational leaders believe that a CMO becomes necessary only if the organization reaches a certain size or complexity. This has likely become an outdated assessment. The healthcare environment is complex, regardless of the size of the organization. Having physician leaders at the table during operational and strategic processes makes a difference for organizations of any size. Size may matter when an institution is considering whether the CMO is a full-time administrative position or a part-time one—but not whether a good CMO will add benefit. And in larger organizations, additional part-time physician leaders may supplement the work of a full-time physician leader. Nevertheless, size and complexity do make a difference. Dyrda (2017) reported that 96 percent of health systems (which do constitute much larger organizations) report having a physician executive.

KNOWING WHAT TO LOOK FOR

Three major issues—title, roles, and responsibilities—pose challenges in filling physician executive positions. For example, is there a real distinction between the titles CMO, vice president of medical affairs (VPMA), chief clinical officer, and chief physician executive? The question may be the ultimate what's-in-a-name? quandary. Many individuals freely admit they really don't know the differences between these titles. Dister (2009) reports that 48 percent of the respondents to a survey thought that the CMO and VPMA positions are essentially the same, whereas 52 percent perceived a difference. Those who perceived a difference indicated that the CMO title was more strategic, had broader responsibilities, and was more externally focused and that the VPMA title was more internally focused and more involved in the day-to-day functions of the medical staff office and medical staff operations.

The distinction between titles may be more of an issue in larger organizations, which may have several physician executives. In these organizations, the CMO (or perhaps the chief physician executive) adopts a more visionary or strategic role and has other physician leaders as direct reports. This arrangement is typically the case at the health-system level, where the CMO title is common and where these individuals are more strategically and externally focused. The health system usually then adopts common physician executive titles across member entities. In smaller organizations, a single individual often fulfills all functions of the role—with either a CMO or a VPMA title, or both of them.

The general organizational management structure can also be a differentiating factor in title selection. For instance, an organization with president and vice president titles may prefer the title of VPMA, whereas an organization with a CEO, chief operating officer (COO), CFO, and CNO will likely prefer to have a matching CMO title.

Role of the Job

Regardless of title, the following functions are typically seen in practically all physician executive positions:

- Oversee medical staff relations and physician engagement
- Oversee the medical staff governance and operations, including credentialing, peer review, and focused professional practice evaluation (FPPE) and ongoing professional practice evaluation (OPPE)
- Oversee quality and risk management
- Coordinate activities of hospital-based medical groups such as hospitalists, radiology, pathology, emergency medicine, and anesthesia
- Supervise medical director roles
- Serve as the clinical face of the organization

- Serve as a senior management officer, offering input into strategy and other C-suite discussions
- Manage budgets of the medical staff office and related departments

The broader CMO role has evolved as the healthcare industry evolves. In many organizations, these additional functions are often seen in physician executive positions:

- Manage the employed physician entity
- Oversee physician recruitment, onboarding, and retention
- Manage selected service lines

As healthcare progressively makes the transition toward value-based care and reimbursement and fulfillment of the triple or quadruple aim, physician leaders' roles and focus must keep pace. These leaders must now be effective change agents, mastering the tenets of change management. They should work to eliminate unwarranted variation, implement best practices, standardize care, and lower their costs. These expectations of the top physician leader often directly conflict with the beliefs of the majority of physicians, who still follow and advocate for the traditional individual autonomy of medical practice. Yet the quality and mechanics of clinical care and accurate documentation are cornerstones of reimbursement and have direct impacts on financial sustainability.

The ability to influence both administrators and physicians alike and consensus building are key skills for success in the current healthcare environment. Encouraging timely responses and sufficient effort ("productivity") was unnecessary when physicians were in independent practice. But in the employed-provider era, these efforts have become commonplace. Healthcare organizations must now focus on balancing productivity expectations with wellness concerns and developing wellness programs. Technological familiarity and aptitude have become a necessity. Healthcare leaders must now manage populations and focus on social determinants of health and other barriers to care that exist outside the organization's walls. Such considerations were not consistently part of hospitals' or practices' past purviews. Today's CMOs have to master the ever-increasing statutory, regulatory, and accrediting parameters and requirements. They should also develop other physician leaders and have succession planning processes in place. Success in the role is often measured as overall organizational outcomes rather than individually identifiable achievements.

Qualifications

Beginning around 2010, the type of individuals who filled these executive physician roles has changed. Traditionally, the person selected was an older, affable, respected medical staff leader approaching retirement and someone who relied on personal relationships built over years of practice. Today, however, CMOs should be well-trained physician executives or individuals who seek management and leadership education. These physicians are better suited to fulfill the expanded, more sophisticated, and still-evolving CMO roles of today. And as is the case for any major executive recruitment, cultural fit is an overriding factor. Cultural fit encompasses how the expectations of the organization, the medical staff, and the C-suite fit with credentials, experience, and personal characteristics of the candidate.

Credentials and Additional Degrees

With more and more physicians pursuing physician executive career paths, many candidates for CMO positions will have advanced degree credentials beyond their medical degrees. Online or distance learning has expanded physicians' abilities to earn an additional advanced degree. Most will seek a master's degree in business administration (MBA), in medical management (MMM), in health administration (MHA), or in public health (MPH), or various degrees in informatics, quality, or patient safety.

The American Association for Physician Leadership (AAPL, which was formerly the American College of Physician Executives, or ACPE) has offered an intermediate path toward advanced education for those aspiring to be physician executives (AAPL 2018). The CPE (certified physician executive) designation indicates additional leadership and management education. This credential requires completion of more than 150 hours of core and elective coursework and culminates in a capstone project or event. The AAPL also collaborates with several prominent universities to offer a path from CPE designation to master's degree completion. The CPE-associated work is applied to the master's degree requirements. Moreover, many physician executives choose to become members of the American College of Healthcare Executives (ACHE) and further advance to Fellow (FACHE). Some organizations also offer physician leadership training programs that do not lead to advanced degrees but offer advanced education for the role, such as the AAMC (Association of American Medical Colleges) CMO Leadership Academy and the AAPL CMO Academy (AAMC 2021). Finally, an increasing number of organizations have designed their own internal programs in physician leadership development, often with both external and internal faculty.

Not all organizations and positions require additional advanced degrees for physician leadership positions. Those that do tend to include positions at the health-system level, academic medical centers, and large teaching hospitals. Positions at smaller nonteaching community hospitals, rural hospitals, and employed-physician networks may not have these requirements. These smaller organizations would still benefit from considering physicians who have shown the drive to complete physician leadership educational opportunities to obtain a greater foundation of administrative knowledge.

Experience

Advanced education with practical leadership and management experience is invaluable in physician executive positions. But besides education, crucible experiences (those that take place when leaders are put into situations they have not confronted before and when there is risk involved with the decisions made) and learning by doing are critical parts of the growth of leaders. Even leadership development programs that provide for case projects do not provide the substantive experiential aspects of learning. Thomas (2008) explains the value of true experience: "Leaders learn how to lead from experience. Formal training can help, but it's no substitute for learning on, and off, the job." As is the case with advanced credentials, the type of preferred professional experience will also vary by organizational type and position level. Positions at the health-system level, academic medical center, and large teaching hospitals usually require a career path of progressive physician executive positions in the organization or other similar organizations. Positions at smaller nonteaching community hospitals, rural hospitals, and employed-physician networks might focus on past experience in similar roles or in medical staff leadership, such as chief of staff.

Personal Characteristics

A list of ideal professional and personal characteristics that CMOs should possess can be quite exhaustive. Although a detailed discussion of these characteristics lies outside the scope of this book, the following are examples of some needed personal characteristics. An ideal CMO

- is reflective; thinks about broad overall goals and strategies; does not shoot quickly from the hip;
- embraces a philosophy of collaboration and teamwork; is able to listen, understand, reflect, and mediate differences on issues; reflects before speaking;

- is passionate about being a positive role model in the local community of physicians;
- has excellent interpersonal and communication skills; can build consensus, given a high premium; has noticeable skills in engaging physicians and finding synergies; maintains a pleasant interactive style;
- is comfortable working in groups, forming teams of physicians and management, with an ease in working with other diverse groups;
- understands how to create change through influence and not through direct authority; and
- is analytical and can draw conclusions from the data.

Leadership Style

Effective leaders must exhibit a leadership style appropriate for the situation at hand. Individuals with a servant leadership and coaching approach are usually more successful CMOs than are those taking an autocratic or directive approach. Servant leaders tend to develop leaders and not followers. The associated personality traits of empathy, foresight, persuasion, and commitment all play well when a leader is dealing with physicians and administrative colleagues alike. In stark contrast, autocratic or authoritarian leaders often try to control all decisions and seldom seek true input from those they lead. These leaders tend to face apathy, distrust, or rebellion from physicians.

Clinical Expertise

As a rule, while all physician leaders should be recognized and respected for their clinical expertise, this skill is seldom the most important one for the job itself. Clinical expertise does engender credibility, but the best physicians are not always the best administrative leaders. Some outstanding physicians cannot seem to translate their clinical reasoning to the administrative setting and skill set, whereas others can make a seamless transition.

CHARACTERISTICS THAT SUPPORT PHYSICIAN ENGAGEMENT

The AAPL lists seven characteristics that define a strong physician leader: "adaptable, ethical, visionary, introspective, vigilant, tactical and knowledgeable" (Sabol 2018). These characteristics form the basis for the association's physician leadership curriculum.

To this list, we can add other attributes and qualities that physician leaders should have to best support physician engagement:

- **Empathy:** The ability to understand the feelings and emotions of others not only improves a leader's interactions with them but also helps the leader drill down to the root causes of suboptimal performance and to build up and develop others.
- **Humility:** Increasingly recognized as a favorable characteristic of physician leaders, humility tends to promote empathy. Humble people speak of *we* instead of *I* and *you*. Egocentrism and narcissism do not bode well for this role.
- **Critical thinking:** Leaders must be able to independently analyze, synthesize, and evaluate information and situations to make rational decisions in an open-minded fashion, driven by the available evidence.
- **Integrity:** Beyond being honest and ethical, a leader must be able to be relied on to deliver what is promised and to promise only what can reasonably be delivered—and diligently work to do so. Respect is earned and does not automatically come with the position. Integrity is integral to gaining respect.

- **Energy:** Positive energy is infectious and is necessary to build consensus and drive change. Human systems also obey the physical laws of entropy, so a constant infusion of energy is required to move systems to higher levels of performance.
- **Flexibility:** Effective leaders must be able to adapt to changing circumstances and to function under ill-defined or uncertain parameters.
- **Creativity:** Maintaining the status quo will not serve organizations well. Beyond continual performance improvement, thinking in new and different ways is a key to adaptability—and survivability—in this ever-changing healthcare environment.

WHERE CANDIDATES COME FROM

When an organization seeks out CMOs or other physician leader candidates, there are advantages and disadvantages to choosing a person from inside the organization. Similarly, outside candidates have advantages and disadvantages.

Like many other questions about physician leadership positions, the decision to pursue internal or external candidates depends on the organization's goals and circumstances when the spot is being filled. Most organizations would still benefit from considering a mix of both internal and external candidates during recruitment, to ensure that they find the best possible candidate.

Internal Candidates

Some organizations have well-developed physician leadership development programs integral to their succession planning. These organizations actively groom physicians to fill future leadership and management positions, including the CMO, and believe that the best fit comes from within.

Internal candidates know the organization. They have been working in the system and know the medical staff, administration, and other organizational staff members. They know the culture and the market. They know the clinical informatics system. Because of this familiarity, they can hit the ground running. Moreover, the organization knows the internal candidate. There is a good grasp on how the candidate is suited to the position and will fit in the organization. There should be few surprises. Finally, internal candidates are less expensive since the organization will incur no expenses associated with recruiting, moving, orienting, and onboarding.

However, internal candidates may have never worked at any other organization and may tend to perpetuate the status quo. They may fail to recognize that their new role is different and that even though they are familiar with the organization, the CMO role in that organization presents a different perspective. Internal candidates can be amazed at how much the actual role and interactions differ from prior perceptions. Moreover, relationships change with the new position, and the transition can be difficult for not only the candidate but also colleagues and peers. Some new CMOs make this transition well, and others not so well.

External Candidates

Organizations may have no option other than to seek a candidate from outside their walls. There may be a gap in the leadership continuum and no heir apparent, or perhaps a change in thought processes is advantageous. External candidates can bring fresh perspectives and experiences not available in a single system of care. Relationships are also defined in the context of the role without the baggage of history or inherent expectations. On the other hand, an external candidate requires a transition period to become familiar with the organization's culture, staff, operations, market, medical staff, and informatics systems.

BUSINESS SUIT OR WHITE LAB COAT? THE CMO'S DILEMMA

Any physician leadership position creates an internal conflict for the physician who holds the role. These leaders have one foot in healthcare administration and one foot in the clinical world. The two worlds have traditionally been pitted against each other—and in many organizations, they still are. Moreover, having one foot in each camp generally means that neither camp fully accepts the person. With which group does the physician leader primarily identify? Does the person work harder for alignment with the administrative group or the clinical one? Both administrators and physicians may view the physician leader as "one of them" (i.e., the enemy) and may hesitate to offer this executive their full trust. Among the clinical staff, the physician leader becomes one of the "suits." While the medical staff elect the chief of staff and still think of this official as one of their own, they view the CMO as someone selected by administration and "one of them." To administrators, the CMO is and always will be a physician. Although physician leaders can prove worthy of acceptance by both camps, approval usually takes time and effort to prove trustworthiness and to gain respect—with the potential for significant internal conflict in the interim.

Related to this internal conflict are the external forces at play in any organizational culture at every level of administrative leadership. Understanding the dynamics of the various groups and how to function in those environments can be a challenge. The functional reality is often entirely different from the clinical physician environment and often entirely different when the physician leader is working within the structure as opposed to observing from the outside. CMOs need to understand and adapt to the differences to succeed in their bilateral role.

Clinical Versus Administrative Career Identities

Few CMOs entered the medical profession to become a health-care executive. Most chose medicine for the patient-care aspects of the profession and strove to be successful in that undertaking. Accepting the CMO position can call career options into question. Most CMOs are internally driven not only to succeed but also to excel. Departing from the clinical realm—even if not done full-time—can create internal conflict in even the most self-confident and secure individuals. Doubts abound: "Will I be successful in executive medicine—or successful enough to meet my personal expectations—despite my individual efforts? Will there be clinical time, and will it be enough to fulfill my clinical aspirations and to stay current and relevant? And can I maintain credibility without sufficient clinical activity as my peers define it?" CMOs often feel grounded by clinical activity. They achieve a sense of balance, and they calm their internal conflict when permitted to remain involved in clinical pursuits. This internal conflict can reach a fever pitch if a physician is considering becoming a full-time executive.

Internal Versus External Validation

As a rule, CMOs need to rely on internal validation; external validation is relatively rare. Their role is typically considered a thankless job. To know or convince themselves that the course is correct and the effort effective, physician leaders may have to rely on indirect evidence. They may, however, have difficulty knowing whether internal perceptions match external opinions. As they mature in the role, receive consistent internal and external validation, and achieve tangible and intangible results, the leaders slowly overcome the internal and external personal dilemmas they feel.

THE CMO CANNOT DO IT ALL

As suggested thus far, installing a CMO does not magically create a pied piper whom all physicians instinctively and automatically follow and who makes everything instantly better. Increased physician engagement does not just happen because an organization has appointed a CMO. The CMO is only one, albeit important, way to engage physicians. The organization cannot look to the physician leader as the sole driver of physician engagement.

Organizations may also benefit from, or may even require, CMOs and other physician leaders at multiple levels, such as those for the system, the individual hospital, and the employed-provider network. The positions at each of these levels serve similar functions, and the individuals should possess similar traits—though their absolute functions will necessarily vary.

Healthcare organizations need physician leadership in other roles, such as medical staff officers, service-line medical directors, and departmental chairs. Investment in the training and development of individuals in these roles or people being considered for these roles will reap organizational dividends that exceed the positional roles and responsibilities. Organizations must groom individuals for leadership and help them attain these roles. The greater the investment in physician leadership training, the greater the return—especially in overall physician engagement and organizational function and performance.

PHYSICIAN LEADERSHIP COUNCILS

Beyond formal individual physician leader positions, organizations can develop greater physician engagement and more positive outcomes through leadership and advisory councils. CMOs can spearhead these groups to provide the benefit of greater physician input. Some of these councils already exist but are underutilized—specifically the medical executive committee (MEC). Organizations tend to use the MEC only for its traditional delegated activities, which are related to clinical quality monitoring and medical staff credentialing. Many CEOs seem to lament dealing with the medical staff's elected leadership as these individuals may not be fully aligned with the administration's mindset. Failing to involve the MEC in strategic planning and tactical objectives development is a missed opportunity to engage the organization's physician membership—and is likely to create more work and suboptimal outcomes down the road.

Similarly, a provider leadership council for the employed-provider network includes employed providers in the problem solving and decision-making, leading to greater engagement and improved outcomes. Miller, McWilliams, and Ansel (2018) suggest that physicians on the councils "take ownership of the performance and success of the network." They recommend that administrators recognize that they "need physicians' help and leadership in (1) discovering operational challenges, (2) developing the solutions, and (3) supporting the implementation of those solutions."

Finally, creating informal cabinets of constituency groups that are lacking in the traditional medical staff structure, like community-based providers, to meet regularly with C-suite members (minimally the CEO, CMO, and CNO) to discuss common issues can build bridges and levels of engagement that marketing and other initiatives cannot attain.

CONCLUSION

Healthcare organizations that embrace physician leadership involvement in all its forms promote physician engagement and enjoy improved organizational performance. The installation of a CMO is often the focal point for engagement. Dye and Sokolov (2013) describe the effort: "Leading physicians is challenging. Physicians, as a class of people, are exceptionally bright, were often at the top of their classes, and have been trained in a highly competitive environment."

Despite the challenges, these individuals, if developed fully as leaders, can have the greatest positive impact on physician engagement.

REFERENCES

American Association for Physician Leadership (AAPL). 2018. "2018 Chief Medical Officer Academy." Accessed January 31, 2021. www.physicianleaders.org/summer-academy-cmo.

Association of American Medical Colleges (AAMC). 2021. "Chief Medical Officers (CMO) Leadership Academy." Accessed January 31. www.aamc.org/professional-development/leadership-development/cmo-leadership-academy.

Dister, L. 2009. "CMO or VPMA: Is There a Difference?" *Physician Executive* 35 (3): 12–16.

Dye, C. F., and J. J. Sokolov. 2013. *Developing Physician Leaders for Successful Clinical Integration*. Chicago: Health Administration Press.

Dyrda, L. 2017. "50 Facts and Statistics on CMOs and Medical Directors." *Becker's Hospital Review*. Published March 9. www.beckershospitalreview.com/hospital-management-administration/50-facts-and-statistics-on-cmos-and-medical-directors.html.

Miller, D. W., T. R. McWilliams, and T. C. Ansel. 2018. *Employed Physician Networks: A Guide to Building Strategic Advantage, Value, and Financial Sustainability*. Chicago: Health Administration Press.

Sabol, E. 2018. "Seven Characteristics That Define a Physician Leader." American Association for Physician Leadership. Published April 26. www.physicianleaders.org/news/seven-characteristics-that-define-a-physician-leader.

Sonnenberg, M. 2018. "Changing Roles and Skill Sets for Chief Medical Officers." American Association for Physician Leadership. Published June 19. www.physicianleaders.org/news/changing-roles-skill-sets-chief-medical-officers.

Thomas, R. J. 2008. *Crucibles of Leadership: How to Learn from Experience to Become a Great Leader.* Boston: Harvard Business Press.

CHAPTER 5

Dyads, Triads, and Quads, Oh My!

Terry R. McWilliams

The best interest of the patient is the only interest to be considered and in order that the sick may have benefit of advancing knowledge union of force is necessary . . . [I]t has become necessary to develop medicine as a cooperative science.
—William J. Mayo, 1910

DR. MAYO'S WORDS still ring true as patient-care delivery, the business of healthcare, and the healthcare industry become increasingly complex. Providing outstanding care and managing the systems that deliver it require increasingly broader and deeper expertise. The transition from volume-based to value-based care delivery and reimbursement models further complicates the required skill mixes and serves as a powerful driver for involving physicians in management dyads and other leadership positions.

Articles on the topic support most healthcare leaders' perceptions that the dyad model of healthcare management is a relatively new phenomenon. However, the Mayo Clinic is credited with creating the model more than a hundred years ago (Buell 2017). Back then, Dr. Mayo and Harry Harwick (who later became one of the Medical Group Management Association founders) united the clinical and administrative sides of medicine to initiate an integrated healthcare management structure—a structure that is still in place across the Mayo system. While Dr. Mayo did not refer to the jointure as a management dyad, he did originate and utilize the concept for healthcare management.

Dyads, triads, and quads (or dual dyads) are variations of management or leadership team structures that strive to leverage the strengths of the team partners to synergistically deliver outcomes better than what any of the individuals could accomplish on their own. The partner combinations vary with the entity managed or led, but all have similar foundations. In this chapter, I develop this leadership model using elements of dyads and then expand the model to include increasing complexity of triads and dual-dyads.

MANAGEMENT DYADS

At its core, a dyad is defined as a pair, but more commonly, the word describes two individuals maintaining a sociologically significant relationship. One example of a dyad is a marriage. In fact, marriage provides an easily understood, real-life analogy for the concept of a management dyad. A marriage represents two unique individuals united for a common purpose, with each partner being jointly committed to the success of that purpose and each bringing individual strengths and weaknesses to the relationship. The better the partners can work together to take advantage of their individual strengths and buoy their individual weaknesses, the greater the chance they will enjoy success in their marriage. Ideally, one partner's skills and demeanor will be complementary to those of the other partner. Successful marriages do not happen by chance. They require the partners to know each other well, exhibit trust and respect, communicate well, develop common understandings of their roles and responsibilities—both individual and shared—and work together to make the union thrive.

As an organizational structure, a management dyad pairs two leaders who are mutually responsible for the performance of an area. Ideally, in this team-based approach to management, the team members directly contribute their strengths to organizational performance through well-defined, mutually supportive individual and shared responsibilities. Each leader contributes equally in a synergistic fashion that avoids redundancies. And the partners must exhibit many of the characteristics outlined previously for a successful marriage: They must know each other well, exhibit mutual trust and respect, develop common understandings, communicate constantly, and work to make the relationship flourish. The American Hospital Association (AHA) underscores that "dyad leadership involves more than a collaborative spirit or collegiality among peers. Clinical partnership goes beyond role clarification and shared accountability structures" (AHA 2018). It is about the relationship—a true partnership.

In a dyad relationship, decisions are made together and the pair owns the overall performance of the area they lead. Information is jointly promulgated. As Zismer and Brueggemann (2010) succinctly state, "Neither [partner] is permitted to delegate responsibility for these common areas or blame the partner for his or her lack of performance in this regard. The success of each is tied to the other." The partners consider and understand the perspective of their counterpart. They speak as one voice, and each partner represents the positions of the other partner when that person is not present (AHA 2018).

To accomplish this level of unity, dyad partners must share a common philosophical approach to leadership and management and a common moral and ethical foundation. They must work closely together and have ready formal and informal access to each other. Their offices are ideally colocated, and the pair are regularly seen together and function collectively to lead and manage their area of responsibility. They must focus on the benefit to the organization and not on self-aggrandizement.

Successful dyad relationships exhibit many other characteristics, perhaps none more important than partnering intelligence. *Partnering intelligence* is the ability to develop trusting relationships while accomplishing mutually beneficial objectives (AHA 2018). One characteristic underlying partnering intelligence is individual emotional intelligence. Emotional intelligence goes beyond straightforward mental acuity and refers to the ability to recognize emotions in oneself or others. In a healthcare dyad management, emotional intelligence means that both partners have a high awareness of—and respect for—each other and how each reacts to various types of issues, struggles, or stresses.

Another important characteristic of the dyad is psychological safety. Beyond trust and mutual respect, psychological safety is characterized by the partner's being "confident in speaking up and being themselves without fear of embarrassment, rejection, punishment, or ostracizing" (AHA 2018). These factors promote an opportunity to grow personally and professionally while knowing the partner has your back.

A management dyad can be effective in various areas and at multiple levels across healthcare organizations. The functional needs of the area or level define the best combinations of dyad partners and their specific responsibilities. One of the most common leadership dyads consists of a clinical member, most often a physician, and an administrative member. The physician, often known as a medical or clinical director, brings expertise in clinical operations, provider relationships, and related issues. The administrator, often known as the administrative director, brings expertise in business operations, finance, and related issues. This combination is particularly prominent in employed-provider networks and in operational areas like cardiac catheterization labs.

Individual and Shared Responsibilities

Although the dyad's responsibilities will vary with the size and complexity of the organization or subunit thereof, they are often consistent with those outlined in exhibit 5.1. This list is not all-inclusive, but it presents an overview, using the previously described physician–administrator dyad as an example.

Exhibit 5.1 Responsibilities of a Physician–Administrative Leadership Dyad

Shared	Physician Member	Administrative Member
• Developing or implementing strategy and associated action plans • Fostering group culture • Promoting, monitoring, and reporting group and individual performances • Quality of care, patient safety • Patient experience • Operational efficiency • Operating budget • Developing internal and external organizational relationships • Optimizing clinical informatics and data analytics systems	• Providing medical staff supervision • Performance review • Discipline • Recruiting, onboarding • Creating, implementing, and monitoring clinical practice guidelines • Driving population health management initiatives • Evaluating clinical outcomes (effectiveness and efficiency) • Supporting administrative member	• Developing operational goals, priorities, responsibilities • Monitoring group financial functions: budgeting, accounting, reporting • Managing and developing human resources consistent with organizational guidelines, established contracts, and legal requirements • Coordinating necessary support functions: marketing, IT, financial • Supporting physician member

In many instances, the physician half of the dyad may not need to commit to a full-time administrative presence and could maintain a degree of clinical activity. However, the physician must dedicate the effort necessary to accomplish the physician's dyad responsibilities. No one—neither the physician, the administrative partner, nor those in the area served—should perceive the physician's dyad responsibilities as a marginal or part-time duty that can be squeezed in between patients or cases. The physician must be granted—and must individually dedicate—the time required to wholly fulfill the intended role.

Benefits of a Management Dyad

Traditional management structures are strictly operational, with clear lines of authority driven by nonclinical administrators. This structure risks a lopsided approach that does not understand the complexities of the clinical environment, the nuances of care, and the collegial relationships that underpin integrated services (Belasen 2019). Physicians and other clinicians rarely have a formal role in the leadership hierarchy and risk becoming disengaged. Organizations change slowly in the traditional model—and often against significant resistance by the physicians who were not involved in the development process.

Traditional management structures still exist in numerous healthcare organizations. Many of these organizations adhere to a philosophy that physicians should "just see patients" or "just practice medicine" and that only business professionals should manage operations—assigned medical staff functions aside. On the hospital side, these organizations prevent physicians—who can be viewed as key customers who drive cost, volume, and efficiency—from providing highly knowledgeable input into clinical and business operations and risk alienating someone who should be an essential partner. Some organizations that recognize the costly impact of this shortcoming may pursue comanagement arrangements with independent physicians in addition to management dyads with employed physicians. On the employed-practice-network side, traditionally managed organizations abrogate leadership roles from the physicians, many of whom successfully managed their own independent practices before acquisition. To be fair, many physicians had tired of the challenges associated with managing their own practices and abdicated the role to the acquiring healthcare organization. Either case underutilizes the full talents of the employed physicians, undervalues the importance of that key internal customer, and misses the great benefits that physician involvement in leadership can bring.

Instituting a management dyad immediately injects physician leadership into the formal management hierarchy and engenders greater physician trust and engagement in group operations (exhibit 5.2). Buy-in also comes naturally as part of normal operations, because physicians are intimately involved in planning, development, and the execution of strategy. Leadership consequently does

Exhibit 5.2 Separate and Shared Interests and Responsibilities in a Management Dyad

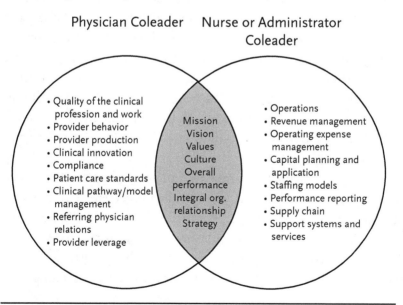

Physician Coleader   Nurse or Administrator Coleader

- Quality of the clinical profession and work
- Provider behavior
- Provider production
- Clinical innovation
- Compliance
- Patient care standards
- Clinical pathway/model management
- Referring physician relations
- Provider leverage

Mission
Vision
Values
Culture
Overall performance
Integral org. relationship
Strategy

- Operations
- Revenue management
- Operating expense management
- Capital planning and application
- Staffing models
- Performance reporting
- Supply chain
- Support systems and services

not have to seek out buy-in separately. Enhanced trust in the system allows the group to move forward more efficiently. So while decision-making might go slightly slower, the implementation of change is faster and more effective—and encounters fewer complications, as most problems were anticipated during design and development.

In addition to providing favorable change agency, management dyads secure the full spectrum of leadership skills needed to deliver strong management across multidisciplinary groups. The pairing allows leaders to be used at the "top of their licenses" and ensures a maximum return on each leader's time and effort. Baldwin, Dimunation, and Alexander (2011) note that "in the dyad model, the time invested up front ensures that the physicians understand the change and have voiced their opinions regarding a potential change."

The mutual support inherent in solid partnerships that promote strong teamwork also lessens stress and reduces the risk of premature burnout inherent in isolated leadership roles, a benefit highlighted by Trandel (2015).

Finally, dyads that include a physician align the physician and support staff reporting structures into a single system, which eliminates physician complaints about reporting to nonphysicians and avoids physician tendencies to subvert the reporting structure by going around the administrative leadership to reach the top. This organizational structure benefit alone can be a unifying feature that promotes more cohesive and effective unit function. All unit members hear a single message, delivered jointly by the dyad, whether both partners or only one is delivering the message at any given time.

All management structures have inherent pros and cons. In the dyad, what is gained in trust, alignment, engagement, and smoother operations may be offset by a potential ambiguity regarding authority and seemingly slower decision-making, but these downsides are often balanced by the ability to implement change faster and more effectively. And performance can be maximized through diligence.

Success with a Management Dyad

Consider the following guidelines when initially implementing a management dyad or introducing a new team member:

- **Establish the structure.** Before filling positions, ensure that the framework under which the dyad will function is in place. Clearly define the organizational structure, reporting relationships, and expected roles and responsibilities through detailed descriptions of the positions.
- **Recruit wisely.** A successful pairing begins with the selection process. The key requirements for suitable candidates go beyond the usual positional competencies. Evaluate the cultural fit between the candidate and the other team member and with the unit they will lead. Both the physician leader and the nonphysician leader must embrace interprofessional collaboration and teamwork (Belasen 2019; Zismer and Brueggemann 2010) over individual leadership. Effective leaders will involve an existing member of the dyad in the selection of the other member.
- **Clearly set functional expectations.** The pair is expected to work synergistically to execute each member's well-defined roles and responsibilities. Leaders need to emphasize that the members are a management team that shares accountability for the unit's performance and that their roles are complementary rather than duplicative. They are not two people doing the same job; nor are they a team in which one member (the administrator) does all the work for review by the other (the physician). Not all aspects of how the pair functions together can be predetermined, but establishing basic expectations is crucial to functional success.

- **Train and mentor the physicians selected for these leadership roles.** Clinical excellence is not enough. The selected physicians ideally aspire to a career as a physician executive in medical administration. Although some educational elements should already be a part of the physicians' curriculum vitae, the physicians should pursue formal (specific courses, graduate education) and informal (independent self-study) learning to ensure continued professional development. Didactic knowledge should be shaped through coaching and mentoring to optimize performance.
- **Train and mentor the administrative member of the dyad.** The selected administrative member should already have the administrative skills required by the position and further professional development to add to that knowledge base. However, the administrative member may not have a firm understanding of dyad management concepts and how to function as a team to achieve results. Coaching and mentoring regarding the management concept are often necessary.
- **Train and mentor the dyad in their relationship.** Even if individually familiar with the concept of a dyad, the members often benefit from joint mentoring and coaching—almost like preemptive marriage counseling—to promote maximum functional success. Opportunities to jointly attend or complete courses related to dyad management will further cement the relationship and enhance collective function. If ignored and left to their own devices, the two members may devolve into separate spheres, rotating independently while revolving in a common central structure. If this occurs, dysfunction will result.
- **Educate the organization.** Make sure that everyone knows about the dyad's roles and responsibilities, staff reporting relationships, and who should be approached with what

issues. Explicitly defining these elements with staff sets realistic expectations. Ideally, those in the reporting structure could approach either dyad member with any issue or concern and the pair could decide the best approach to take and the roles of each partner in the process. Reliable execution fulfills expectations and yields success.

- **Delegate authority, and hold the pair accountable.** All the previously listed actions set the stage for allowing the dyad to make decisions, exercise its delegated authority, and be held accountable for its actions and results. Establish realistic goals that mirror the stated expectations and that can accurately measure progress in their spheres of influence. Regularly review progress to promote success and accountability.

- **Be patient.** Successful, systematic implementation and utilization of the dyad model does not magically occur overnight. Although some dyads succeed by solely relying on individual team dynamics, most of them need time and significant investment to generate a culture that ensures widespread adoption of a thriving, systematic approach.

When properly implemented and executed, management dyads can have a profoundly positive impact on organizational success.

Physician–Nurse Dyads

An extremely common dyad in hospitals and health systems is the physician–nurse dyad. This combination can start at the top with the CMO–CNO pair leading initiatives, chairing standing or ad hoc committees (such as joint practice committees), and jointly contributing to strategic and operational discussions. The physician–nurse pairing is also a popular construct for service-line leadership at both the hospital and health-system levels.

In 2018, the AHA released a white paper outlining the benefits of the physician–nurse dyad and delineating fundamental characteristics of all dyads. The paper was developed in conjunction with key stakeholders, including the AHA Physician Alliance, the American Organization of Nurse Executives, and the American Association for Physician Leadership (AAPL). In addition, the AHA convened a forum consisting of highly respected physician and nurse executive teams to explore factors leading to successful physician–nurse executive dyads and to inform the white paper's content. The paper advocates utilizing the physician–nurse partnership at all hospital levels, "from the executive level to the bedside," to leverage the clinical synergy necessary to "achieve strategic objectives and deliver excellent patient care" as organizations make the transition from volume to value and continue to emphasize patient safety.

The success of the physician–nurse dyad greatly depends on the participants' willingness to overcome their historical professional differences and to focus on the common benefit of all. Although temporary leadership partnerships had been formed for specific initiatives and although longer-term coleadership arrangements were present in some joint practice committees or operational areas, the degree of involvement was usually unequal and relied too heavily on the nurse leader. While some of these relationships may have evolved to become true long-term dyads, their underlying design and intent were readily distinguishable from the mutually responsible and accountable intent of a true dyad.

An important consideration of traditional physician–nurse relationships is the traditional medical director position. Some organizational leaders point to medical director roles as evidence that dyads have existed in their organization for a long time. As noted earlier, while some relationships between the medical director and nursing director may have evolved into a true dyad, many involved only perfunctory involvement of the medical director in actual decision-making and the operational functioning of the involved unit. Many medical directors were only required to be available as necessary, when specific questions arose or when a problem came up with a physician.

Even worse, some medical directors were appointed in name only—the title was created to permit direct compensation to influential physicians on the medical staff. Paying physicians to be medical directors without spelling out their duties was commonplace before the Stark laws were enacted. But Stark compliance alone does not guarantee that medical director roles rise to the level of that required in true dyadic function. For instance, many medical directors do not dedicate a set amount of time to the role; they instead try to answer questions or provide other input around and between their full clinical activity. These individuals restrict their role to simply answering questions when their input is felt to be necessary—with the nurse director doing all the work and remaining exclusively responsible for the function of the unit. Many medical directors who fill this type of role believe that they have no true authority over their physician peers, let alone over the nonphysician members of the unit. While medical directorships are a mechanism to directly involve physicians in leadership and increase physician engagement in a functional area, few of these positions rise to the level of involvement, time commitment, responsibility, and accountability inherent in a dyad.

MANAGEMENT TRIADS

Management triads are dyads with a third, equal member in the relationship. As in dyads, the composition will vary according to the circumstances, but the conceptual framework is the same.

A common triad in hospitals and health systems is formed with the inclusion of an administrator in the physician–nurse dyad. The administrator assumes operational responsibilities from the original pairing and creates a clinical operations team with the physician–nurse pair. Like dyads, triads can be found at all levels of an organization, including the C-suite (CMO–CNO–COO), individual service lines, and clinical operational units. The triad concept recognizes that traditional physician and nursing education and training curricula lack significant attention to business operations. For this reason, adding business expertise to the group can strengthen it and improve outcomes—as long as all the shared responsibilities, such as those shown in exhibit 5.1, apply equally to the new member. A similar outcome results when a financial officer joins the physician–nurse dyad to augment financial and business development acumen to the clinical operations. Examples are a CMO/CNO/CFO triad and a medical director/nursing director/financial director triad. The benefits of these types of additions often persist even when either or both clinical members of the team achieve an advanced degree in business or healthcare management.

Less common in the hospital and health system environment is the addition of a nurse to a physician–administrator dyad to augment the clinical operations aspect of the team. Fewer of such triads exist, because the underlying physician–administrator model is less common than the physician–nurse dyad in these areas.

In contrast, the employed-provider network commonly advocates the use of a physician–administrator dyad as a base construct. To develop a triad in this environment, the leadership can add a financial officer to the physician–administrator dyad, thereby augmenting the business operations side of the network. Another scenario adds an APP (advanced practice provider) director to the physician–administrator team in employed-provider networks that have a substantial proportion of APPs in the provider mix. The addition of such a director also augments the clinical-operations side of the network. A third, less common combination is the addition of a nurse to the dyad to focus on RN, LPN, and medical assistant perspectives; provide unique insight for programs such as care management; and augment the clinical-operations side of the network.

MANAGEMENT QUADS—OR DUAL DYADS

As the name implies, management quads consist of four equal partners. This construct is more clearly depicted as a dual dyad: two dyads working synergistically to manage the organization. In

Exhibit 5.3 Structure and Responsibilities of a Management Quad (a Dual Dyad)

| Director of nursing and clinical operations | Director of medical operations | Director of business operations | Director of finance and revenue cycle |

- Clinical workforce develvement
- Patient care and safety standards
- Quality data and metrics
- Clinical workflow optimization
- Policy and process improvement

- Provider performance management
- Oversight of clinical and financial key performance indicators
- Compliance
- Provider behavior
- Referral network coordination
- Internal organization relationships

- Budget and capital planning
- Financial analysis of acquisitions and recruiting
- Lean supply chain
- Operating expense management
- Performance reporting

this model, a physician, a nurse, an operations manager, and a financial officer—the equivalent of the CMO, CNO, COO, and CFO—collaborate to lead the organization by contributing their respective individual strengths to achieve their combined roles and responsibilities (exhibit 5.3).

While some might argue that the preceding description would apply to most C-suites, the difference lies in the degree of interaction and interfunctionality. In most C-suites, these leaders function relatively independently in their daily activities and focus primarily on their individual areas of responsibility outside of weekly operations meetings with the CEO. The positions are not designed to function as dyads, with one dyad concentrating on clinical operations (the physician–nurse team), the other dyad concentrating on business operations (the operations manager–finance director team), and the two dyads interacting regularly to ensure an intimately combined function. Highly functioning C-suites tend to evolve into this type of relationship but were not designed that way.

As described by David James, MD, JD, and CEO of Memorial Hermann Medical Group, this management construct worked very well at his group (James 2016). Dual dyads increased physician engagement, employee retention, operational efficiency, and key performance indicator achievement while decreasing the investment (subsidy) per provider full-time employee.

CONCLUSION

Management dyads in all their variations can be highly effective leadership and management constructs. They take advantage of individual member strengths to synergistically propel their area of responsibility to a higher functional state and achieve enhanced outcomes—including greater physician engagement and trust in the organization.

REFERENCES

American Hospital Association (AHA). 2018. "A Model for Clinical Partnering: How Nurse and Physician Executives Use Synergy as Strategy." Published August 1. www.aha.org/system/files/2018-08/plf-issue-brief-clinical-partnering.pdf.

Baldwin, K. S., N. Dimunation, and J. Alexander. 2011. "Health Care Leadership and the Dyad Model." *Physician Executive Journal* 37 (4): 66–70.

Belasen, A. 2019. *Dyad Leadership and Clinical Integration: Driving Change, Aligning Strategies*. Chicago: Health Administration Press.

Buell, J. 2017. "The Dyad Leadership Model: Four Case Studies." *Healthcare Executive* 32 (5): 33–40.

James, D. 2016. "Increasing Physician Leadership Through Dual Based Dyadic Management." Paper presented at ACHE Congress on Healthcare Leadership, Chicago, March 14.

Mayo, W. J. 1910. "Quotations from the Doctors Mayo." Mayo Clinic History and Heritage. Accessed January 22, 2021. https://history.mayoclinic.org/toolkit/quotations/the-doctors-mayo.php.

Trandel, E. 2015. "Advocating for Dyad Leadership at Your Organization?" Advisory Board. Published March 26. www.advisory.com/research/physician-executive-council/prescription-for-change/2015/03/dyad-leadership-slides.

Zismer, D. K., and J. Brueggemann. 2010. "Examining the 'Dyad' as a Management Model in Integrated Health Systems." *Physician Executive Journal* 36 (1): 14–19.

CHAPTER 6

Assessing Physicians for Leadership

Kevin M. Casey

An All-Too-Common Scenario

The hospital administrative team was looking for a new CMO, and of all the potential candidates, one stood out. As a well-respected "silverback" physician near the end of a long career, the candidate wanted to slow down and move into an administration role. For the admin team, this appeared to be an easy choice. Six months into the role, this physician no longer practices clinically but is ineffectual in the CMO role. The medical staff has become more disillusioned than before and less engaged with the organization and its leadership. The once-respected physician's reputation is greatly diminished. But having left clinical practice and with nothing else to do, the physician must now continue to serve as the CMO.

After one contentious meeting with hospital physicians, an administrator was overheard asking, "What should we have looked for? What qualifications and experiences should we have required to ensure a great CMO?"

FOR DECADES, PHYSICIAN LEADERSHIP roles have been viewed as a rite of passage for physicians who had long tenures on the medical staff and who were approaching a time when they might want to slow down. Often more an acknowledgment of historical service and loyalty, the appointments given these physicians would sometimes put them into difficult situations. In these leadership roles, they had neither the experience nor the skill set to successfully navigate the needs of the healthcare team. And in hindsight, this pattern is not what is best for the other administrators, the other providers, the staff, the patients, or even the physician. Considering that physicians receive no formal instruction in leadership in medical school or residency and that the skills and approaches taught and reinforced during their training years may conflict with necessary leadership skills, it is a wonder that some physicians have succeeded in leadership roles at all.

Although they are seen and labeled as leaders in healthcare, most physicians, because of their lack of leadership training, are poorly equipped to assume the role today. Thankfully, this situation appears to be changing. Some medical schools and residencies now offer training in leadership, and healthcare organizations are providing physician leadership development programs. However, these efforts are not enough, as education alone without exposure or experience is inadequate preparation.

Moreover, the importance of assessing, training, and retaining the best physician leaders cannot be overstated. Hiring the right physician leaders is one of the greatest determinants of physician and staff engagement, quality, and patient experience in healthcare.

THE CONUNDRUM

Physicians historically have been instructed and rewarded for certain behaviors and attitudes. Those have included autonomy, determination, a focus on the individual patient (exclusively), confidence, and paternalism. Naturally, these leanings can lead to a natural command-and-control leadership approach. And unfortunately, these tendencies are also contrary to what leaders in healthcare need to demonstrate to be successful today. Healthcare administrators need to choose physician leaders with an understanding that to succeed, the organization must invest in leadership development for those who move into these roles.

NONNEGOTIABLE CHARACTERISTICS

Many physicians may not be naturally suited for leadership and will require additional management and leadership training. Before investing the time and money to do this, the organization needs to identify the characteristics most indicative of a physician's leadership potential. There are a few "nonnegotiable" characteristics that should be looked for in any candidate for a leadership role (and probably in any person to be hired at all).

Intrinsic Motivation for the Work of Leadership

The first nonnegotiable is a drive to lead. While this may seem to be power-seeking, it is nevertheless a key factor for the effective work of leadership. Perhaps better labeled *ambition*, this characteristic is a significant requirement for effective leadership. Beeby (2017) puts it simply: "Ambition is necessary for a great leader."

If candidates do not demonstrate a strong desire to make positive differences in their leadership roles, they are unlikely to be successful. The connection between intrinsic motivation and leadership potential cannot be overemphasized. Zarian (2015) writes, "Intrinsically motivated leaders have the passion and purpose that extends beyond the immediate external goal for leading. Their desire to lead is like a well that overflows for the passion for leading others to achieve a mission, and their intrinsic desire to lead does not dry out once that goal has been fulfilled." Fortunately, ambition is one of the easiest nonnegotiable characteristics to identify.

Respect as a Clinician

Physician leaders, no matter what their roles, are always being judged by other physicians on how they perform as clinicians. For this reason, physician leaders must, whenever possible, continue to do some clinical work. Keeping their hands in this kind of work will help them retain a kinship with the other physicians and the nurses they are leading and affords some balance to the administrative work that they perform (more on this later). If you are hiring someone with an established clinical history in your facility, the physician might already have a well-established clinical reputation. If the physician is from outside the facility, it is wise to have them provide some type of clinical care in service to the healthcare entity.

Prior Experience

For any candidate, prior experience is often one of the best indicators of future performance. Candidates who show ambition as discussed earlier, who have sought out and served in committee leadership roles, who have served as de facto practice administrators in their practices, or who have served on outside boards or other civic leadership roles usually have the best proclivity toward being effective leaders.

THE THREE Cs OF LEADERSHIP

Anyone under consideration for a leadership position (physician or otherwise) should also be evaluated for the *three Cs*: character, chemistry, and capacity. Each characteristic is briefly discussed in the following sections, with examples of questions that might help reveal the presence of each. Those evaluating potential physician leaders must ensure that the candidate has all three Cs from the beginning. As is true of any person in a new environment, reputation is cemented in the first few weeks and is difficult to change later. A lack of one or more of the three Cs will make the person's leadership journey much more difficult and likely unsuccessful.

Character

When hiring someone it is important to first assess for integrity, or "character." There is no other quality that, when present, will prevent difficulties in your institution before they manifest. Any person who is not reliable and accountable for their actions provides an endless number of headaches for a leader. A person falsely denying they did something or claiming to have done something they did not do erodes any trust anyone might have in that person. Someone who cannot be trusted is a person that is difficult to lead and even more difficult to follow. It is not unrealistic to say that if you get the "character" aspect of the hiring process right, 98 percent of your potential problems disappear before they even begin.

In interviews, people's character might be revealed by how they talk about themselves and how they answer questions. Some examples are provided in exhibit 6.1.

Chemistry

Chemistry, in this discussion, refers to interpersonal skills, the ability to work on a team, and social intelligence. Unfortunately, because of the training and work expectations placed on physicians, a significant number of these professionals are unskilled in this area. Many are additionally unaware that they are unskilled, or they overlook the importance of these skills. Chemistry is not to be confused with introversion versus extroversion. Many people believe that extroverts make

Exhibit 6.1 Response Examples: Character

Question or Observation	Response Showing More Character	Response Showing Less Character
"Tell me about some successes you have had recently."	Uses "we," "the team," or other phrases that imply credit to others as well.	Uses "I," "me," or "my" as the person most responsible (instead of "we").
"Tell me about a time when you experienced failure and what you learned from it."	Uses "I," "me," or "my" as the person most responsible (instead of "we").	Uses "we," "the team," or other phrases that put blame on others as well.
"When is it OK to lie?"	Gives a considered response that demonstrates a greater good. (My personal response is to share an example of an older woman who had severe burns across the majority of her body. As I was preparing to intubate her, she asked, "Am I going to be OK?" in a scared voice. Knowing full well that she was not, I still reassured her.)	"Never," because almost everybody does lie, usually as a white lie.
"Tell me about a time when you were aware that another manager had embellished budget or quality numbers. What did you do?"	Describes an effort to tactfully confront the manager in a private setting to correct the exaggeration.	Responds with either "I have really never seen that" or "I would call it out on the spot even if it were in a public meeting."
"What are you most proud of in your life?"	Describes an accomplishment that benefits others much more than it benefits the respondent.	Describes any individual accolade or accomplishment.

better leaders, but much research says differently. There are multiple examples of both introverts and extroverts who are lacking in social intelligence. The preference of extroversion or introversion is more of a consideration of the type of role for which the person is being considered (extroverts might make better large-group salespeople while introverts may not). If a hiring team correctly gets both the character and the chemistry factors of the hiring process, then most potential problems are likely to disappear before they can manifest themselves.

The chemistry of internal candidates is probably known, but for outside candidates, the example questions in exhibit 6.2 might be useful. However, the best way to determine interpersonal and social skill of a potential hire is to perform the due diligence of calling references, coworkers, and associates and asking them direct questions about the candidate's chemistry.

Exhibit 6.2 Response Examples: Chemistry

Question or Observation	Response Showing Good Chemistry	Response Showing Little Chemistry
"Tell me about a recent disagreement you had with someone. What was it about, what was the outcome, and what have you learned from it?"	Describes a misunderstanding that was recognized and addressed without blaming, and explains the commitment made to provide better clarity in the future.	Gives any response that denigrates another person's character or capabilities.
"How would your coworkers describe you?" Best if asked about particular groups of coworkers (e.g., floor nurses, office staff, fellow residents)	Gives descriptions that demonstrate both strengths and characteristics that, if overbearing, might be a negative.	"They like me" or, even worse, "We don't really get along."

(continued)

(continued from previous page)

Question or Observation	Response Showing Good Chemistry	Response Showing Little Chemistry
"Do you do things with your coworkers outside work?"	"Yes, we get together socially with our significant others occasionally/ frequently."	"Not really, we aren't really interested."
"Have you told your coworkers you are interviewing?"	"Yes, they are sad that I might be leaving but are supportive."	"No, because it will make my life much more difficult if they knew."

Capacity

Capacity refers to many dimensions of the candidates. One of the most important capacities is time: Does the candidate have enough time to dedicate to the position? Many physicians struggle to have enough time to see more patients, do electronic charting, and maintain their social and family lives all while attempting to avoid burnout. But as most have been high performers with often little recognition of their own limitations, physicians frequently think they can accomplish more than is realistic. What's more, those who would like to give up working clinically to move into full-time executive roles primarily to reduce their workload have the potential to make mistakes that might adversely affect the institution.

Another aspect of capacity is the basic set of skills necessary for the position. While many of the skills of leadership might be best learned on the job, other leadership skills are necessary on day one. Because leadership roles are generally public-facing positions, the ability to communicate in a clear and concise manner free from medical jargon is a must. Additionally, all physician leaders should have some familiarity with hospital organizational structure and the relationship between the board, administration, medical staff, and the function of the bylaws.

Capacity also relates to a desire and an ability to adapt and learn (or to add two more Cs, a *critical curiosity*). Healthcare is changing at an ever-increasing rate, from both internal and external forces (evidence the COVID-19 pandemic). Today's physician leaders need to be able to learn new skills, let go of preconceptions or previously learned knowledge, and look with a critical eye toward improvement. This critical eye should apply to structures, processes, and, maybe most important, their own knowledge base and current skill sets. All leaders owe it to themselves and to the people they lead to continue to grow as leaders. Exhibit 6.3 suggests some questions leaders might ask when assessing physicians' capacity for leadership.

Exhibit 6.3 Response Examples: Capacity

Question or Observation	Response Showing Better Capacity	Response Showing Less Capacity
"How do you plan to organize your current workload with the needs of this position?"	Demonstrates consideration of the needs of both current and future workloads, ideally with detailed descriptions.	"I am really efficient. I'll just get them done."
"What additional skills or training do you think might be helpful for you to succeed in this role?"	Reflects an understanding of the limits of their own experiences and current knowledge and skill sets.	"None, really."
"What are your plans for the first (30, 60, 90) days in this role?"	"I plan on meeting key people and listening to their thoughts and concerns to develop an organized approach to what needs to be addressed and in what order."	"I'm going to fix X."

Exhibit 6.4 The Nonnegotiables That Lead to Leadership Effectiveness

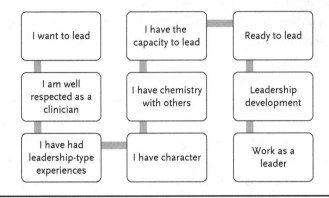

The three Cs approach to assessing potential leaders requires candidates to demonstrate self-awareness of both strengths and weaknesses. Not only is self-awareness invaluable, but one cannot lead successfully without character, chemistry, and capacity. Finally, exhibit 6.4 shows how all six characteristics (the three nonnegotiables and the three Cs) ultimately enable a person to take on a leadership role.

WORKING CLINICALLY

Whenever possible, physician leaders should ideally still perform some type of clinical work while in leadership roles. The feasibility of continuing to practice will often be driven by the organization's size and the physician's specialty. Obviously, the CMO of a $4 billion multihospital system may see little opportunity to practice, whereas the CMO of a critical access hospital may easily practice one day a week. Morgan and colleagues (2020) suggest that "fostering balance among physician leaders' clinical and leadership responsibilities is not a one-size-fits-all task. In particular, it is relevant that perspectives and features of balance varied across leadership type and clinical specialty." Moreover, they also explain, the observation that many clinical leaders "believed patient care aided them in fulfilling their leadership responsibilities is informative to both physician leaders and organizations seeking to foster physician leadership."

For effective leadership, physician leaders should sometimes be seen in arenas visible to the people being led. Physicians judge other physicians according to how they perform clinically. Strong clinicians are often given grace for missteps in administrative capacities, but weaker clinicians will not be given nearly as much latitude.

When considering outside candidates for physician leadership roles, the recruiting team must ask about the person's clinical performance. In the relatively small world of medicine, weaker clinicians are quickly recognized. Weaker clinical skills almost certainly make leading more difficult for the healthcare entity and the leader.

Working clinically often provides tremendous benefit for physician leaders as well. The administrative tasks and approaches are, in many aspects, different from what the physician has been taught and is accustomed to. Having time to go back and practice in a familiar arena—a place of demonstrated comfort and competence—allows physician leaders some balance with the growth challenges of administration. Exhibit 6.5 compares aspects of clinical and administrative work.

Exhibit 6.5 Differences Between Clinical and Administrative Perspectives

Clinical	Administrative
Years of training; career starts in early 30s	Fewer years of training; career starts in early to mid-20s
A *standard of care* for a given condition; decision-making is V-shaped; information reduced to a single best course of action	Many choices on how to address a situation; decision-making is W-shaped; information reduced to multiple options

(continued)

(continued from previous page)

Relatively quick, objective evidence of success or of movement in the right direction	Many actions require months to years to see the consequences, good or bad
Days off duty	Always on call
Patients often say thank-you	Rarely thanked, but often asked to address other people's issues, concerns, or crises
Usually a sense of accomplishment at the end of a day	Tasks often unresolved and need to be addressed over longer periods
Professional camaraderie and respect	Often viewed with distrust by physicians and labeled "a suit" or "a turncoat"

Because of the benefits shown in the first column in exhibit 6.5, physician leaders who work clinically enjoy feeling able to lead and to tend to their emotional health. Additionally, physician executives who work clinically are often much more successful in creating engaged workforces.

PHYSICIAN EXECUTIVE SKILLS

The nonnegotiables and the three Cs discussed so far in this chapter are characteristics that any leader, physician or otherwise, should possess before being considered for a leadership role. Dye and Garman (2014) provide an additional portrayal of other skills and competencies that physician leaders should develop (exhibit 6.6).

Not all these competencies need to be completely developed before a person starts in a leadership role; some can be developed and strengthened while the person is leading. The astute administrator will frequently assess all leaders for opportunities for growth in these competencies. There are three main methods (the *three Es*)

Exhibit 6.6 Exceptional Leadership Competency Model

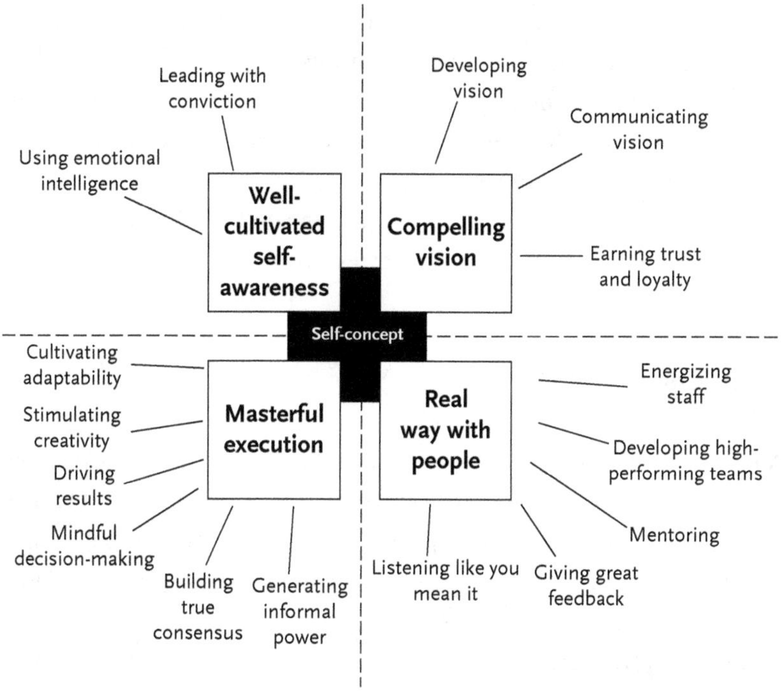

Leading with
conviction

Developing
vision

Communicating
vision

Using emotional
intelligence

Well-cultivated self-awareness

Compelling vision

Earning trust
and loyalty

Self-concept

Cultivating
adaptability

Energizing
staff

Stimulating
creativity

Masterful execution

Real way with people

Developing high-performing teams

Driving
results

Mindful
decision-making

Mentoring

Building
true
consensus

Generating
informal
power

Listening like you
mean it

Giving great
feedback

Source: Dye and Garman (2014).

for helping leaders develop competencies: education (knowledge), experience (skills), and exposure (mentors). The best return on the investment in a leader's development occurs when the method corresponds with the skill to be developed and the individual's preferred learning style.

Education (Knowledge)

In some instances, physician leaders are asked to lead in areas where they have little knowledge. For example, one physician was preparing a plan for a healthcare system to internally fund the doubling of its emergency medicine residency program and was tasked with providing a pro forma financial analysis for the project. Despite the physician's many years of education, the term *pro forma* was not recognized. After spending many evenings searching "how to make a pro forma" online, the physician soon learned that there was a large gap in his knowledge base. The discovery prompted him to earn an MBA, which has more than paid for itself over and over again. This investment in education, to compensate for a knowledge gap, has been instrumental in any successes this physician has had since.

Experience (Skills)

With the lack of administrative and leadership education and experience provided to physicians, there are, not surprisingly, tasks to which they have not been exposed. While a dearth of experience is not a true knowledge gap, the lack of familiarity makes some people less confident and more reluctant to execute an action. In supportive environments with few negative consequences if tasks are not performed well, physicians can develop skills more readily. This approach is analogous to the first two steps in the classic "see one, do one, teach one" adage for learning surgery. An after-action debrief by a skilled, respected leader on what went well and which areas require improvement is crucial. Despite what some might believe, physicians crave feedback, both good and bad, as much as anyone else does. This feedback is vital to leadership development.

Exposure (Mentors)

Sometimes, new leaders just don't know what "right" looks like. If they have never chaired committees, sat in on board meetings, or participated in strategy discussions, they may not be comfortable leading in those arenas or know what is expected of them. Having new leaders sit in on meetings as observers; having premeetings, where expectations are explained; and providing them ideas about the purpose of the role allows them to be more successful (another example of an administrative version of "see one, do one, teach one"). The identification of mentors, formal or otherwise, also helps newer leaders address questions and concerns that are not obvious to the outside observer.

EARLY IDENTIFICATION OF PHYSICIAN LEADERS

To develop physician leaders, other leaders should provide new leaders with less impactful opportunities before placing them in roles of greater responsibility. One physician was employed at a health system where an associate director of a department suddenly resigned. There was no obvious replacement, but four internal candidates, none with formal leadership experience, articulated interest. Because no candidate was a clear front-runner, the four developed a shared-governance leadership model. The associate director responsibilities were divided into four categories, one assigned to each of the interested persons along with an appropriate amount of time to dedicate to the responsibilities.

The results were interesting. One of the candidates discovered very quickly that he did not have enough patience and tolerance to serve in an administrative role at the facility and resigned from the responsibility shortly afterward. A second physician recognized that administrative work is not a way to "get paid more to work less." When the contrast between clinical and administrative work became obvious to him (see exhibit 6.5), he decided to no longer pursue this type of leadership opportunity. Although the experiences of these physicians might be considered unfortunate, they are, in fact, great successes for both of them and for the healthcare system. Two people who thought they wanted to pursue an administrative leadership title and position found out quickly that they did not enjoy the roles as much as they thought they would. Both were able to resign from the role and course-correct their careers, with no significant harm to the system or themselves. The other two physicians have gone on to greater leadership roles, and while they were in this shared-governance leadership model, they could take advantage of the three Es to further develop their leadership knowledge and skill sets.

STRENGTHS VERSUS WEAKNESSES

Some leadership development theories suggest that it is a good idea to immerse newer leaders in areas where they are not skilled, or areas of weakness, to force them into becoming a more well-rounded leader. This approach may be useful for areas in which leaders have no prior experience and might have a latent strength, but it is counterproductive in an area that is truly a weakness. No one is a complete leader, as there is no single definition of the term *leader*. Individuals have different acquired and innate capabilities, many of which can be moved along a scale to some degree. But some capabilities cannot be changed.

Why is it better to place a new leader in a position of strength rather than try to improve on the person's weakness? For any given skill set, imagine a horizontal scale of ability numbered from 0 (low) to 100 (expert). Exhibit 6.7 presents an example using the skill set of stimulating creativity.

Our new leader starts off with a score of 25 on this skill set, a score that means 75 percent of leaders are presently more adept at inspiring creativity. If the leader has never experienced a creativity-stimulating atmosphere before, the individual might have a latent but untested skill and the opportunity for great improvement

---

Exhibit 6.7 Stimulating Creativity

0	10	20	30	40	50	60	70	80	90	100
		X								

---

could be present. However, if the leader has little innate ability or growth capabilities in this area, it will be difficult to move the X much more than 10 points to the right. Even with this amount of growth, 65 percent of leaders will still be more skilled at stimulating creativity. The leader will continue to struggle, recognize underperformance, and suspect that others recognize it as well. This situation does not serve the best interests of the healthcare system and can be cruel to the leader.

A much more effective approach is to allow the leader to work in dimensions in which the person is gifted and skilled. The new leader can grow from a score of 60 to 70 and succeed. Designing and hiring teams that have complementary strengths and weaknesses allows for greater success, increased job satisfaction, and much greater engagement of the team members and followers.

CONTINUED GROWTH

A core component of every job description should be succession planning. One of the best ways to ensure continued success in a role and in an institution is to insist that every leader identify and develop potential successors for their role. Succession planning works for many reasons. Clearly the best way to learn and become proficient at something is to teach it to others. Teaching others how to perform one's own position improves the teacher's performance in the role as well. When leaders are expected, as part of their stated responsibilities, to identify and prepare potential successors, the leaders become more proficient in their positions. This practice also increases the level of engagement for both the person in the leadership position and the identified successor or successors. Engagement rises with good relationships, and the mentor and mentee structure should be built on mutual respect. Such respect will also help prevent both the current and the potential leader from looking elsewhere to use their talents. Moreover, good leaders move to new positions either inside or outside the healthcare system. Having a prepared successor allows for a much smoother transition when someone does change roles and for prior successes to continue to be built on.

To invest in the continued growth of leaders, healthcare systems might structure their teams so that each leader has at least one mentor and is responsible for preparing at least one successor. The guidance "from above" (from mentors) and the responsibility for someone "below" (for a potential successor) provides balance for the leader. Having a role model to emulate and a mentee to guide, a leader has more opportunities to remained engaged in the work and with the system.

CONCLUSION

The most successful healthcare institutions have strong physician engagement, and having the right physician leaders in place is one of the best determinants of this level of engagement. Most physicians are not taught leadership skills but are wrongly assumed to already have them. In assessing potential physician leaders in its institution, the leadership needs to identify early on candidates who have the three Cs (character, chemistry, and capacity) and a strong desire to make a positive difference. Once these potential leaders are identified, they should have small opportunities to demonstrate their leadership abilities and learn more of them. Such opportunities will help prevent larger-scale mistakes while enabling the new leaders to identify strengths and to grow.

The three ways physicians develop leadership competencies (through education, experience, and exposure—the so-called three Es) can be evaluated, and any shortfalls in the three Es can be transformed into strengths or recognized as areas to avoid. One way to guide these transformations is through mentorship. Potential leaders—and all leaders—benefit from being both a mentor and a mentee in that these relationships support the "see one, do one, teach one" method for continued growth and engagement.

With physician leaders, it is important to identify potential early, then allow opportunities for growth to become better leaders, and to invest in them through their service. There is no more important investment in healthcare and none that will provide a greater return.

REFERENCES

Beeby, T. M. 2017. "What Role Does Ambition Play in the Success of a Leader?" Penn State Presidential Leader Academy. Published September 24. https://sites.psu.edu/academy/2017/09/24/what-role-does-ambition-play-in-the-success-of-a-leader.

Dye, C. F., and A. N. Garman. 2014. *Exceptional Leadership: 16 Critical Competencies for Healthcare Executives*, 2nd ed. Chicago: Health Administration Press.

Morgan, J. W., A. S. Detsky, J. A. Shea, and J. M. Liao. 2020. "Physician Leaders' Perspectives About Balancing Clinical and Leadership Responsibilities." *American Journal of Managed Care.* Published July 6. www.ajmc.com/view/physician-leaders-perspectives-about-balancing-clinical-and-leadership-responsibilities.

Zarian, S. 2015. "Intrinsic and Extrinsic Motivations to Lead." *LeAD Labs* (Claremont Graduate University blog). Published September 22. https://research.cgu.edu/lead-labs/2015/09/22/motivations-to-lead/.

CHAPTER 7

Supply-Chain Issues

Scott B. Ransom

Understand and harness the principles of disruptive innovation.
—Clayton Christensen, *The Innovator's Dilemma*, 1997

A 40-HOSPITAL HEALTH SYSTEM, developed through a series of acquisitions in the twenty-first century, began to experience significant financial challenges from payer pressure and increasing costs. The health system CMO and chief supply officer discussed with the chief of orthopedic surgery the potential for significant financial opportunities related to orthopedic implants. The group decided to create an action plan. The goal was to reduce the cost of hip and knee implants while maintaining or improving overall quality and patient access. After deep analysis of the literature and other evidence as well as significant expert opinion from health system orthopedic surgeons, nursing, supply chain, and others, the group reduced the number of preferred implants from 14 to 6 for the hip and from 9 to 5 for the knee. After negotiating with its suppliers, the health system reduced the number of preferred implants to 3 each for knee and hip replacements.

The CMO and chief of orthopedic surgery developed a plan to engage all orthopedic surgeons in the health system. Their approach began with meetings with approximately three dozen key orthopedic and nursing opinion leaders who have major influence with the more than three hundred orthopedic surgeons and nursing leaders across the health system. This step was critical for the CMO and surgery chief to learn perspectives of, and to earn buy-in from, many key decision-makers before disseminating the information further. Following the one-on-one meetings, these opinion leaders met three times over six weeks to review relevant analysis and literature, discuss the issue, share perspectives, and finalize an approach. The hospital-based chief of orthopedic surgery and at least one local opinion leader met at least twice with each of the 32 hospitals' orthopedic surgery departments that completed implant surgery. The first meeting was used to elicit people's perspectives on the preferred implant approach. In the second meeting, the executives finalized this input and shared two gainsharing approaches—one for the employed physicians and the other for affiliated and volunteer physicians.

With a select group of opinion leaders, legal counsel, and a vice president of finance, the CMO and chief of supply chain developed a gainsharing approach from their analyses and group input. Employed physicians could easily understand the approach of gainsharing, whereby each surgeon could earn additional income if the individual supported the preferred items. Affiliated physicians, on the other hand, realized their gainsharing benefit in the form of earning additional resources to their various departments. They could apply these resources, for example, to continuing medical education, research assistants, scribes to facilitate both office and hospital work, and other support to improve the orthopedic surgeon's environment and workflow at each of the hospitals.

The quickest to adopt the orthopedic implant approach were the employed-physician group and two early adopting hospitals with completely voluntary medical staff. Leadership was careful to ensure that the gainsharing distribution was transparent for both the physicians and the hospitals that earned the support as well as for individuals who earned no support. The gainsharing distributions were provided every other month, and as the program gained traction, additional physicians began to use the preference items. The progressive adoption required 18 months to reach 72 percent compliance with the preferred hip and knee implants. All totaled, the health system's financial gain for the implant program, net of orthopedic surgeon gainsharing distributions, was approximately $42 million for the first year of the program and $63 million savings for the second year.

A few key parts of this supply-chain transformation contributed to the success of the implant preference program. First, several orthopedic surgeons had to be trained on the surgical techniques for procedures that used the preferred implants. Second, to ensure senior leadership support, the program tied 40 percent of each hospital's chief of orthopedic surgery administrative bonus directly to implant preference utilization. Third, each of these chiefs was provided detailed monthly data, including the number and percentage of specific implants used, length of stay, cost, complications, and other quality outcomes. Fourth, monthly reports were disseminated to each orthopedic surgeon; the reports contained the surgeon's own data and information according to hospital, region, the entire health system, and nationwide best-practice hospitals to ensure full transparency. Finally, the health system regularly provided all orthopedic surgeons a blinded report of the gainsharing distributions to prove the hospitals' commitment and to further incentivize orthopedic surgeons to comply with the program in the future (Kiewiet 2020).

Overall, the implant preference program was considered a success by the health system as well as the majority of orthopedic surgeons. The approach and lessons learned were then applied to cardiology and neurosurgery implants across the health system.

TRADITIONAL EFFORTS TO IMPROVE THE SUPPLY CHAIN

Providing more cost-efficient care has become a priority in healthcare. Independent of the reimbursement approach, hospitals continue to look for areas to reduce unnecessary costs while maintaining or improving quality of care. Hospitals have historically tried to reduce supply-chain costs through several avenues. They have negotiated better deals with vendors for their needed products, taking advantage of volume discounts by joining group purchasing organizations with other hospitals. Hospitals have also reduced inventories and created a more just-in-time purchasing approach and have modified their product choices for nonclinical items. Physician leaders must also focus on how pandemics and other crises might affect the requirements for such supplies as personal protective equipment (PPE), ventilators, and pharmaceuticals (Anderson 2020). Although many traditional approaches are valuable, leading-edge hospitals are beginning to engage physicians and clinicians in efforts to optimize the choice of, use of, and access to medical products and surgical implants to reduce costs while providing excellent quality and access.

Whether hospital revenues come through a traditional fee-for-service or value-based reimbursement methodology, the reduction of supply costs is good for the bottom line. For fee-for-service, the hospital typically gets paid more for more medical services but will generally be paid the same for each of those services, independent of product cost. For example, a hospital receiving payments based on a diagnosis-related group will generally get paid the same for a hip replacement whether it chooses a more expensive or less expensive hip implant. Similarly, value-based reimbursement approaches are looking to improve patient service by improving quality while reducing costs. Thus, a hospital paid on value will certainly be better off by reducing unnecessary supply costs as long as the product maintains or improves quality (Rehman, Scholosser, and Schneller 2016).

Hospital leaders often hesitate to engage physicians in discussions about optimal product choice or utilization. Because affiliated private practice physicians often choose which hospital to send their patients to, hospital leaders might feel concerned about putting undue pressure on these physicians. They worry that the physicians might sent their patients elsewhere, thereby shifting market share to competitors (Kiewiet 2020). On the other hand, hospitals must support their physicians in improving quality while reducing unnecessary costs to maintain sustainability and margin, drive the quality agenda, and create greater value for their communities. Although all hospitals are interested in improving quality and reducing costs, only a few have created a successful approach to lead physician engagement in better product choice and utilization.

ENGAGING PHYSICIANS IN OPTIMIZING SUPPLY UTILIZATION

While hospitals have chosen to work with physicians and clinicians in optimizing product choice through a variety of approaches, no organization has perfected its optimization methodology. As this observation suggests, the drive for optimal supply utilization and availability is much more art than science. Leading-edge hospitals have engaged physicians through various approaches. For example, hospitals maintain a balanced vision of quality, efficiency, access, and cost and conduct systematic literature reviews and product assessments to provide their physicians with the available knowledge and expert opinions on the topic. They also create greater transparency on cost and quality factors affecting supplies and, especially, physician preference items such as surgical implants and pharmaceuticals. These hospitals also provide physician and department data on key metrics related to quality, efficiency, and cost (e.g., supply cost per case, implant cost per case). Coaching and training are other parts of leading-edge hospitals' efforts, providing one-on-one physician coaching opportunities with highly credible physician peers and experts and the necessary training for using the preferred products. In deciding on the preferred products, these hospitals establish policies to reduce conflicts of interest, such as inappropriate personal or financial relationships with vendors. Finally, the hospitals provide financial incentives to better align the goals of improving quality and reducing cost through gainsharing, pay for performance, and related methods (Schneller and Eckler 2020).

BALANCING QUALITY, EFFICIENCY, ACCESS, AND COST

Physicians are generally suspicious of administration's goals for driving change and optimizing supply choice. Leaders must focus on optimizing supply utilization through a balanced view of improving or maintaining quality of care, efficiency, access, and cost. Leaders who begin the discussion with cost and financial issues are effectively dead on arrival and have little hope of actively engaging physicians for future discussions on product and supply optimization. While nearly every clinician engagement study shows that physicians modify their practice according to financial incentives, most physicians do believe they are looking out for the best interests of their patients. For this reason, starting the discussion by focusing on improving quality is usually the best approach.

A balanced discussion that begins with patient quality will at least support an initial conversation with physicians. But even when best practices prove that alternative approaches are best for their patients, physicians may struggle to change their professional-practice habits and surgical techniques, which were often established during their training. Administrators who are looking to lead physicians to new supply choices must begin the discussion with patient quality to start on the moral high ground and then make the transition to a discussion of efficiency and cost factors (Cardinal Health 2020).

While most institutions complete these discussions through one-on-one or small group meetings, others have taken more systematic approaches by facilitating physician engagement with supply-chain leaders. For example, a top academic medical center started its own group purchasing organization. The group aimed to build dialogue between physicians and supply-chain leaders to support collaborative decisions and to improve clinician satisfaction and patient outcomes. A key part of this approach was to have the clinical community evaluate products being considered for purchase through a lens of clinical evidence and patient needs. In addition, this forum encouraged physicians to see the bigger picture, including the betterment of the system as a whole.

One area of success was a collaboration between spinal surgeons and their supply-chain colleagues. The two groups collaborated to secure a $3.3 million in contracted savings on spinal implant products from 14 vendors. The contracting department informed vendors that the health system would pay only a certain price for each product while the spinal clinical community evaluated each implant's importance to patient care. Ultimately, the group's assessments supported the arguments for lower prices, helping the contract department to save approximately $800,000 net of gainsharing and other expenses.

SYSTEMATIC LITERATURE REVIEWS AND PRODUCT ASSESSMENTS

Before engaging physicians on supply choice, healthcare leaders should always get the facts. They should conduct a comprehensive literature review before meeting with physicians. The leaders need to understand the science, the current state of knowledge, and expert opinion on the product's quality, efficiency, and cost. Generally, practicing physicians are not up-to-date on the science and expert opinion for many or most supply choices. It is therefore the administrator's responsibility to be armed with the most credible information available about a product, including what others are saying about product choices.

A comprehensive literature review should include sources such as PubMed, specialty society reviews, Google searches for presentations and opinion articles on the topic, commercial and vendor materials, and Cochrane and other systematic reviews. Leaders conducting this review should seek to determine the most credible sources (e.g., preferring a double-blind, randomized trial over a financially driven opinion article supported by vendors). In conducting the review, administrators should make sure they understand the positive and more challenging aspects of the various products and have efficiently organized the materials from most to least credible sources to efficiently summarize the fact base for the physicians or clinicians.

The administrator must then compare the products that are currently on formulary and used at their institution with the range of alternatives, including hospital-specific cost differences. This product review should get down to the per-patient level so that physicians can appreciate the cost and quality differences for an individual patient. While product cost is often difficult to determine with the various deals, incentives, and volume discounts, it is the responsibility and challenge of the administrator to summarize these product choice differences so that physicians can understand the financial consequences of their decisions in terms they understand (e.g., for an individual patient). In addition, if the healthcare organization is considering a new product that may have significant volume discounts, it is absolutely appropriate to share how physicians' choices affect current and future quality, cost, access, and financial elements of care (Snowdon 2018).

Finally, leadership needs to prepare a simple summary of the quality, efficiency, and cost impact of the physicians' decisions so that they can quickly understand the consequences. As a matter of principle, it is often best to place products that have been proven to reduce patient quality in a completely different, "not acceptable" category so that physicians can easily appreciate that the administration also aims for good quality of patient care. The golden rule of the summary is to keep it extremely simple, with data presented on a per-patient basis. A one-page summary in a large and easy-to-read font is always better than a lengthy, complicated article. Physicians appreciate supporting materials and data, but the administrator should keep the core presentation to the physician and clinician simple and straightforward. It should boil down the cost and quality implications to one standard patient. For example, the cost of using product A on the patient is X dollars, and its resulting quality is no different from that of current products.

Furthermore, the summary should highlight for the physicians how reducing the number of vendors can provide the hospitals with

Exhibit 7.1 Reducing the Number of Products Can Support Better Pricing Negotiations

Total client spending on spine implants, by vendor, in millions of dollars

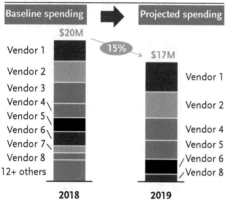

- Reducing the number of vendors from more than 20 to 8 can reduce spending on spine implants due to improved negotiated prices
- Reducing the number of implants in the hospital also reduces total inventory costs by reducing inventory volume dedicated to spine implants

better leverage in pricing negotiations. The benefits of consolidating vendors can easily be presented to physicians in the form of simple data comparison. Exhibit 7.1 was used to show a group of spine surgeons that reducing the number of vendors had significant impact on the bottom line without compromising quality.

TRANSPARENCY OF DATA

Administrators should provide accurate and reliable information to physicians to support optimal supply decisions. Information can be shared in meetings or documents, but the most common approach to data dissemination is through one-on-one or two-on-two meetings with one target physician or clinician along with a highly regarded physician colleague or external expert. The messenger or messengers are important to credibility. A transparent, believable message can make or break the initial discussion, setting the stage for future dialogue and providing evidence that supports change.

Group meetings with a few physicians can help the administration earn their support for the better supply choice, but the meetings do require significant preparation. To ensure a receptive audience, the presenter should already have discussed the materials and presentation with all key decision makers and opinion leaders individually. By having a one-on-one discussion before a group meeting with the most vocal opinion leaders, the presenter may get feedback that will help them target the desired individuals in the larger meeting and otherwise improve the presentation; the one-on-one will also encourage the testing of certain assumptions and facts. With proper meeting preparation, the presenter will be far more likely to have a receptive audience, especially if a few of the opinion leaders are prepped with good questions and supportive feedback. Preparation for these high-stakes meetings cannot be overemphasized. Countless well-intended leaders have gone into these group or department meetings alone, with no preparation or built-in support. Often, such meetings result in a loss of credibility for the messenger and the message.

High-quality documents and supportive literature can be distributed to physicians and clinicians, but a summary, with information supporting the point of view, is a more user-friendly format for busy physicians. More is generally not better when sharing information with busy people. By summarizing key materials and explicitly stating the main point, the brief document is much more likely to help physicians understand the goals and eventually support the approach.

Many administrators are surprised that few physicians know or understand the cost or quality implications for many of the physicians' product decisions. For this reason, physicians and clinicians need transparent information on cost and quality. As previously noted, it is best to relay this information on a per-patient level so that the physicians can easily see the implications. While patient-level data often requires significant work by the administrator, this information will be critical to support transparency in the context of patient care.

One academic medical center encouraged significant transparency through the use of a grand rounds sessions to highlight the facts about priority pharmaceuticals and products. The medical center commissioned an impartial faculty member with a background as an epidemiologist to complete a comprehensive review on all relevant competing products. After the review was summarized and presented to the entire department, an active discussion ensued regarding the evidence base as well as the advantages and disadvantages of each competing product. The discussion focused on quality, cost, and efficiency. After this preliminary discussion and dialogue (20 to 30 minutes), representatives from the top competing products were invited to provide short presentations to the entire department. The presenters compared their product with alternatives and left time for questions and answers. At the end of the meeting, the chairperson facilitated a discussion to help the entire department agree on one or more preferred product options. These departmental recommendations were forwarded to the Pharmacy and Therapeutics Committee and to all physician faculty and residents. This highly engaged approach proved very useful to ensure transparency, disseminate the facts, facilitate discussion, and support final recommendations on the product choice in a relatively efficient time frame (e.g., generally within the confines of one 2-hour grand round).

If done properly, sharing physician-specific data is an extremely powerful tool for engaging physicians and supporting change. A physician's cost and quality data may be compared with the physician's peers, hospital outcomes, health system performance, external benchmarks, and international best practices. As physicians are often competitive, accurate and credible data on how they compare with others can be a very powerful way to encourage change and promote physician engagement.

Before data is shared with physicians, the administration must ensure the accuracy and reliability of the primary data sources, the analytical approach, and the benchmark sources. Lower-performing physicians often first attack the data, so all normal objections and challenges must have immediate answers to support the data and the credibility of the messenger. The lower-performing physicians are also likely to attack the messenger. To reduce these likely personal attacks, the administration often prefers to have two highly credible messengers with complementary skills to discuss the data with physicians. Specifically, one messenger would ideally be a physician with good credibility in the discipline (e.g., a medical director, chairperson, an opinion leader, an external expert), and the second messenger would be highly knowledgeable about the analysis, data sources, and fact base (e.g., a medical director, a vice president of medical affairs, a researcher, an administrator). The goal is to provide information that is highly credible to reduce the potential for personal attacks so that the physician can thoughtfully consider options to improve a product choice to both improve quality and reduce cost.

A few hospitals have created tools to collect and disseminate information to key stakeholders and physicians. For example, a large 40-hospital health system created a supply variance tool that measured targeted supply use by hospital and by physician (see, for example, exhibit 7.2). This tool was used to provide a physician-specific report that compared their product use with a blinded list

Exhibit 7.2 Supply Consumption for Health System Physicians

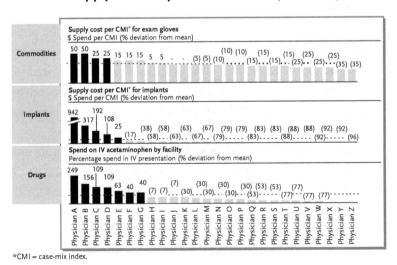

*CMI = case-mix index.

of peers as well as hospital and health system averages and best practices, national benchmarks (where available), and known international best practices. In addition, each administrator was provided a report on supply utilization, down to the physician level, for the administrator's areas of responsibility. This data tool was found to be extremely powerful in aligning physician and administrator goals with those of the hospital.

Another example of an approach is highlighted by Stanford Medicine. The organization experienced challenges with aligning physicians to specific product choices to improve quality, cost, access, and efficiency outcomes. To create evidence-based solutions, Stanford created a Value-Based Selection Committee to review efficiency and efficacy and to make recommendations on optimal product choice. This committee facilitated the transition from a physician-centric culture to one that focuses on quality, cost, and outcomes. In addition, the committee distributed information and supported one-on-one and small group communications so that physicians could make better, more informed decisions to optimize their care approach. This committee realized savings in excess of $12 million the first year and began reducing clinical variation leading to better patient outcomes.

PHYSICIAN COACHING

Physician-specific data can be presented to a variety of stakeholders, but a blinded graphical representation of key quality, cost, access, and efficiency data often works best for engaging a physician (see, for example, exhibit 7.3). Ideally, the data would compare the individual physician's data with peer data, department average or best practices, health system best practices, and external benchmarks and best practices. Well-presented data can quickly and efficiently show how the physician's numbers compare with those of the various groups. For credibility and balance, physicians must be able to see areas where they excel and areas that are more challenging for them.

Exhibit 7.3 Examples of Physician Data Compared at Various Levels (Peers, Hospital, Regional)

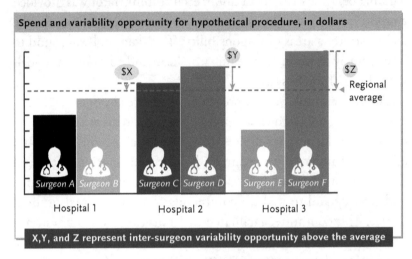

Spend and variability opportunity for hypothetical procedure, in dollars

$X

$Y

$Z

Regional average

Surgeon A | Surgeon B | Surgeon C | Surgeon D | Surgeon E | Surgeon F

Hospital 1   Hospital 2   Hospital 3

X, Y, and Z represent inter-surgeon variability opportunity above the average

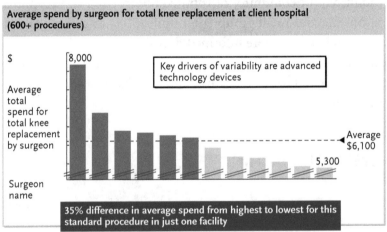

Average spend by surgeon for total knee replacement at client hospital (600+ procedures)

$

8,000

Average total spend for total knee replacement by surgeon

Key drivers of variability are advanced technology devices

Average $6,100

5,300

Surgeon name

35% difference in average spend from highest to lowest for this standard procedure in just one facility

To build comfort and rapport with the physician, the administrator or other leader should share positive messages first and save the more challenging ones for later in the discussion.

Once the physician understands the analysis and generally agrees with the data, the discussion often shifts to how better-performing physicians achieve their outcomes. At that time, the leader should share best practices with the physician and allow for significant discussion. In this conversation, the physician may share any concerns with the analysis or with changing product choice to best practices. For example, a new hip implant may require a different technique that is not fully understood by a surgeon and may require additional training. Other concerns may arise. If, for example, a cardiologist has a financial stake in a preferred product, the leader must have an open discussion and remind the physician of hospital policies. Still other concerns, such as physicians' continuing disagreement with the data and best practices, often require follow-up meetings to help physicians become comfortable with the recommendations and more engaged with the decision-making.

GROUP MEETINGS

After key physicians have had one-on-one discussions and an opportunity to review blinded physician-specific data, it is often helpful to present the same data at a department meeting to reinforce messaging and establish hospital guidelines. These group meetings go far in creating greater transparency with, and peer pressure on, physicians, encouraging them to embrace the desired product choices. While these meetings use the same credible physicians and other individuals knowledgeable about the details of the analysis as the primary messengers, wise leaders will also ask physicians who were generally positive during the one-on-one meetings to share their perspectives. The department meeting presents the opportunity for everyone to share ideas on the opportunities and challenges and to consider the best ways to train physicians unfamiliar with the product or how best to adopt the recommended best practice.

For example, an orthopedic center used this group-discussion tactic to reduce cost variability and establish best practices in its product choices. The initial review of the data revealed that two types of hip implants were being used; the more expensive implants were coated with vitamin E to promote bone growth. The supply-chain team presented the data, and the surgeons presented a review of the literature. The literature revealed that the coated implants were ideal for patients younger than 70, whereas patients older than 70 received no benefit from the more expensive product. The orthopedic surgeons agreed to use vitamin E–coated implants only on younger patients to save money while maintaining quality expectations.

CLINICIAN TRAINING FOR BEST PRACTICES

Because physicians often continue the same patient-care approach they learned in residency and fellowship, many of them require training to adopt new surgical implants, devices, and related products. This training should ideally be offered at the hospital or another convenient location, with a minimum of practice disruption and conflict. The environment must avoid anything that would cause hostility, professional conflict, and embarrassment. Understanding that some physicians have conducted some procedures the same way for decades, the organization must develop training opportunities for these physicians in a manner that is highly professional and that complements their existing expertise. For this reason, the organization should seek out highly credible peers or external experts as trainers.

REDUCING CONFLICTS OF INTEREST

As personal and financial conflicts are reasonably common in medical and surgical practice, health systems must have institutional policies and procedures to prioritize best practices that optimize patient outcomes while maintaining cost-efficiency. Some surgeon entrepreneurs create their own surgical implants and other devices that should be evaluated for cost-effectiveness and for how they compare with best practices. Similarly, it is not uncommon for surgeons to be hired by pharmaceutical and product companies as medical experts or presenters with the explicit goal of encouraging the use of their products. Furthermore, some physicians may have a spouse, family member, or close friend selling a particular product that poses conflicts with best practices and cost-effective outcomes.

For example, a highly regarded physician scientist from a top academic medical center invented, and began using, a pharmaceutical product whose cost ran in the high five figures. Hospital leadership led by the CMO reviewed and found that other products were available at much lower cost and with better demonstrated patient outcomes. Because of the prestige of this physician scientist, the issue eventually went to the full board of directors, who decided to eliminate the product from the formulary and block it from future use. The medical center learned that the physician received compensation from the pharmaceutical company for this invention. This compensation naturally made it difficult for him to objectively appreciate the consequences.

Organizations must have well-defined policies and procedures that address these conflicts. These policies and procedures should be in compliance with those of the American Medical Association and other professional societies and with any applicable state guidelines.

FINANCIAL INCENTIVES

Several examples of pay-for-performance and gainsharing methods encourage physicians to align with hospital or practice goals. While organizations that employ their physicians generally have the greatest latitude in legally supporting these financial incentives, many types of gainsharing incentives can better align affiliated physicians as well.

For example, a hospital used gainsharing incentives to encourage eligible orthopedic surgeons to use implants that the available literature showed were high quality and that were more cost-effective from the hospital's perspective. The incentive provides physicians a percentage of the upside to the hospital to support personal income. These arrangements, however, must be reviewed by highly qualified attorneys before implementation, to avoid Stark and other inurement violations. Another hospital agreed to provide its cardiology division a percentage of the financial gain if the group used the preferred implants and other supplies so that the division could invest in new equipment, purchase books for residents and students, and support educational programs and guest speakers. This financial contribution to the division was found to meet all legal requirements because it encouraged higher-quality practices and a better-trained workforce.

As noted, organizations with employed physicians and faculty have the greatest leeway in using financial incentives to improve quality of care and efficiency. For example, a medical school faculty was encouraged to improve patient quality metrics with efforts that included the adoption of several best practices. These included the use of preferred implants and pharmaceuticals, maintaining length-of-stay targets, achieving blood-transfusion goals, and ensuring measurable levels for patient satisfaction. The medical school believed that a balanced approach to providing financial incentives through a broad definition of quality (e.g., financial quality, service quality, clinical quality) improved its competitiveness. These incentives have proven very effective in driving practice changes because of the balanced emphasis on key goals and only financial outcomes.

THE PHYSICIAN LEADER'S ROLE

It is the physician leader's role to evaluate access for common lifesaving products and pharmaceuticals and to anticipate product utilization spikes that can occur during such rare situations as pandemics and disasters causing mass casualties. Again, leaders should look at data to understand how past spikes in demand may be related to season, special events, and local or national trends. In addition, institutions need to anticipate how they would respond efficiently to these rare disasters or pandemics—for example, through a rapid sourcing of products—and they should review these plans regularly.

Consider the real example of the COVID-19 pandemic. Organizations must anticipate the unusually high product utilization for such items as healthcare worker PPE or lifesaving pharmaceuticals and respond to this demand as early as possible. While no physician leader could have anticipated the near-immediate, extraordinarily high need for PPE during the pandemic, an organization's leadership must know the supply channels to rapidly access various supplies and pharmaceuticals in case of an unusual demand (O'Rourke 2014). As they did during the COVID-19 crisis, physician leaders must often push nonclinical leaders to respond to the likely need for these products as disease prevalence increases. Physician leaders may also be required to problem-solve dramatic national shortages by seeking products from nontraditional vendors and even become inventors to create alternatives. During the height of the COVID-19 crisis, many leaders were required to seek products from unknown and often more suspicious vendors because traditional sources were unavailable.

Furthermore, the pandemic required many health system leaders to invent product alternatives to solve short-term shortages. For example, several hospitals responded to the shortages of PPE by inventing their own solutions from day-to-day products such as garbage sacks and store-bought cloth to create alternatives. And a number of other health systems devised creative solutions for sterilizing typically onetime-use products (e.g., masks and other PPE) with ultraviolet light and other means to solve some extreme shortages of these products. In summary, the physician leader should ensure that a tracking system exists to identify inventory concerns for critical items as an early warning signal to alert the organization about unanticipated supply challenges for protective equipment and products used for emergencies. While maintaining an adequate supply may have cost implications, it is key to maintain reasonable supply levels to promote patient care and healthcare worker safety.

CONCLUSION

As summarized in exhibit 7.4, engaging physicians in optimizing product choice, access, and utilization requires a deliberate and

Exhibit 7.4 Role of Physician Engagement in Optimizing Product Choice to Drive Quality and Cost Benefits

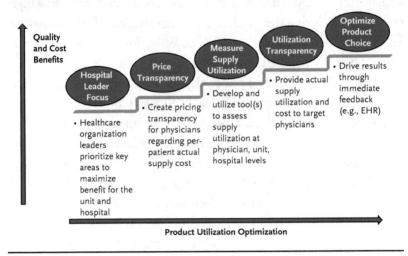

consistent approach; however, the healthcare organizations that continue the journey targeting priority products have the opportunity to improve patient outcomes as well as reduce necessary variation and costs.

REFERENCES

Anderson, M. 2020. "5 Ways Rural Hospitals Can Secure PPE." *Becker's Hospital Review*. Published May 21. www.beckershospitalreview.com/supply-chain/5-ways-rural-hospitals-can-secure-ppe.html.

Cardinal Health. 2020. "3 Tips to Take Control of Your Supply Chain." *Becker's Hospital Review*. Published August 3. https://www.beckershospitalreview.com/supply-chain/3-tips-to-take-control-of-your-supply-chain.html.

Christensen, C. M. 1997. *The Innovator's Dilemma: When New Technologies Cause Great Firms to Fail*. Boston: Harvard Business School Press.

Kiewiet, S. 2020. "Supply Chain Knowledge Is Important for Orthopedic Surgeons." *AAOS Now*. Published March. https://aaos.org/aaosnow/2020/mar/managing/managing01.

O'Rourke, D. 2014. "The Science of Sustainable Supply Chains." *Science* 344 (6188): 1124–27.

Rehman, A., M. Scholosser, and E. S. Schneller. 2016. "Physician Leadership in Supply Chain: The Missing Link." *Becker's Hospital Review*. Published August 15. www.beckershospitalreview.com/supply-chain/physician-leadership-in-supply-chain-the-missing-link.html.

Schneller, E. S., and J. Eckler. 2020. "Supply Chain Management, What's in It for Me? What Physicians Gain from Supporting Supply Chain Teams." American Association of Physician Leadership. Published July 22. www.physicianleaders.org/news/supply-chain-management-whats-in-it-for-me-what-physicians-gain-from-supporting-supply-chain-teams.

Snowdon, A. W. 2018. "Clinically Integrated Supply Chain Infrastructure in Health Systems: The Opportunity to Improve Quality and Safety." *Healthcare Quarterly* 21 (3): 19–23.

CHAPTER 8

The Roles of Boards of Trustees

Bhagwan Satiani and Mary Dillhoff

ALTHOUGH PHYSICIAN ENGAGEMENT has become a prized objective, many hospitals have failed to achieve this goal. Governance of health systems has become so much more complicated. The ultimate responsibility for engagement rests with the health system or hospital CEO and the board. The board of trustees has its hands full with multiple weighty tasks. The boards are also faced with an explosion of regulations; legal mandates; public dissatisfaction with the cost of care, access to services, and calls for transparency related to price; outcomes; and quality-of-care measures. Consider the cumulative effect of the number of hospitals in the United States and the thousands of their boards that could have an impact on the lives of physicians. If they work in tandem with physicians, the engagement of physicians to achieve a better future for healthcare delivery should be achievable.

In 2020, there were 6,146 hospitals in the United States. Of these, the majority (5,198) were community hospitals, that is, nonfederal short-term general hospitals, including academic hospitals (AHA 2020). About two-thirds of community hospitals are nongovernmental not-for-profit (NFP) hospitals. In contrast to for-profit hospitals, the board members of NFPs are not responsible to private owners or shareholders but instead answer to the community that the hospital serves.

While hospital board members do not provide patient care or manage hospital operations, they do have a fiduciary responsibility to provide oversight, particularly over patient safety and quality of care. Integrated Healthcare Strategies, a healthcare consulting firm, has condensed the board's duties down to three fiduciary duties (care, loyalty, and obedience) and six core responsibilities: financial oversight, oversight of patient safety and quality, setting strategic directions, board development and self-assessment, management oversight, and advocacy. Patient safety and quality and management oversight are probably the most important (Becker's Hospital Review 2016).

Considering the various duties and responsibilities of hospital boards, they play an important role in many aspects of physician–hospital relations. In this chapter, we will review the current state of hospital boards, the roadblocks to physician representation, what hospital boards need to do to engage physicians, and in turn how physicians can seek board positions and be successful.

BOARD REPRESENTATION IMPORTANT AS PART OF PHYSICIAN ENGAGEMENT

As Bryan Oshiro, MD, medical director of Health Catalyst, astutely notes, physicians are the bedrock of healthcare solutions: "Every strategy to fix problems in healthcare today revolves around the buy-in of one critical group—the physicians" (Oshiro 2015). Reviewing a 2016 Gallup study, Guptta (2017) notes that only 33 percent of workers are engaged in their work. And with large numbers of physicians switching to working as employees, they are certainly not an exception to Guptta's observation.

Physician engagement is purported to be vital for high-performing healthcare systems since it improves health outcomes and reduces cost (Milliken 2014; Taitz, Lee, and Sequist 2012). Many studies have shown that high physician engagement correlates with patient safety, a reduction in healthcare disparities, and improved overall organizational performance (Hall et al. 2016; Prins et al. 2010; Taitz, Lee, and Sequist 2012).

However, the exact metrics regarding what *engagement* means are wide-ranging. Perriera and colleagues (2019) separate engagement activities from a hospital standpoint into either micro- or macro-level activities. Micro-level engagement activities refer to those at the patient level, whereas macro-level activities occur at the system level. Macro involvement includes community contributions, population health, or board participation.

Physicians and other clinicians must be viewed as an important part of macro engagement for many reasons. Since many board members are laypeople, with no inside knowledge of healthcare, they rely on hospital administration, other members, or clinicians on the board to inform them of possible solutions to healthcare issues brought to the board. The board has a fiduciary responsibility to establish a broad organization strategy, allocate financial resources, oversee internal auditing and risk management, recruit future board members, and select and evaluate senior executives. However, the board's duty to focus on patient safety and quality of care is paramount.

Physicians, on the other hand, were until recently mostly independent and were considered customers of the hospital. As more and more hospitals employ physicians, health systems are under more pressure to engage them, especially since hospitals expected that these physicians would become true partners fully committed to the health system's mission. The previous existing transactional relationship has changed to one of interdependence and, hopefully, partnership.

WHY HOSPITAL BOARDS NEED A PHYSICIAN PRESENCE

Since one of the board's primary responsibilities is to ensure quality of care and patient safety, it stands to reason that physicians and other clinicians with expertise in these areas should be board members with voting privileges, not just in an advisory capacity (Bader et al. 2008). A report from the Governance Institute showed that of the 14 CEOs and 57 board members queried, 59 percent stated that the additional expertise would help the board in its deliberations (Governance Institute 2012).

Bai and Krishnan (2015) looked at the US Department of Health and Human Services database on NFP hospitals in California from 2004 to 2008 and found that the absence of physicians on hospital boards was associated with a decrease of 3 to 5 percentage points in three out of four measures of care quality. This result was obtained using regression analysis, which controlled for various hospital characteristics. Hospital size, church affiliation, urban location, and system affiliation were positively associated with quality of care; the proportion of Medicaid patient revenue and poverty level of the county in which the hospital is located were negatively associated with quality of care.

Jiang, Bass, and Fraser (2008) have demonstrated a link between board oversight of quality and reduction in mortality rates. The study also showed that having physicians involved in the board quality committee further enhanced the quality of care.

A survey by Jha and Epstein of a thousand board chairs of US hospitals showed that less than half rated quality of patient care as one of the two top priorities, with the better performers more inclined to view quality as a priority (Jha and Epstein 2010). In contrast to financial performance, which was on the board's agenda 93 percent of the time, quality performance was an agenda item only 63 percent of the time.

These results highlight the importance of physician participation in hospital governance and indicate areas for hospitals, boards, and policy makers to focus on to enhance medical quality management. For this to happen, healthcare organizations need their physicians to be engaged.

Current State of Physician Representation on Hospital Boards

The typical NFP hospital in a 2009 survey had 14 to 17 board members, of whom 12 were *independent*, or not employed by the hospital. The average hospital board had 2 physicians as part of the board (Prybil et al. 2012). In another review by Satiani and Prakash (2016), who looked at 14 large health systems, 80 percent of board members were not healthcare providers, 14 percent were physicians, and 6 percent were nurses.

In a 2018 American Hospital Association (AHA) survey, the average board size was 14 members, compared with 13 in 2014 and 12 in 2011 (AHA Trustee Services 2019). Between 2011 and 2018, the average overall board size increased by 16 percent. About 49 percent of system boards reported including outside members, compared with 17 to 27 percent in system subsidiary hospitals and freestanding hospitals.

The recent AHA survey of 1,316 CEO respondents showed that 70 percent of hospitals had at least one physician on their board in 2019 compared with 75 percent in 2014. Of those surveyed, 64 percent were in NFP hospitals (AHA Trustee Services 2019). The survey also pointed out that in systems that had physicians on their board, independent members more often had voting privileges than did those who were employed by the hospital. Hospital boards also appeared to be getting older, with the proportion of members younger than 50 years decreasing from 29 percent to 22 percent between 2005 and 2018.

We collated board member composition of the top ten health systems in the Midwestern United States (exhibit 8.1). Cleveland Clinic and Mount Carmel System were excluded from the table because the hospital boards for the two were subservient to a larger main health system board over the entire organization. These subservient hospital boards often deal with local hospital and quality issues but cede to the health system board for broader issues. Physicians constituted only about 16 percent of these hospital boards.

Exhibit 8.1 Board Member Composition of Top Ten Health Systems in the Midwestern United States

Institution	Private or Academic	Size (beds)	Total Board Members	Board Physicians (% of board members)	Board Nurses	% Members in Healthcare	Notes
University Hospitals Cleveland Medical Center	Academic	1,032	26	1 (4)	0	4	1 PhD; ex officio 2
Wexner Medical Center	Academic	1,133	10[b]	0 (0)	5	0	ex officio 2
Christ Hospital	Private	538	17	2 (12)	0	12	
Promedica Toledo	Private	859	21	5 (24)	2	33	1 PhD
Ohio Health Riverside	Private	1,059	23	4 (17)	0	17	
Kettering Medical Center	Private	410	16	0 (0)	0	0	1 PhD
University of Cincinnati	Academic	555	15	2 (13)	0	13	1 PhD
Bethesda North Hospital	Private	365	13	3 (23)	0	23	1 PhD
			136				**Total physicians: 16%**
Cleveland Clinic[a]	Private / academic	6,026	31[c]	24 (77)	1	81	1 PhD elected
Mt. Carmel Hospital[a]	Private	53	12	10 (83)	0	83	

[a] Excluded from totals. See text.
[b] Number includes 5 board-appointed members.
[c] Number includes 20 board-appointed members.

Diversity of Hospital Boards

In terms of engaging physicians of different ages, race, gender, or ethnicity, the news is not encouraging. The AHA survey reports that overall, boards are 83 percent white and more than 70 percent male (exhibit 8.2). Some 58 percent of boards in 2018 reported at least one member who was a racial or ethnic minority, compared with 53 percent in 2014. From 2005 to 2018, the proportion of women on boards increased from 23 percent to 30 percent. Boards surveyed by the AHA indicated an increasingly aging membership. The percentage of board members age 50 or younger has decreased from 29 percent in 2005 to 22 percent in 2018. Disturbingly, 73 percent of CEOs were not making extra efforts to recruit younger members to their boards.

Increasing diversity on boards is not just about looking at demographics such as age, race, ethnicity, or gender. There is enough data now to show that broadly defined diversity does improve performance (Palmquist 2015). Diversity training is usually the major response to any criticism about a lack of diversity. Dobbin and Kalev (2018) show that the effects of an isolated diversity program last only for a couple of days, mostly because of the program's focus on controlling managerial behavior and because of negative messaging consisting of such implied threats as lawsuits.

Exhibit 8.2 Hospital Board Demographics in the United States

Type of system	Physician/Nurse Representation	Independent Members	Gender Composition (Male)	Racial Composition (White)
Faith based (n = 179)	11%/9%	49%	60%	83%
Secular S (n = 95)	18%/2%	82%	79%	82%

Source: Compiled from Prybil et al. (2012).

Hospitals and boards should instead take advantage of proven efforts that succeed in weaving overall diversity, including gender or racial representation, throughout the organization (Dobbin and Kalev 2018).

There has been some progress toward narrowing the diversity gap in healthcare. Robert Wood Johnson University Hospital's board asked the CEO to create a three-year plan to develop junior employees and create a mentorship program and resource groups to enable like-minded workers to share ideas (Livingston 2018). This strategy improved the percentage of minorities on the hospital's leadership team to 32 percent in 2015, from 4 percent in 2012. Minority share of the board itself increased from 17 percent in 2011 to 22 percent in 2015. These efforts won the hospital the AHA's Equity of Care Award in 2015.

ROADBLOCKS TO INCREASING PHYSICIAN REPRESENTATION

One reason given as a roadblock to having adequate physician participation on hospital boards appears to be Internal Revenue Service (IRS) regulations and the 2002 Sarbanes-Oxley governance rules, which define the independence of board members more stringently. These restrictions have led many public companies to change their board-member selection process (Addison-Hewitt Associates 2002). In addition, Beaudry (2010) reports that the Panel on the Nonprofit Sector has stated that "a substantial majority" of the board of a public charity, usually meaning at least two-thirds of its members, should be independent.

An independent board free from influence is therefore mandated by Sarbanes-Oxley, the IRS, and federal and state laws. Organizations require that the majority of board members and all members of compensation and audit committees be "independent." This means that board members can have no direct or indirect material conflict of interest. This restriction has direct bearing on physician board members and prohibits hospitals from packing the board with "conflicted" physicians. The implication is that members must not receive direct compensation as an employee or that, if they do, their total compensation should be less than $10,000 as an independent contractor during that tax year (Beaudry 2010; Proskauer Rose LLP 2017). Even though the law may not apply to NFP hospitals, they have chosen, in the interest of safety, to follow the requirements for independent board members.

Physicians on administrative staff serving on a board are prohibited from participating in decisions when there is any question of inurement or private benefit to them, such as compensation. The IRS considers employees and most active members of the medical staff to be "insiders," and it limits the number of insiders serving on the board to no more than 49 percent of the entire board. These regulations and laws are the reason that many clinician board members are listed as ex officio (seated because of their position on the medical staff) and nonvoting members.

The large increase in hospital-employed physicians creates a problem for hospitals that need independent directors on their boards. IRS regulations require an NFP organization to state on IRS Form 990 the number of board members who are independent. Most NFP hospital board members serve without compensation. Only about 10 to 15 percent of the members are compensated, although government-sponsored hospitals compensate about 16 percent of board members (Becker's Hospital Review 2011; Governance Institute 2015).

Hospital CEOs may also be concerned with physicians' increased access to board members—access that the executives fear may undermine their authority. In addition, hospital administration also is wary of unfiltered communication between a physician and a board member. Part of the concern is that the physician might send mixed messages. One of us (Bhagwan Satiani) has been on a large NFP hospital board and observed efforts to limit one-on-one access to board members for fear of mixed messaging or undue influence.

MISCONCEPTIONS THAT ARE HOLDING PHYSICIANS BACK FROM BOARDS

Many nonphysician board members and administrative executives believe that most physicians lack the knowledge base, in terms of leadership and business skills, to fully comprehend the complex issues being debated at the board level. They point out that the best clinicians are seldom taught the skills needed to contribute at the board level.

This reasoning probably does not hold anymore, considering the increase in the number of physicians getting certifications, graduate degrees, experience in related industries such as pharmaceuticals and health insurance, and roles with significant management responsibilities in hospitals. Accountable care organizations (ACOs) are a perfect example of entrepreneurial physicians becoming involved in the business side of healthcare. Muhelstein, Tu, and Colla (2020) reported that in 2018, approximately 45 percent of all ACOs were led by physician groups, compared with 25 percent led by hospitals and 30 percent jointly led.

These ACO numbers show that many more physicians are capable of not only providing expert medical input but also understanding the business aspects of healthcare discussed at board meetings. All these capabilities make physicians attractive to hospitals as board members, and physician membership on hospital boards can improve physician engagement.

Even if physicians are ex officio and nonvoting members, they are not prevented from speaking up on patient care and any other issues important to them. Indeed, it is important for the CEO to make sure physicians are seen as independent and committed to patient care and quality of care. Since 80 percent of hospitals are NFP, the IRS limits the membership of insiders (employed or active staff physicians) to less than half. According to the IRS's Section 4958 "rebuttable presumption of reasonableness" criteria, the compensation committee cannot include physician insiders (Brauer et al. 2002).

Unfortunately, the average number (2.7) and median number (1) of physicians serving on boards as of 2015 have not changed significantly from the 2013 report of an average of 2.5 and median of 1 physician (Governance Institute 2015). However, because the trend of physicians acquiring business education has taken off since around 2010, a change in physician board participation may be reflected in future surveys.

A ROADMAP FOR PHYSICIANS WANTING TO SIT ON HOSPITAL BOARDS

Let us review what boards are looking for in physicians interested in serving on hospital boards. In the AHA survey mentioned, 42 percent of CEOs reported that their selection committees used an approved set of competencies in selecting board members (AHA Trustee Services 2019). The top five knowledge, skills, and behavior competencies used to select board members were an information-seeking approach (80 percent); innovative thinking (73 percent); knowledge of business and finance (66 percent); knowledge of healthcare delivery and performance (62 percent); and community orientation (60 percent).

More physicians are acquiring further knowledge and experience in healthcare management or business. An MBA is one path. The MBA curriculum must be broad and include financial management, budgets, strategy, communications, health insurance, population healthcare, working in teams, and healthcare delivery. However, not all MBA programs include enough education in the business of healthcare to provide a good base for understanding and functioning appropriately at the hospital board level (Satiani et al. 2014). In our experience, the most valuable behavioral competencies to teach physicians are nonclinical good people skills.

Then, it is important for physicians to serve on multiple committees or task forces, including finance, ethics, and patient safety and quality, to acquire broad knowledge beyond clinical practice.

Serving on the medical staff executive committee as chair and having interactions with top management and a few board members is also desirable. A hospital executive as a mentor can help fill in gaps in knowledge.

While compensation for serving on a for-profit board is not uncommon, it is unusual for NFP boards. Furthermore, members of NFP boards are not only expected to serve as unpaid volunteers but also expected to donate and assist in fundraising for the hospital development foundation. Most physicians, particularly specialists early in their careers or those in the middle of their careers and considering top executive positions, may not be interested in a board position because of a significant commitment of time and the resulting loss of income. However, serving on a board may be a good path to take for others who are still practicing, because it is a way to learn the intricacies of healthcare management, become familiar with the challenges, and make contacts in the industry.

Many board actions related to physicians such as credentialing and privileging are routine and may be boring for most board members partly because they might assume that the executive and medical staff office have done their job appropriately. It is the rare item that slips through the screening process. In this case, physicians are needed to speak up at the board meeting, to protect the public, the physician's rights, or the hospital's mission if there are questions about inappropriate actions. They may possess inside knowledge and may in the long run prevent public harm and save the hospital from lawsuits.

HOW TO ENGAGE PHYSICIANS FROM A BOARD PERSPECTIVE

All of healthcare leadership would be wise to heed this observation by the Advisory Board Company: "Physicians go where they are invited, stay where they are well treated, and grow where they are cultivated."

If physician engagement is one of the goals of improving performance of hospitals, increased physician representation on hospital boards within regulatory limits is a must. In a 2010 online survey of a thousand physicians by PricewaterhouseCoopers, 56 percent pointed to the lack of adequate physician representation and physician leadership as a factor in their absence of trust in hospital relationships (Gamble 2011).

For decades, an appointment to a hospital board was a matter of prestige in the community, complimentary meals, often-free trips to resorts, and signing on to most if not all agenda items put forward by hospital administration. Board trustees had minimal time commitments, they had no fixed terms, and conflicts of interest were often tolerated. For one of us (Bhagwan Satiani), experience as a board member meant that when there was a conflict such as a construction bid, the affected board member would leave the room before discussion and a vote took place. This practice, however, was routine because members all knew each other well. These conflicts need to be handled before the board meeting.

Things have changed dramatically in healthcare. Pressure now comes from many directions, including governmental regulations, multiple stakeholders, local politics, and the press focused on conflicts of interest or incidents related to patient safety. People's time commitment on the board is now also significant. Members are also exposed to some liability, regardless of insurance, and certainly bear some risk to their reputations (Orlikoff 2018). Conflicts of interest are now declared ahead of election or appointment to the board.

Board members are selected not only for their influence but also for their expertise in any number of healthcare-related areas that give the hospital a competitive advantage. Physician leaders as board members also provide the hospital a competitive advantage, especially as value-based care becomes an increasing part of reimbursement and as population health management turns out to be a critical aspect of successful healthcare organizations.

Hospitals are attempting to find physician leaders or retired physicians who come from outside their organization and who have the skills or experience that would bring a fresh perspective to a board. As discussed, however, despite these efforts, the data shows that physicians continue to be poorly represented on hospital boards. No matter how much healthcare-related education is passed down to "lay" board members, the perspective and professionalism of clinicians on the ground cannot be duplicated or replaced.

With the explosion in technical knowledge in medicine, board members need to have a trusting relationship with physicians on and off the board. Physician engagement is not just the job of the executive staff; it should be a priority for the entire board. Healthcare reform has already led to increased physician employment by hospitals, and it is clear to both parties that their individual goals and objectives can only be fully realized if there is mutual trust and true alignment of interests. The health system should lay out clearly as one of its priorities why it needs physicians as board members.

Recruiting and Engaging Physicians for Participation on the Board

Oshiro (2015) details practical and effective strategies to encourage physician trust, buy-in, and, therefore, engagement. He emphasizes how hospital and board leadership needs to speak of physicians as partners: "In addition to great leadership, physicians also need to see the organization as a partner, a partner they can believe in. A partner that will help them. A partner that will not only work to improve the lives of their patients, but all of the lives the organization comes into contact with, including the lives of the physicians." Here are eight practical ways to recruit physicians for membership on hospital boards:

1. Hospital executives should be searching for physicians who are committed to the organization's mission, who exhibit

leadership skills, and who are inclined to think strategically (high-potential candidates). These physicians should be started on the road to ultimately be considered for a board seat.

2. Selected physicians can also shadow senior executives as if the physicians were MHA students. They can then, depending on their interests, be placed on committees and task forces and be given duties so that leadership can judge their performance. These approaches do not have to be a formal program.

3. As scientists, many physicians may not respond to emotional arguments. Data is a powerful motivator for most of them. If physicians are shown data and best practices related to improving services and driving down adverse events, for instance, they will usually want to be part of the solution. Some will then want a bigger role than a committee membership.

4. A formal leadership program will spark interest in many physicians who may at some point wish to advance professionally.

5. For most physicians, the board is a mythic black box where everything is done in secret. The board can ask for physicians to come to every board meeting and brief members on important clinical issues or advances in research. It can then ask the physicians to stay over for the meeting and observe how issues are addressed. Invitations like these break the seal around the black box and allow the board to hear different voices and possibly view future physician leaders. This approach also advances board transparency among physicians beyond just those seated on the board.

6. The board and administration wisely appreciate that merely seating the CMO on the board may sometimes not represent all physicians or even the majority. For instance,

the majority of CMOs are primary care physicians and may not be in tune with specialists. Different opinions, particularly on quality issues, may be needed.

7. If employed physicians are compensated on a wRVU (work relative value unit) basis and if the health system emphasizes productivity, then physicians should be rewarded for participating in system activities by allotting wRVUs or other credits for these activities.

8. Since the number of employed physicians on the health system board is limited, the organization can recruit independent physicians who have demonstrated suitable skills and experience in varied areas. Management may have to pay fair compensation for them to spend time on the board, but their contribution to the board is worth the expense.

HOW TO SUCCEED AS A PHYSICIAN BOARD MEMBER

More than 90 percent of physicians surveyed by consulting firm PricewaterhouseCoopers said they should be involved in such hospital governance activities as serving on boards to assist in performance improvement (AHA 2011). Participation or chairing hospital committees does not necessarily give physicians an accurate and expansive view of how a hospital board functions. Before contemplating accepting a nomination for a hospital board, physicians should examine their motivation and values and whether they will be able to fulfill the time commitments necessary (exhibit 8.3).

Here are some basic recommendations for physicians planning to participate in board deliberations:

- Understand policies and procedures related to the board.
- Remember that the board's function is to govern, not to manage.

Exhibit 8.3 Brief Checklist for Physicians Considering a Seat on a Hospital Board

Motivation	Assess your motives for presence on the board Are you committed to the mission? Prestige comes with the appointment, but do you truly have a desire to serve and benefit the community?
Values	Do you have shared values with the board you wish to be serving on?
Time	Do you understand how much time is required, including time for off-site strategy or board education meetings? Will you have enough time to commit to discharge your obligations?
Skills and expertise	Do you have the appropriate skills and expertise to contribute to the board? Are there special skills you bring to the board?
Experience	Have you had enough nonclinical experience, such as experience in business; an executive role; or experience in strategy, finance, or quality and patient safety?

- Review the responsibilities of being on the board; attend all onboarding meetings to familiarize yourself with legal obligations, declaration of conflicts, and voting responsibilities.
- Learn the background, interests, and expertise of the executive staff and all the board members.
- Come prepared to discuss issues on the agenda for each meeting.
- Speak up politely and respectfully, but be sure to be honest and to represent both your patients and your physician colleagues with integrity.
- Volunteer for a committee where you think you can contribute.

- Be sure to network and be friendly with the board members and the administrators so that you have someone to turn to for advice; offer your contact information in case they wish to reach out to you for a medical staff perspective.

HOW *NOT* TO SUCCEED AS A PHYSICIAN BOARD MEMBER

Having sat on a large health system board, one of us (Bhagwan Satiani) has seen inexperienced physicians seated on the board. Their presence reflected poorly on other physicians. Here are some suggestions for overcoming the problematic tendencies of a few physician board members:

- Do not come to meetings thinking you are the authority on anything. Do not try to dominate discussions; get familiar with others' expertise before participating in discussions.
- Do not disparage people or actions, since you lack a full perspective of the issues.
- Do not hesitate to speak up when there is going to be a vote on a significant clinical issue affecting the patients, patient safety, or quality. Remember, you are representing the community, the patients, and your coworkers in addition to being loyal to the board.
- Try not to go behind the CEO's back to board members without first raising the issue with the executive.
- Do not bring material to distribute without having it screened by the executive staff, who will make sure it is relevant and accurate.
- Confidentiality of board proceedings is necessary, so be careful about disclosing protected information.

CONCLUSION

With the growing complexity of healthcare, health systems need qualified, engaged clinicians, especially physicians, to be active partners on their governing boards. Efforts to engage physicians must start at the very top, which is the health system board, and must permeate throughout the organization.

Engagement efforts need to be genuine. These should include the encouragement of active participation by physicians, whether independent or employed, to provide clinical expertise and technical knowledge to benefit the community the hospitals serve.

Thus far, hospitals have been unsuccessful in efforts for diversity on their boards. To move forward in step with the rest of the business world, healthcare leaders need to apply extra effort to encourage, train, and mentor high-potential physicians as partners in improving the health of our communities.

Physician engagement in the health system and hospital needs to be a priority for the hospital board. Engagement should occur on all three fronts: operationally, strategically, and economically.

Physicians recognize that partnering with organizational and board leadership can deliver better and more efficient care. They are hoping that they can help lead the system and not simply work for it.

ACKNOWLEDGMENT

We are grateful to Carson Dye, FACHE, for valuable suggestions to improve this chapter.

REFERENCES

Addison-Hewitt Associates. 2002. "The Sarbanes-Oxley Act." Accessed March 11, 2021. www.soxlaw.com.

American Hospital Association (AHA). 2020. "Fast Facts on U.S. Hospitals." Accessed December 31. www.aha.org/statistics/fast-facts-us-hospitals.

————. 2011. *Physicians on Hospital Boards: Time for New Approaches*. Chicago: American Hospital Association.

American Hospital Association (AHA) Trustee Services. 2019. *National Health Care Governance Survey Report, 2019*. Published March. https://trustees.aha.org/system/files/media/file/2019/06/aha-2019-governance-survey-report_v8-final.pdf.

Bader, B. S., E. A. Kazemek, P. R. Knecht, and R. W. Witalis. 2008. "Physicians on the Board: Conflict over Conflicts." *BoardRoom Press*. Published February. http://static1.squarespace.com/static/5487509fe4b0672ae6c16f81/t/54a427c0e4b0631d0c423dd2/1420044224443/Physicians-on-the-Board-Conflict-over-Conflicts.pdf.

Bai, B., and R. Krishnan. 2015. "Do Hospitals Without Physicians on the Board Deliver Lower Quality of Care?" *American Journal of Medical Quality* 30 (1): 58–65.

Beaudry, L. 2010. "Tax-Exempt Organizations and the Independent Governing Board." Reinhart Boerner Van Deuren, Attorneys at Law. Published February 26. www.reinhartlaw.com/knowledge/tax-exempt-organizations-independent-governing-boards/.

Becker's Hospital Review. 2016. "50 Best Practices for High-Performing Health System Boards." Published January 12. www.beckershospitalreview.com/hospital-management-administration/50-best-practices-for-high-performing-health-system-boards.html.

————. 2011. "Survey: 15% of Non-Profit Hospitals Compensate Board Members." Published November 9. www.beckershospitalreview.com/compensation-issues/survey-15-of-non-profit-hospitals-compensate-board-members.html.

Brauer, L. M., T. T. Tyson, L. J. Henzke, and D. J. Kawecki. 2002. "An Introduction to I.R.C. 4958 (Intermediate Sanctions)." Internal Revenue Service. Accessed February 6, 2020. www.irs.gov/pub/irs-tege/eotopich02.pdf.

Dobbin, F., and A. Kalev. 2018. "Why Doesn't Diversity Training Work? The Challenge for Industry and Academia." *Anthropology Now* 10 (2): 48–55.

Gamble, M. 2011. "7 Tips for Physician Representation in Hospital Governance." *Becker's Hospital Review*. February 18. www.beckershospitalreview.com/hospital-physician-relationships/7-tips-for-physician-representation-in-hospital-governance.html.

Governance Institute. 2015. *21st-Century Care Delivery: Governing in the New Healthcare Industry*. San Diego, CA: The Governance Institute.

———. 2012. *Dynamic Governance: An Analysis of Board Structure and Practices in a Shifting Industry*. San Diego, CA: The Governance Institute.

Guptta, K. 2017. "Gallup: American Workers Are Unengaged and Looking Elsewhere." *Forbes*. Published March 8. www.forbes.com/sites/kaviguppta/2017/03/08/gallup-american-workers-are-unengaged-and-looking-elsewhere/.

Hall, L. H., J. Johnson, I. Watt, A. Tsipa, and D. B. O'Connor. 2016. "Healthcare Staff Wellbeing, Burnout, and Patient Safety: A Systematic Review." *PLOS One* 11 (7): e0159015.

Jha, A., and A. Epstein. 2010. "Hospital Governance and the Quality of Care." *Health Affairs* 29 (1): 182–87.

Jiang, H. J., L. C. Bass, and I. Fraser. 2008. "Board Oversight of Quality: Any Differences in Process of Care and Mortality?" *Journal of Healthcare Management* 54 (1): 15–29.

Livingston, S. 2018. "Fostering Diversity for the Next Generation of Healthcare Leaders." *Modern Healthcare*. Published October 13. www.modernhealthcare.com/article/20181013/NEWS/181019970/fostering-diversity-for-the-next-generation-of-healthcare-leaders.

Milliken, A. D. 2014. "Physician Engagement: A Necessary but Reciprocal Process." *Canadian Medical Association Journal* 186 (4): 244–45.

Muhelstein, D., T. Tu, and C. Colla. 2020. "Accountable Care Organizations Are Increasingly Led by Physician Groups Rather Than Hospital Systems." *American Journal of Managed Care* 26 (5): 225–28.

Orlikoff, J. 2018. "Time for a New Model of Governance." AHA Trustee Services. Published July. https://trustees.aha.org/transforminggovernance/articles/time-for-a-new-model-of-governance.

Oshiro, B. 2015. "6 Proven Strategies for Engaging Physicians—and 4 Ways to Fail." *Health Catalyst Insights*. Published March 5. www.healthcatalyst.com/proven-physician-engagement-strategies.

Palmquist, M. 2015. "The Advantages of a Diverse Board." *Strategy+Business*. Published June 18. www.strategy-business.com/blog/The-Advantages-of-a-Diverse-Board.

Perriera, T. A., L. A. Perrier, M. Prokopy, L. Neves-Mera, and D. D. Persaud. 2019. "Physician Engagement: A Concept Analysis." *Journal of Healthcare Leadership* 11: 101–13.

Prins, J. T., J. E. H. M. Hoekstra-Weebers, S. M. Gazendam-Donofrio, G. S. Dillingh, A. B. Bakker, M. Huisman, B. Jacobs, and F. M. M. A. Van Der Heijden. 2010. "Burnout and Engagement Among Resident Doctors in the Netherlands: A National Study." *Medical Education* 44 (3): 236–47.

Proskauer Rose LLP. 2017. "Independent Directors and Tax-Exempt Organizations." DC Bar Pro Bono Center. Updated July. www.probonopartner.org/wp-content/uploads/2016/01/Independent-Directors-and-Tax-Exempt-Organizations-DC-Bar-0717.pdf.

Prybil, L., S. Levey, R. Killian, D. Fardo, R. Chait, D. R. Bardach, and W. Roach. 2012. *Governance in Large Nonprofit Health Systems: Current Profile and Emerging Patterns.* Lexington, KY: Commonwealth Center for Governance Studies.

Satiani, B., and S. Prakash. 2016. "It Is Time for More Physician and Nursing Representation on Hospital Boards in the US." *Journal of Hospital & Medical Management* 2 (1): 1–6.

Satiani, B., J. Sena, R. Ruberg, and E. C. Ellison. 2014. "Talent Management and Physician Leadership Training Is Essential for Preparing Tomorrow's Physician Leaders." *Journal of Vascular Surgery* 59 (2): 542–46.

Taitz, J. M., T. H. Lee, and T. D. Sequist. 2012. "A Framework for Engaging Physicians in Quality and Safety." *BMJ Quality & Safety* 21 (9): 722–28.

CHAPTER 9

Quality: A Cornerstone of Physician Engagement

John Byrnes

The process of creating healthy organization–physician relationships is critical to organizational success. Partnerships in process improvement can nurture these relationships and mitigate burnout by meeting physicians' psychological needs. To flourish, physicians need some degree of choice (control over their lives), camaraderie (social connectedness), and an opportunity for excellence (being part of something meaningful). Organizations can provide these opportunities by establishing constructive organization–physician relationships and developing physician leaders.
—Steven Swensen, Andrea Kabcenell, and Tait Shanafelt, "Physician–Organization Collaboration Reduces Physician Burnout and Promotes Engagement," 2016

WHY ADDRESS QUALITY in a book on physician engagement? Consider this: Can a robust quality and safety program be the cornerstone of a successful physician engagement strategy? To what extent are physician engagement and quality related? Does one element drive the other?

Consider three facts. First, physicians ascribe to the Hippocratic Oath, which is often interpreted as "I will first do no harm." While these are not the exact words of the oath, the Greek translation is better phrased as, "Abstain from whatever is deleterious and mischievous." While this admonition may seem stale, it is nonetheless a part of every physician's foundation.

But then consider a second fact. Physicians are the people who make the majority of clinical decisions and guide practically all the actions that affect clinical quality. Physicians and clinical quality are as related as milk and cookies. Oshiro (2015) describes this relationship well: "Making significant improvements is not an achievement organizations can do without physician engagement, though. They need physicians to be on board. Why? The reality is that physicians play a large role in the complex mechanisms of healthcare delivery. From providing frontline care to filling leadership positions, physicians drive 75 to 85 percent of all quality and cost decisions. That's a mighty large percentage, which translates to significant financial losses if physicians are disengaged and don't participate in improvement initiatives." The relationship between physician engagement and clinical quality is clear-cut. It is strong; it is 100 percent correlated; it is critical.

And not only is quality directly correlated with physician engagement, but in light of the same logic, so are patient safety and patient experience. As Kramer (2019) explains, "An emotional connection with the patient can be just as important as an accurate diagnosis. Though individual providers take the Hippocratic Oath, its provisions on warmth, sympathy, and humanity are a road map for improving overall culture." Consider also the findings from Press Ganey, a firm that conducts thousands of surveys and is an expert voice on both physician engagement and patient satisfaction. In a white paper on engagement, the company writes, "Patients have front-row seats to an organization's cultural successes and failures. They can tell whether employees and physicians are engaged or would rather be working somewhere else. Being surrounded by engaged caregivers reinforces to patients that they are in a safe place and affects how they evaluate their care" (Press Ganey 2013).

Finally, a third fact that cannot be ignored is that physicians and institutions face the risk of medical malpractice suits. Although this risk presents a negative reason for equating physician engagement

Exhibit 9.1 Quality, Safety, and Patient Experience as Related to Physician Engagement

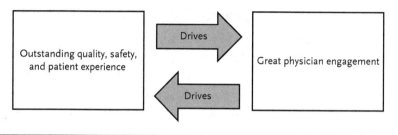

and quality, it is nonetheless an important factor. Low physician engagement can be related to stress, which can cause quality issues that expose both physicians and organizations to medical malpractice risks. Shanafelt and Noseworthy (2017) write that "physician distress has also been linked to physician prescribing habits, test ordering, the risk of malpractice suits, and whether or not patients adhere with physicians' medical recommendations."

To conclude, clinical quality and physician engagement are most likely closely related. The relationship is shown in exhibit 9.1.

The following case study illustrates the matter of driving physician engagement and quality simultaneously.

Case Study: Board Retreat

During a recent board retreat where the outside speaker was focusing on clinical quality improvement, many of the physicians in attendance seemed surprised at how much they as individual clinicians affected quality. They had mostly viewed quality as an organizational function, something that was relegated to the hospital quality committee and the quality officer. They had not fully reflected on how they as individual physicians drive quality. While the discussion continued, they began to recognize that their impact on quality came from

(continued)

(continued from previous page)

two basic mechanisms: the orders they write and the medical decisions they make. During a break at the retreat, two physicians approached the speaker, visibly troubled. They were concerned about how much effect they had on the outcomes of their patients and wanted to know what more they could do to learn about and improve their performance. Toward the end of the retreat, the speaker asked all the physicians if they believed that they could or would now play a larger leadership role in improving care for their patients. Hands raised around the room, showing 100 percent buy-in and the physicians' sincere willingness to help lead clinical projects in their organization. Moreover, they wanted to begin immediately!

Later that day, many of the physicians were asked what, among all the things they had heard during the retreat, motivated them to volunteer to now lead improvement projects in their organization. Unanimously, they indicated that it was the realization that they as individuals have an impact on nearly all the clinical outcomes. This new awareness clearly provided the motivation.

This case study should be an important wake-up call for all readers. This encounter (which is not fictitious) demonstrates physicians' passion for quality and, as a result, their zeal to be engaged. As noted, patient quality and physician engagement are tightly linked. The moral of this story is this: When physicians understand their impact on clinical quality, they will engage with and lead improvement projects. In this case, and in less than a day, an entire room of physician board members became highly engaged in their organization's journey toward better quality. Why? They understood that they are personally responsible for their patients' outcomes—through the orders they write and the medical decisions they make.

HOW PHYSICIAN CULTURE AND ATTRIBUTES DRIVE ENGAGEMENT AND QUALITY

In designing physician engagement programs, healthcare leaders should consider the elements of physician culture and other physician characteristics that can help drive clinical quality and engagement. Exhibit 9.2 shows these key traits. We will next look at them in detail.

A Desire to Be Involved

Simply asking physicians to help is one of the best ways to put to good use their desire to be involved. One method a healthcare leader used was clear-cut. It went something like this: "Dr. Rodriguez [a surgeon], I need your help to lead an improvement team focused on reducing surgical infection rates. Your expertise will be essential to designing our care guidelines, and your standing with your peers will help a lot with collaboration among the docs. Can you help out?" As most readers know, the old adage of "Just ask; all they will do is say yes or no" can go far in leadership.

Asking for help also takes advantage of another key characteristic of physician culture: Physicians want to be involved in decisions that affect their practices, their patients, and their organizations.

Exhibit 9.2 Common Physician Culture and Attributes That Drive Engagement and Quality

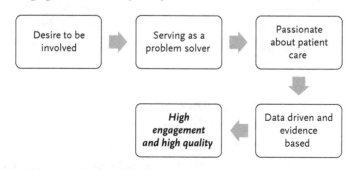

This desire to have some influence in decisions lies at the core of physician culture. And nothing gets a physician closer to having some influence than does working on improvement teams to design evidence-based guidelines, order sets, and the clinical dashboards that physicians will use to improve their clinical outcomes.

But, the number one mistake that leaders can make is to engage physicians only *after* decisions that affect their practice have already been made. Like most people, physicians don't like when things are done to them without their input and involvement. To ensure greater physician engagement, always invite them to lead or at least participate in an improvement team from the beginning. They are busy professionals, but many will make time for this important work.

> The number one mistake that leaders can make is to engage physicians *after* decisions that affect their practice have already been made.

A Problem-Solver Attitude

Another aspect of physician culture can be used to drive engagement on quality projects: Physicians are problem solvers. It is what they are trained to do, and it is what they do every day—with every patient they see. When physicians understand that the goals of a clinical project are to eliminate complications, mortality, and readmissions, they are ready to engage. To meet these goals, they will need their problem-solving skills. If every improvement project is clearly a problem-solving exercise, quality and physician culture will be fully aligned. And when these two are aligned, physician engagement is almost always guaranteed.

> Physicians are problem solvers. It is what they are trained to do.

Compassion About Patient Care

Ritchie (2019) writes that "when health care providers take the time to make human connections that help end suffering, patient outcomes improve and medical costs decrease. Among other benefits, compassion reduces pain, improves healing, lowers blood pressure and helps alleviate depression and anxiety." The benefit of physician compassion may be one of the strongest arguments for the link between physician engagement and patient quality. Rarely does any conversation with a physician not include the topic of patient care. And consider this side benefit, described by Emma Seppälä (2019): "Compassion for patients is associated with lower medical expenditures."

> Physicians are compassionate about patient care.

A Data-Driven Mindset

Physicians are data driven. They use data every day to make decisions for every patient. They are trained in the scientific method and know how to analyze and interpret data. So when data sets and dashboards are used to drive clinical improvement, physicians are well suited for the task. But with this expertise comes the expectation that the data is accurate and that the quality department staff will be transparent and will disclose potential weaknesses inherent in a data set. Physicians do not expect perfection, but they will quickly identify the flaws in a dashboard, especially when the information is reported for a familiar medical condition or surgical procedure. We will next look at how data can be a tool that fosters fabulous engagement or, when things go wrong, disengagement and a loss of trust.

Data's Role in Engagement and Disengagement

Data can be the best or the worst tool to promote physician engagement. Key to its role with physicians is how organizations: (1) involve physicians in the design of data dashboards, (2) shift ownership of data and dashboards to physician leaders, (3) support physician leaders in the dashboard rollout, and (4) troubleshoot data integrity issues when they occur. Let's review this process in some detail, as the approach will determine how well it goes.

Involving Physicians in Dashboard Design

As discussed, physicians want to be involved in everything that affects their practice. For this reason, they must be included at the beginning of any dashboard design session. Here are some key steps to get off to a good start:

1. Assemble a physician-led dashboard design committee.
2. Ask the medical director or chair of a department to chair the committee.
3. Before the first meeting, (a) fully brief the physicians on the purpose of the project and (b) share several dashboard examples from other organizations and ask them to bring examples of their own.
4. For every meeting, always supply quality-improvement and analytic staff who are subject-matter experts in data sources, validation, and so forth.

The foregoing steps guarantee a good start to a data and dashboard development session. Following these steps will give physicians ownership of the dashboard and will instill a sense of trust between the quality department staff and physicians. Ownership and trust are key to the physicians' buy-in and ongoing support. Leaders make a common mistakes when they present a prototyped dashboard to the physicians as a completed design. This approach will fail every time and guarantees wholesale disengagement, as the physicians will be inclined to reject anything they had no part in developing.

Supporting Physician Leaders During Dashboard Rollout

After the dashboard prototype has been designed and the data validated by quality department analysts, the next step is the rollout. Keep in mind that the rollout reaches a broader group of physicians, those whose performance will be contained in the dashboards. Because of its wide reach, the rollout must be done correctly for positive engagement.

The rollout includes at least five goals. First, the physicians must fully understand the dashboard content, especially the definition of each measure. Because the definitions can be complicated, no one should rely solely on the measure's name. For instance, certain criteria must be met to code the record for "respiratory failure following surgery." Physicians need to understand when this complication is coded and reported on the dashboard. Because of the complexity, every physician dashboard meeting should always include a data analyst. They are the experts, so take full advantage of their support.

Second, the physicians need to understand how the dashboards will be used. When dashboards are used to drive improvement, track adherence to evidence-based practices, or educate physicians about their performance, then they will feel engaged. However, if dashboards are used in any punitive manner, such as for finger-pointing or "bad-apple chasing," then physicians will be disengaged.

Third, the physicians should understand when a *statistically significant* change in performance occurs. Month-to-month variation in performance is inherent in clinical care patterns. However, physicians do not want to react to every minor change in performance. *Statistical process control charts*, with their built-in rules for identifying significant changes, provide a ready-made solution.

Fourth, physicians must know how the dashboards will be used throughout their organization. For example, who will see physician level data? Administration? Other physicians? Nursing leaders and staff? The board of directors? The medical executive committee (MEC) or any of the various quality committees, including peer review committees? A policy that is approved by the MEC is a good safeguard. A good policy will state exactly who will see physician-level performance information and exactly how it will be used in the organization. A good rule to follow is this: Use data for measurement and learning *but not for judgment.*

Finally, leaders should limit access to physician-level data. Most organizations limit initial access to individual physician-level data to the physician or physicians listed on the report. The information is usually blinded to the group, and only the individual physicians involved know their own personal performance. As improvements are implemented and performance improves, many physicians are usually comfortable unblinding the data to their peers and department chair. And given 12 months to see improvements, physicians may actually ask to have this "objective" performance data added to their peer-review file. After all, they did much of work to improve performance; why shouldn't it be used in credentialing and privileging?

In summary, if the leaders cover the following topics with the physicians in the dashboard rollout meetings, positive engagement will result (this list was adapted from Byrnes [2015]):

1. Introduce members of the design committee—always include physicians.

2. Review the development process for the prototype—it included physicians.

3. Discuss the sources used for the dashboard measures.

4. Explain how validation and audits are used to verify accuracy.

5. Explain the physicians' role in improving data accuracy throughout the next year.

6. Review the types of measures included—process versus outcome measures.

7. Review the definitions of the measures.

8. Proactively address common objections physicians usually voice about data integrity.

9. Introduce statistical process control (SPC) charts—how measures will be trended over time (e.g., 24 rolling months)—and how statistically significant changes will be determined.

10. Discuss common-cause and special-cause variation, that is, discuss how to determine when a change is significant.

11. Review the accepted uses for each level of dashboard (system rollup, hospital comparisons, and physician level) and which groups will have access to each.

12. Review the protection in place for physician peer-reviewed data.

13. Review how physician attribution is assigned—a formal MEC approved policy is a must.

14. Tell physicians that they may not like the initial results. If they have not measured their performance previously, it is unrealistic to expect great performance.

15. Seeing less-than-great performance means they should investigate the information (with quality department assistance to investigate), uncover any data errors, validate the performance, or take some or all of these actions.

16. Ask for the physicians' help in making the data more accurate with each monthly update.

The last point is particularly important, because 100 percent accuracy is impossible when a group is developing clinical dashboards. There are just too many variables that rely on human input, and humans are inherently error-prone. Transparency on this one issue will result in great engagement, probably more positive than most leaders could have imagined.

The following example script illustrates a successful approach to starting the discussion with physicians:

Databases are dependent on humans to construct and maintain them. We've used the best data sources [name them—finance, cost accounting, coding, electronic health record, chart review] we have available. But no data set will ever be perfect. For quality improvement projects, we strive for 90 to 95 percent accuracy. The databases we are using, especially the administrative data, has been extensively validated. After all, our administrators use it to run the business side of our organization. But we *now need your help* to identify problems with the data (inaccuracies) that our teams did not catch. This step relies on your clinical expertise and the insight you have into your practice. When you identify a measure that seems out of line with your clinical experience, we will pull the charts, review the coding and database entries, and share the results with you and the team. Sometimes, it's a data issue, which we will correct, or it can be close to true performance. In that case, and in the spirit of *data for learning and not for judgment*, together we will help design new care processes to improve our performance. Sound good?

The rollout meeting can be an hour or two of discussion and clarification. Spend as much time as necessary, and be 100 percent transparent about the data sources and how the dashboard has been produced. When the physicians understand that the leaders and quality team are sincere and supportive and have no punitive intent, clinical dashboards will become the primary tool driving improvement. This is physician engagement at its best, but all these topics need to be addressed up front, with full transparency, and in a spirit of collaboration. With this collaborative, honest approach, true trust will start to emerge.

CELEBRATING SUCCESSES

Celebrating successes by recognizing the frontline physicians, advanced practice providers, nurses, and clinical support staff who have done all the work is not just the right thing to do; these demonstrations of gratitude and recognition are the *fuel of engagement*. In *The Quality Playbook* (Byrnes 2015), I express the importance of celebrating people's successes: "Demonstrations of gratitude—a pat on the back or verbal thank you—[are] potent energizers for your program. Over the years, the celebrations I've held have generated such enthusiasm and goodwill that they fueled individual and group motivation for months (if not a full year) into the future. If I can say only one thing about this topic it's this: Always celebrate your [front lines'] successes in quality and safety, *always*."

REWARDS AND RECOGNITION

The most successful healthcare leaders know that they should recognize their people for doing great things. But all recognition must be sincere, unique, and from the heart. It cannot be a cookie-cutter solution or feel forced or trivial. Actions reflected by comments like "Every leader sends out *x* number of thank you cards a week," or "We're doing rounds every Wednesday at 10 a.m. so that we can thank *a*, *b*, and *c*" are not the right approach. That is not how widely successful recognition programs are built. One book with many ideas for recognition is Bob Nelson's *1501 Ways to Reward Employees* (Nelson 2012). The book offers unique, heartfelt solutions to provide sincere recognition in a world where it can be very rare.

Award Ceremonies

Annual award ceremonies provide so much engagement and enthusiasm that one organization's executive team deemed these forums an essential element of its quality (and engagement) programs. In a few years, the organization's Annual Synergy Awards ceremony grew to seven hundred physicians, staff, and their spouses in attendance. The rules are simple. Anyone in the organization can nominate a quality or safety team for several categories of awards. But one requirement must be met: The team must demonstrate significant improvement in a set of clinical, safety, or experience measures over the past 12 months. For each award category, the nominated teams are introduced by video vignettes (professionally produced) that highlight their members and the improvements made. When the winning team is announced, the members come up on stage, receive an elegant crystal award piece, and are personally thanked by members of the executive team, usually the CMO, CQO, and CNO.

What makes the Annual Synergy Awards even more special? At some point in the program, the spouses are invited to stand. They receive a heartfelt thank-you from the MC and then a standing ovation from the crowd. This organization has received much feedback since the ceremony was begun, but it can be summed up in the words of one attendee: "The awards are nice and the food great, but what makes the event so special to them is that they can share the evening (and their accomplishments) with a loved one and that their leaders are there as well."

Public Recognition

Public recognition for exemplary performance is a great way to thank those responsible, including physicians, clinicians, staff, and volunteers, and to further solidify the engagement of your physicians. For example, a hospital just received a Watson Health 100 Top Hospitals Award, which uses a balanced scorecard composed of clinical, operational, and financial metrics for 2,600 hospitals in the United States (IBM Watson Health 2020). This award places a hospital in the top 4 percent of those included in the study. Such an impressive accomplishment needs to be celebrated widely. The following sections present some ways to recognize those who contributed.

Sunday Newspaper

A full-page tribute placed in the Sunday newspaper has always been a crowd-pleaser. It must thank and congratulate all the physicians, staff, and hospital volunteers involved. However, don't make the mistake of turning it into an advertisement for the organization. The announcement has only two purposes: recognition of, and thanking, the front line. A good gesture is to place at the bottom the signatures of the chair of the board, CEO, chief of staff, CMO, CNO, and CQO. A public tribute like this highlights the values of the organization and the importance of all the frontline caregivers, and it creates a tremendous sense of pride among everyone.

Personalized Letter from the Board Chair and CEO

Who can imagine getting a letter at home thanking them for their contributions at work? Can they further imagine that the letter details the patient outcomes they personally helped improve? And what if it is signed by the board chair, the CEO, the CMO, and the department chair? Such a letter says that their efforts have been recognized and that the highest organizational and physician leadership is grateful for the effort. Now *this* is guaranteed to make an impression.

To be successful with such an effort, leaders should ask everyone to personally sign the letters. Signature stamps send just the opposite message. And mail them to the recipient's home. Do not use interoffice mail. It's in the same category as signature stamps. There are many reports of these being shared with family and being hung on refrigerators at home.

When should these letters be sent? At the end of each calendar year, for every metric that has shown improvement, and to every team member responsible for making those improvements, leaders should send a letter.

Commendations from the Board of Directors

Commendations are reserved for truly spectacular quality or safety improvements. Examples include a children's hospital that reduced serious safety events by 90 percent, a department that achieves CABG (coronary artery bypass graft) surgery mortality rates that are 25 percent of the predicted rates, and a medical group that has 90 percent of its HEDIS (healthcare effectiveness data and information set) measures in the top decile seven years in a row. These real examples from just one US healthcare system show, amazingly, exactly what is possible.

For extraordinary accomplishments like these, a formal resolution and commendation from the board of directors is appropriate and a powerful way to recognize excellence. It should be signed by the board chair and board quality committee chair. When the quality team coleads, both committees should receive the commendation, and after the update at the board of directors, the chair should reaffirm the resolution and present (the often surprised) leaders with the framed commendation. Word spreads like wildfire through the organization, the commendation is hung at the nursing station, and physician engagement is improved yet again.

Service-Line Annual Reports

Similar in size and quality to a corporate annual report, a service-line annual report is a document sent to an organization's surrounding communities. It highlights the services provided by the line and includes pictures of physicians, nursing leaders, and frontline staff. And of course, it includes a lot of information on the clinical outcomes (mortality, complication rates, costs, etc.) of the service line. Because of its wide distribution, this report is a powerful way to recognize everyone who contributed to the outstanding performance of the hospital or health system. Service-line annual reports are also distributed throughout the organization, helping drive pride in the organization and, of course, the engagement of all caregivers, including physicians.

A Simple Thank-You

A sincere thank-you is one of the nicest ways to recognize individuals. When a healthcare environment can be full of blame and bad-apple chasing, this small act begins to turn the corner toward a new culture of appreciation and respect for hardworking caregivers. Many will say that a thank-you is just common sense, and that is true. But leaders often forget this simple but meaningful act during their busy days on the front line.

When delivered in person, a thank-you feels great. When it is written on a nice card with sincerity and not as an obligation, a thank-you certainly goes a long way to improve physician engagement.

But a word of caution: Thank-yous can be overused. Too many of them, in too many meetings, from too many leaders can have a detrimental effect. After a while, an excess of thanks starts to feel hollow—the words feel insincere and start to hurt reputations. The repetition can generate resentment and disengagement in staff and physicians. The bottom line? There should be no forced schedule for sending out thank-you cards. Only use them when they are well deserved. Sure, set a monthly goal, but don't overdo it. The same guidelines apply to thanking an entire group at the beginning or end of meetings. Just don't overdo it. And when making rounds, be sure your thanks are sincere, heartfelt, and well deserved. Find the right balance, and this recognition will be appreciated. It will move engagement one more step in the right direction.

CONCLUSION

The chapter began by asking, "Why address quality in a book on physician engagement?" It should be very clear that a robust quality and safety program can be the cornerstone of a physician engagement strategy. In fact, many of the most successful health systems have used quality as the primary strategy to begin or enhance physician engagement in their organizations. Properly designed quality programs appeal to the physician mindset—one that is involved, leadership-driven, compassionate about patients, problem-solving, and focused on data. When they are engaged at the beginning of projects, physicians are happy to be involved and appreciate that their voices are heard. They believe they have a true position in the organization. They move from caring for one patient at a time to affecting the lives of thousands through their improvement work. When their efforts are recognized and celebrated through small and large events, physicians become loyal partners of the organization. In summary, quality fuels engagement and improves physician relations, and because of that engagement, quality moves organizations to levels of excellence they never thought possible.

REFERENCES

Byrnes, J. 2015. *The Quality Playbook: A Step-by-Step Guide for Healthcare Leaders.* Bozeman, MT: Second River Healthcare.

IBM Watson Health. 2020. "Watson 100 Top Hospitals Snapshot Report." Published April 21. www.ibm.com/downloads/cas/ REAWOAOD.

Kramer, M. 2019. "7 Physician & Staff Engagement Strategies to Boost Patient Experience." *Calibrater Health.* Published December 2. www.calibrater.com/physician-engagement-strategies-patient-experience.

Nelson, B. 2012. *1501 Ways to Reward Employees.* New York: Workman.

Oshiro, B. 2015. "6 Proven Strategies for Engaging Physicians— and 4 Ways to Fail." *Health Catalyst.* Published March 5. www. healthcatalyst.com/proven-physician-engagement-strategies.

Press Ganey. 2013. "Every Voice Matters: The Bottom Line on Employee and Physician Engagement." Accessed February 11, 2021. http://images.healthcare.pressganey.com/Web/ PressGaneyAssociatesInc/%7B605442db-1e4f-4d26-8e7f-5512e6f61bd3%7D_PI_Every_Voice_Matters.pdf.

Ritchie, L. C. 2019. "Does Taking Time for Compassion Make Doctors Better at Their Jobs?" NPR. Published April 26. www.npr.org/sections/health-shots/2019/04/26/717272708/does-taking-time-for-compassion-make-doctors-better-at-their-jobs.

Seppälä, E. 2019. "Doctors Who Are Kind Have Healthier Patients Who Heal Faster, According to New Book." *Washington Post*. Published April 29. www.washingtonpost.com/lifestyle/2019/04/29/doctors-who-show-compassion-have-healthier-patients-who-heal-faster-according-new-book.

Shanafelt, T. D., and J. H. Noseworthy. 2017. "Executive Leadership and Physician Well-Being: Nine Organizational Strategies to Promote Engagement and Reduce Burnout." *Mayo Clinic Proceedings* 92 (1): 129–46.

Swensen, S., A. Kabcenell, and T. Shanafelt. 2016. "Physician–Organization Collaboration Reduces Physician Burnout and Promotes Engagement: The Mayo Clinic Experience." *Journal of Healthcare Management* 61 (2): 105–27.

CHAPTER 10

Disruptive Physician Behavior

Lily Jung Henson

That is just the way they are. It is a help to a doctor, especially to one who is full of crotchets, to have as an assistant, a nurse who "knows his ways" and who is not disturbed by his explosions of impatience.
—K. Dewitt, "Practical Points on Private Nursing," 1900

DISRUPTIVE PHYSICIAN BEHAVIOR has long been a known and tolerated issue in healthcare. The chapter epigraph describes physician misbehavior more than a hundred years ago, and, unfortunately, little has changed. Fibuch and Robertson (2019) wrote that "disruptive physician behavior appears to be a continuing and serious problem." Disruptive behavior is still common in modern healthcare organizations, partly because of the presence of high-performing individuals working in stressful environments, partly because of a reluctance to coach respected senior clinicians, and sometimes because of the potential for the loss of the business generated by physicians. But disruptive behavior by physicians or other members of the healthcare team is a well-recognized, direct contributor to a dysfunctional healthcare environment. Such an environment interferes with a culture of safety by endangering patient care, lowering patient satisfaction, decreasing the healthcare team's morale, and increasing the risk of malpractice claims. And simply put, the more an environment allows disruptive physician behavior, the lower its physician engagement will be.

DISRUPTIVE BEHAVIOR DEFINED

The American Medical Association (AMA) defines disruptive behavior as "personal conduct, whether verbal or physical, that negatively affects or that potentially may negatively affect patient care" (AMA 2009). Porto and Lauve (2006) describe physician behavior issues as including "profane language, name calling, sexual comments, racial/ethnic jokes, outburst of anger, throwing equipment, criticizing other caregivers, comments that undermine a patient's trust in other caregivers, intimidating behavior and failing to adhere to organizational policies." The Institute for Safe Medication Practices (2004) further includes "passive activities such as refusing to answer questions, return phone calls or pages, [and] condescending language of voice intonation, and impatience with questions" as disruptive acts.

Note that the label *disruptive* should not be used to describe all physicians critical of issues in a healthcare system. According to the AMA (2009), "Criticism that is offered in good faith with the aim of improving patient care should not be construed as disruptive behavior." However, behavior that causes other healthcare teammates to feel uncomfortable about presenting their perspectives can cause patient harm, so it is incumbent on physicians to recognize the impact of their behavior on others.

SCOPE OF THE PROBLEM

The preceding descriptions are certainly familiar to most healthcare practitioners as scenarios frequently encountered at work. For example, a 2011 survey conducted on behalf of QuantiaMD and the American College of Physician Executives (now the American Association for Physician Leadership) found that 70 percent of the physicians surveyed noted that disruptive physician behavior occurred at least once a month in their organizations, and more than 10 percent described it as occurring daily (MacDonald 2011). In addition, 25 percent of physician respondents acknowledged that they themselves had exhibited disruptive behavior at least once in their professional lifetimes. Despite these discouraging statistics, Santin and Kaups (2015) found that only 3 to 5 percent of physicians were responsible for the majority of physician behavioral issues.

Although physician misbehavior has long been tolerated and even ignored, there is a perception (perhaps based in reality) that healthcare administrators are more likely to ignore the perpetrators who are high producers of revenue. Keogh and Martin (2004) note that 38.9 percent of respondents report that "physicians in my organization who generate high amounts of revenue are treated more leniently when it comes to behavior problems than those who bring in less revenue." A US Department of Veterans Affairs study of 102 hospitals with 4,530 nurses, physicians, and administrators noted that 77 percent had witnessed disruptive behavior in physicians, with a preponderance of the poor behavior coming from physicians in high-stress specialties such as surgery, obstetrics, and cardiology (Rosenstein and O'Daniel 2008b). In a *Seattle Times* series, Baker and Mayo (2017) detail the impact of a highly productive neurosurgeon's disruptive behavior on a hospital system. The physician's mistreatment of staff was allegedly tolerated by the hospital administration and was related to several problems, including physician and nursing turnover, multiple malpractice lawsuits, and federal agency investigations.

CAUSES OF DISRUPTIVE PHYSICIAN BEHAVIOR

Leadership needs to understand the underlying causes of physician misbehavior to prevent and manage further issues. Medical training has endured a long history of "education by humiliation" (Kasselbaum and Cutler 1998). For years in medical school and residency, many trainees have been subjected to abusive behavior by their senior residents and attendings and have accepted this abuse as part of the training process. Generations of premedical and medical students have read Samuel Shem's 1978 novel, *The*

House of God. Fictional but based on real life, the book prepared them for emotional abuse by their superiors, with the recognition that once the students had landed on the other side of training, they too had earned the right to abuse those beneath them. Chen (2012) describes this perpetuating abuse phenomenon in a 2012 *New York Times* article, "The Bullying Culture of Medical School." Sheehan, Sheehan, and White (1990) surveyed a third-year medical school class regarding perceptions of mistreatment and professional misconduct in training and noted that three-fourths of the students described becoming more cynical as a result of their mistreatment. Kasselbaum and Cutler (1998) label this result a "transgenerational legacy" that indoctrinates physician trainees into a culture of cynicism and abuse.

Medical training is also a time to identify potential behavioral issues. Papadakis and colleagues (2005) studied 235 physicians who had been disciplined by 40 state medical boards over a 13-year period. Disciplinary action by a medical board was strongly associated with prior unprofessional behavior in medical school. Behaviors most strongly linked to disciplinary action included severe irresponsibility and a severely diminished capacity for self-improvement. Early identification of, and remediation for, these individuals during training may reduce the incidence of behavioral issues later on.

Obviously, not all physicians go on to have behavioral problems, but some personality traits have been described as more commonly associated with disruptive behavior. Hicks and McCracken (2012) note that those with minimal sociability, low personal trust, and low personal contentment are more likely to exhibit behavioral problems. Physicians who have low levels of emotional self-control and who tend to question the motives of others are more likely to act out. Reynolds (2012) describes Axis I and II disorders associated with disruptive behaviors. These conditions include bipolar, depression, substance abuse, attention deficit, intermittent explosive, circadian rhythm disruption, and dementia disorders. Axis II disorders include paranoid, narcissistic, passive-aggressive, and borderline personality disorders. The presence of drug and alcohol abuse contributes to 10 percent of disruptive behaviors (Weber 2004).

Another contributing factor is physician burnout. A 2020 Medscape survey reported an overall physician burnout rate of 42 percent. Physicians describe frustration with greater regulatory burden, decreasing physician reimbursement, and the EHR. Older physicians have particular difficulty adjusting to a healthcare environment different from the one they are used to. Personal issues such as relationship stressors and monetary concerns can increase the likelihood of disruptive behavior. Anxiety over litigation, real or perceived, can also contribute to physician misbehavior (Rosenstein 2016). Interestingly, the specialties most associated with physician burnout (family medicine, internal medicine, and emergency medicine) do not correlate with those more closely associated with disruptive physician behavior (surgery, obstetrics, and cardiology).

Leaders must recognize that organic illness can manifest itself as behavioral issues. Aging physicians without prior behavioral issues who come to the attention of medical leadership should be evaluated for cognitive decline and associated depression. Consider the following example.

Case Study: When Illness Causes Behavioral Problems

A 69-year-old general surgeon who had been on the medical staff for 30 years with no prior incidents in his medical staff file had an incident report filed by the OR director. When the surgeon had been asked to talk to the family of a patient in the waiting room, he failed to do so, and the family filed a complaint. She noted that the staff had repeatedly reported observing the surgeon acting confused in the surgery department and asking for directions to the waiting room. When

(continued)

(continued from previous page)

he was interviewed by the CMO, he looked disheveled, and his clothes were musty-smelling. He repeatedly asked for clarification of why he was being interviewed. His case was reviewed by the medical staff leadership council, which referred him for neuropsychological evaluation. The results noted mild to moderate cognitive impairment. On further discussion with the leadership council regarding concern over his ability to safely care for patients, the surgeon opted to resign his medical staff privileges.

CONSEQUENCES OF DISRUPTIVE PHYSICIAN BEHAVIOR

In 2000, the Federation of State Medical Boards (FSMB) stated that disruptive physician behavior "creates a hostile environment that interferes with the physician/patient relationship" by shifting "the physician's focus from the patient . . . result[ing] in errors in clinical judgment and performance . . . increas[ing] apprehension and anxiety of the physician's patients . . . who may witness such outbursts and inappropriate behavior . . . decreased effectiveness of the entire health team ... [who] may be intimidated and anxious, causing a loss of their clinical focus and productivity . . . decreas[ing] effective communications among the health care team" (FSMB 2000).

The Joint Commission (2008) issued a sentinel event alert about the connection between disruptive physician behavior and a threat to quality patient care. The alert stated that "intimidating and disruptive behaviors can foster medical errors, contribute to poor patient satisfaction and to preventable adverse outcomes, increase the cost of care and cause qualified clinicians, administrators and managers to seek new positions in more professional environments."

Behavioral issues subvert an organization's ability to develop a culture of safety. Tolerance of this behavior prohibits the development of a cohesive multidisciplinary team and people's ability to speak up about safety concerns. The consequence is poor patient outcomes and potentially serious safety events (Rosenstein and O'Daniel 2008a). In addition, when staff tend to create workarounds to reduce physicians' outbursts, decreased efficiency and productivity often result. Staff attendance and retention are also often adversely affected by misbehaving physicians (Rosenstein 2002). On top of the negative impact on staff morale, disruptive physician behavior is also noted by patients. When their questions and concerns are ignored, patient satisfaction is low. Increasingly, physician misbehavior is also a liability for healthcare organizations because of staff complaints of a hostile work environment and because patients equate bad interactions with physicians to poor quality of care.

PREVENTION OF DISRUPTIVE PHYSICIAN BEHAVIOR

The AMA (2016) remarks that "physicians have a responsibility to address situations in which individual physicians behave disruptively, that is, speak or act in ways that may negatively impact patient care, including conduct that interferes with the individual's ability to work with other members of the health care team, or for others to work with the physician." AMA policy asserts that it is the responsibility of the organized medical staff—not of a hospital's administrative body—to deal with disruptive behavior. The complexity of the current healthcare industry would suggest the need for a more comprehensive approach to the problem of disruptive physician behavior.

At a System Level

Leape and Fromson (2006) remark that a systems-level approach is needed to effectively and promptly respond to physician performance failures, because individual organizations lack the capacity to ensure the safety of the public. The authors call on the FSMB, the American Board of Medical Specialties, and the Joint Commission to collaborate on expanding programs for deficient physicians.

In 2000, the FSMB adopted the recommendation of the Special Committee on Professional Conduct and Ethics that medical "boards' ability to discipline physicians whose behavioral interactions with physicians, hospital personnel, patients, family members, or others creates an environment hostile to the delivery of quality health care or otherwise interferes with patient care" be strengthened from a statutory standpoint (FSMB 2000). For example, the Washington State Medical Quality Assurance Commission stated that "when the Commission receives a complaint concerning a practitioner exhibiting inappropriate and disruptive behavior, the Commission will consider such behavior as a threat to patient safety that may lead to violations of standards of care or other medical error . . . and take appropriate action, including possible suspension, to promote and enhance patient safety" (Farrell 2012). Similarly, the Georgia Composite Medical Board has "the authority to refuse license, certificate, or permit or issue discipline; suspension . . . to an applicant . . . engaged in any unprofessional, unethical, deceptive, or deleterious conduct or practice harmful to the public, which conduct or practice need not have resulted in actual injury to any person" (Georgia Composite Medical Board 2020).

In 2009, the Joint Commission established a new leadership standard that addressed disruptive behaviors (Joint Commission 2009; Schyve 2009):

- The hospital or organization must have a code of conduct that defines acceptable and disruptive and inappropriate behaviors.
- Leaders must create and implement a process for managing disruptive and inappropriate behaviors.

In addition, the Joint Commission's standards in the medical staff chapter have been organized as six core competencies to be addressed in credentialing; these competencies include interpersonal skills and professionalism (Joint Commission 2017b, 2020). Readers are also encouraged to occasionally review the Joint Commission's website (www.jointcommission.org) because of frequent posts and articles that provide guidance on dealing with medical staff behavior challenges.

The Joint Commission (2017a) also issued a sentinel event alert about "the essential role of leadership in developing a culture of safety, which calls upon healthcare leaders to prioritize patient safety and demonstrate a commitment to the organization's safety culture through everyday actions." Specifically, the commission noted that leaders needed to address "intimidating and unsettling behaviors (which cause) emotional harm, including the use of inappropriate words and actions or inactions."

DNV (prior to March 1, 2021, was DNV GL), another healthcare accrediting organization, also addresses disruptive behavior in its standard "MS.14 Corrective or Rehabilitation Action" by requiring that "the medical staff bylaws shall provide a mechanism for management of medical staff corrective or rehabilitative action . . . [which] may result from unprofessional demeanor and conduct . . . An officer of the medical staff, CEO, or any officer of the board may initiate the process for corrective or rehabilitative action. All hospital staff should be instructed in the process to follow when a practitioner is conducting him/herself in an unprofessional manner or presents signs of impairment that would jeopardize the safety and quality of patient care" (DNV GL 2020).

At an Organizational Level

Culture of Respect
Holloway and Kusy (2010) say that to create an environment that does not tolerate physician misbehavior, organizations need to

change from a "culture of toxicity" to a "culture of respect." This transformation requires an organization to commit to large-scale values development with stakeholders, team assessment and norm building, and individualized feedback, including criteria for acceptable interpersonal behavior. Changing a culture is not a simple task. It requires defining what an organization considers professional behavior and providing training in team dynamics, relationship, and stress and anger management.

The growth and influence of physician leaders is also critical to managing disruptive physician behavior. CMOs and medical staff leaders have the ability to discern if a disruptive physician has a legitimate complaint about a process. They can either help to address the physician's concerns or, as peers, to coach the physician about the appropriateness of the behavior in question. Consider the following case study.

Case Study: A Problematic Individual

An agency OR nurse asked to be reassigned because he was uncomfortable with the atmosphere of the OR in which he was assigned. The 40-year-old orthopedic surgeon had made derogatory remarks about some staff members' race and sexual orientation while he was operating. An investigation by human resources revealed that this hostile atmosphere was a common theme in his OR, but the staff who were usually assigned to work with him in the OR had become used to his behavior and chose to ignore his comments. When the surgeon met with the CMO to discuss the complaint, the surgeon initially denied that he had done so, but when presented with evidence to the contrary, he acknowledged that he did regularly use those slurs but that "no one minded." He went on to complain about the OR leadership team and

(continued)

(continued from previous page)

its management of the OR and described how he had to "do everything himself" to get his patients to the OR table and ready for surgery. Later in the day, security identified this physician as the individual videotaped on surveillance cameras in the hospital cafeteria entering the closed cafeteria and taking two cans of beverages without paying for them. The medical staff leadership council reviewed his case and mandated that he participate in a physician behavioral program focusing on professional boundaries and disruptive behaviors.

Allowing Physicians to Be Involved

Rosenstein (2017) suggests that giving physicians a voice, whether it be through surveys, town halls, department meetings, specialty task forces, or one-on-one conversations, will help direct their input constructively rather than ignoring them until they want to act out their frustrations in the workplace. Physicians are well-intentioned, dedicated healthcare professionals who like to fix problems, and a physician's corrective efforts are sometimes not recognized for their original intent. The ability to contribute to a positive change in their work environment has been shown to help reengage physicians and reduce burnout.

Monitoring and Tracking

Organizations must be able to identify and track physician behavioral issues. Most healthcare organizations now use an incident-reporting system that allows monitoring of instances of physician misbehavior. For many years, disruptive behavior was tolerated and not documented. The lack of documentation led to difficulty in pursuing decisive corrective actions when the behaviors finally became intolerable for an organization.

Define Disruptive Behavior

Leadership must define unprofessional behavior in the organization's medical staff bylaws, so that clear criteria exist to pursue consequences for any unacceptable behavior. In addition, by using the credentialing process to have physicians sign off on a code of conduct, organizations create a mechanism to hold physicians accountable later on if they misbehave.

MANAGEMENT OF DISRUPTIVE PHYSICIAN BEHAVIOR

Physician leaders describe managing disruptive physician behavior as time-consuming and emotionally draining. Some administrators think that it is simply easier to terminate misbehaving employed physicians than it is to attempt to change their behavior. Yet in light of the overall cost of training and recruiting physicians, it is incumbent on hospital leaders to prioritize rehabilitating physicians if possible. Moreover, not all misbehavior is caused by the same factors. Sorting out the causes requires patience and aligning the goals of the medical staff and executive leadership.

Behavioral issues have to be addressed in a timely fashion. Quick attention allows the leader to bring the event into the offending physician's active consciousness and is more likely to help the physician recognize the behavior and immediately change it. Kaufmann (2005) describes the importance of listening to the physician's side and offering empathy for the person's perspective. The leader should also follow up and investigate any of the physician's concerns that may have led to the negative behavior. This follow-up helps develop trust between the physician and the leader and helps the physician feel heard.

The importance of documentation of the discussion cannot be overemphasized. The tracking of this and subsequent actions allows for the progression of disciplinary action as needed if the behavior persists.

THE VANDERBILT MODEL

Hickson and colleagues (2007) describe Vanderbilt University School of Medicine's comprehensive approach to identifying, measuring and addressing unprofessional behaviors (exhibit 10.1). The model focuses on four graduated interventions:

1. Informal "cup of coffee" conversations for single incidents
2. Nonpunitive "awareness" interventions when data reveals patterns
3. Leader-developed action plans if patterns persist
4. Imposition of disciplinary processes if the plans fail

When unprofessional events recur despite an initial conversation with the offending physician, "an awareness intervention" (level 1) should occur. At this level, the leader presents data that corroborates the behavior pattern. An estimated 2 to 3 percent of the medical staff

---

Exhibit 10.1 Promoting Professionalism Pyramid

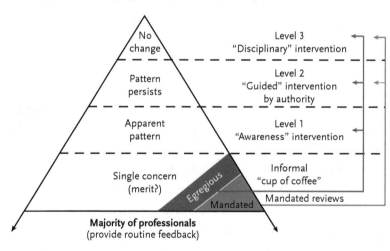

Source: Adapted from Hickson et al. (2007).

---

display disruptive behavior often enough to be noted by leadership (Hickson et al. 2007).

Those who fail to respond to this effort then require "an authority intervention" (level 2). This intervention entails a performance improvement plan. Progressive failure leads to termination of privileges (level 3).

Case Study: When Joking Is Not Joking

An ICU nurse of German descent complained that a senior surgeon told her she was acting "like a Nazi" when she pressed him to follow hospital procedure on managing a post-thoracotomy patient. When counseled on the incident, the surgeon indicated that he had been joking and was actually complimenting her on her style. Several months later, a hospital supply-chain worker wearing a hijab reported that this surgeon had taken a box cutter off the worker's cart while they were riding in an elevator together, held it up to her face, and asked, "Are you a terrorist?" When interviewed, the surgeon responded again that he had been making a joke and did not intend to intimidate her. The medical staff leadership council referred him to a training course on professional boundaries.

Corrective action plans usually entail training programs that consist of training in personality and relationship management, developing personal skills, and team collaboration. Readers are encouraged to review the comprehensive Federation of State Medical Boards (2016) Directory of Physician Assessment and Remedial Education Programs for more resources on corrective action plans.

Hicks and McCracken (2012) and Marton and Pister (2016) suggest that individual coaching can also be effective in physicians with adequate emotional intelligence to be open to more self-awareness.

These physicians learn to reflect on how their responses affect others and modify their behavior.

For physicians whose behavioral issues may be partly due to burnout, the Mayo Physician Engagement Model may allow them to become more actively engaged in addressing the environmental drivers of burnout. As defined by Shanafelt and colleagues (2015), this model employs a sequence called "listen, act, develop, repeat." Leaders *listen* to an overwhelmed physician to identify and understand what is causing distress. They *act* by helping the physician identify and operationalize solutions to address these causes. As the leaders help in this way, the physician is *developed* through performance improvement. The physician and leader *repeat* the process to identify the next round of improvement work to eliminate the causes of burnout.

CONCLUSION

Disruptive physician behavior is common; it impinges on an organization's culture and can diminish physician engagement. Physician misbehavior leads to patient harm, patient and staff dissatisfaction, staff turnover, and potential legal issues. The causes of the misbehavior are many. They include exposure to abuse in training, underlying personality traits, stresses of professional and personal life, alcohol and drugs, and organic disease. To eliminate disruptive physician behavior systemically, leaders must, among other actions, recognize that the behavior can be a root cause for patient harm, and they must establish clear expectations for processes to address the problem. Intervention with physicians who exhibit disruptive behavior can be incremental; the level of the intervention should be based on the success of the response. While much of these recommendations seems like common sense, the healthcare industry clearly needs much more attention paid to the issue even if it only involves a few bad performers. Ultimately patient quality and safety will improve, as well as physician engagement.

ACKNOWLEDGMENT

Both Lily Henson and Carson Dye wish to acknowledge the special input on this chapter provided by Gerald Hickson, MD, Joseph C. Ross Professor of Medical Education and Administration at Vanderbilt University. Dr. Hickson is the Founding Director of the Center for Patient and Professional Advocacy (CPPA) and the Vanderbilt Health Affiliated Network (VHAN), beginning January 1, 2020. Dr. Hickson is an internationally recognized expert in patient safety, medical malpractice, and its causes and prevention.

REFERENCES

American Medical Association (AMA). 2016. "Physicians with Disruptive Behavior." Opinion 9.4.4. Code of Medical Ethics Opinion. Accessed February 12, 2021. www.ama-assn.org/delivering-care/ethics/physicians-disruptive-behavior.

———. 2009. "Report of the Council on Ethical and Judicial Affairs: Physicians with Disruptive Behavior." Opinion E-9.045. Code of Medical Ethics. Accessed February 28, 2021. www.ama-assn.org/sites/ama-assn.org/files/corp/media-browser/public/about-ama/councils/Council%20Reports/council-on-ethics-and-judicial-affairs/i09-ceja-physicians-disruptive-behavior.pdf.

Baker, M., and J. Mayo. 2017. "High Volume, Big Dollars, Rising Tension." *Seattle Times*. Published February 10. https://projects.seattletimes.com/2017/quantity-of-care/hospital.

Chen, P. W. 2012. "The Bullying Culture of Medical School." *New York Times*. Published August 9. https://well.blogs.nytimes.com/2012/08/09/the-bullying-culture-of-medical-school.

DeWitt, K. 1900. "Practical Points on Private Nursing." *American Journal of Nursing* 1 (1): 14–17.

DNV GL. 2020. "DNV GL Healthcare Standards and Requirements." Accessed July 29. www.dnvgl.us/assurance/healthcare/standards.html.

Farrell, M. 2012. "Practitioners Exhibiting Disruptive Behavior." Washington Medical Quality Assurance Commission. Published February 24. https://wmc.wa.gov/sites/default/files/public/documents/MD2012-01PractitionersExhibitingDisruptive Behavior.pdf.

Federation of State Medical Boards (FSMB). 2016. "Directory of Physician Assessment and Remedial Education Programs." Updated January 4. www.fsmb.org/siteassets/spex/pdfs/remedprog.pdf.

———. 2000. "Report of the Special Committee on Professional Conduct and Ethics." Published April. www.fsmb.org/siteassets/advocacy/policies/report-of-the-special-committee-on-professional-conduct-and-ethics.pdf.

Fibuch, E., and J. Robertson. 2019. "Bringing Value: Dealing Fairly with Disruptive Physicians." American Association for Physician Leadership. Published March 8. www.physicianleaders.org/news/bringing-value-dealing-fairly-disruptive-physicians.

Georgia Composite Medical Board. 2020. *Official Code of Georgia Annotated, Title 43, Chapters 34 and 34A,* § 43-34-8 (7). Accessed July 27. www.medicalboard.georgia.gov.

Hicks, R., and J. McCracken. 2012. "Personality Traits of a Disruptive Physician." *Physician Executive* 38 (5): 66–69.

Hickson, G. B., J. W. Pichert, L. E. Webb, and S. G. Gabbe. 2007. "A Complementary Approach to Promoting Professionalism and Addressing Unprofessional Behaviors." *Academic Medicine* 82 (11):1040–48.

Holloway, E. L., and M. E. Kusy. 2010. "Disruptive and Toxic Behaviors in Healthcare: Zero Tolerance, the Bottom Line and What to Do About It." *Medical Practice Management* 25 (6): 335–40.

Institute for Safe Medication Practices. 2004. "Intimidation: Practitioners Speak Up About This Unresolved Problem—Part 1." *ISMP Medication Safety Alert!* 9 (5): 1–3.

Joint Commission. 2020. "Medical Staff and Bylaws." In *Accreditation Guide for Hospitals*. Accessed February 28, 2021. www. jointcommission.org/-/media/deprecated-unorganized/imported-assets/tjc/system-folders/topics-library/171110_accreditation_guide_hospitals_final.pdf.

———. 2017a. "The Essential Role of Leadership in Developing a Safety Culture." Sentinel Event Alert 57. Published March 1. www. jointcommission.org/resources/patient-safety-topics/sentinel-event/sentinel-event-alert-newsletters/sentinel-event-alert-57-the-essential-role-of-leadership-in-developing-a-safety-culture.

———. 2017b. "Medical Staff Essentials Sample Pages." Accessed February 28, 2021. www.jointcommission.org/-/media/tjc/idev-imports/blogs/mse17_sample_pages__l__toc_intro_pp1to7pdf.pdf.

———. 2009. "Leadership Standard LD.03.01.01, EP 4 and EP 5." In *The Joint Commission Leadership Standards*. Oak Brook, IL: Joint Commission Resources.

———. 2008. "Behaviors That Undermine a Culture of Safety." Sentinel Event Alert 40. Published July 9. www. jointcommission.org/resources/patient-safety-topics/sentinel-event/sentinel-event-alert-newsletters/sentinel-event-alert-issue-40-behaviors-that-undermine-a-culture-of-safety.

Kasselbaum, D., and E. Cutler. 1998. "On the Culture of Student Abuse in Medical School." *Academic Medicine: Journal of the Association of American Medical Colleges* 73 (11): 1149–58.

Kaufmann, M. 2005. "Management of Disruptive Behavior in Physicians." *Ontario Medical Review* 72 (10): 59–64.

Keogh, T., and W. Martin. 2004. "Managing Unmanageable Physicians: Leadership, Stewardship and Disruptive Behavior." *Physician Executive* 30 (5): 18–22.

Leape, L. L., and J. A. Fromson. 2006. "Problem Doctors: Is There a System-Level Solution?" *Annals of Internal Medicine* 144 (2): 107–15.

MacDonald, O. 2011. "Disruptive Physician Behavior." Published May 15. www.kff.org/wp-content/uploads/sites/2/2013/03/quantiamd_whitepaper_acpe_15may2011.pdf.

Marton, K., and K. Pister. 2016. "Coaching: A Useful Approach to Disruptive Behavior." *Physician Leadership Journal* 3 (1): 55–57.

Papadakis, M. A., A. Teherani, M. A. Banach, T. R. Knettler, S. L. Rattner, D. A. Stern, J. J. Veloski, and C. S. Hodgson. 2005. "Disciplinary Action by Medical Boards and Prior Behavior in Medical School." *New England Journal of Medicine* 353 (25): 2673–82.

Porto, G., and R. Lauve. 2006. "Disruptive Clinician Behavior: A Persistent Threat to Patient Safety." *Patient Safety and Quality Healthcare.* Published July–August. https://psnet.ahrq.gov/resources/resource/4100.

Reynolds, N. T. 2012. "Disruptive Physician Behavior: Use and Misuse of the Label." *Journal of Medical Regulation* 98 (1): 8–19.

Rosenstein, A. H. 2017. "Physician Dissatisfaction, Stress, and Burnout, and Their Impact on Patient Care." In *Distracted*

Doctoring: Returning to Patient-Centered Care in the Digital Age, edited by P. J. Papadakos and S. Bertman, 121–42. Cham, Switzerland: Springer International Publishing.

———. 2016. "Human Factors Affecting Disruptive Physician Behaviors and Its Impact on the Business of Medicine." *Journal of Business and Human Resource Management*. Published August 14. www.physiciandisruptivebehavior.com/admin/articles/58.pdf.

———. 2002. "Nurse–Physician Relationships: Impact on Nurse Satisfaction and Retention." *American Journal of Nursing* 102 (6): 26–34.

Rosenstein A. H., and M. O'Daniel. 2008a. "A Survey of the Impact of Disruptive Behaviors and Communication Defects on Patient Safety." *Joint Commission Journal on Quality and Patient Safety* 34 (8): 464–71.

———. 2008b. "Managing Disruptive Physician Behavior." *Neurology* 70 (17): 1564–70.

Santin, B. J., and K. L. Kaups. 2015. "The Disruptive Physician: Addressing the Issues." *Bulletin of the FACS* 100 (2): 20–24.

Schyve, P. M. 2009. "Leadership in Healthcare Organizations: A Guide to Joint Commission Leadership Standards." Joint Commission. Accessed February 28, 2021. www.jointcommission.org/-/media/deprecated-unorganized/imported-assets/tjc/system-folders/topics-library/wp_leadership_standardspdf.pdf.

Shanafelt, T. D., G. Gorringe, R. Menaker, K. A. Storz, D. Reeves, S. J. Buskirk, J. A. Sloan, and S. J. Swensen. 2015. "Impact of Organizational Leadership on Physician Burnout and Satisfaction." *Mayo Clinic Proceedings* 90 (4): 432–40.

Sheehan, K. H., D. V. Sheehan, and K. White. 1990. "A Pilot Study of Medical Student 'Abuse': Student Perceptions of Mistreatment and Misconduct in Medical School." *JAMA* 263 (4): 533–37.

Shem, S. 1978. *The House of God.* New York: Richard Marek Publishers.

Weber, D. O. 2004. "Poll Results: Doctors' Disruptive Behavior Disturbs Physician Leaders." *Physician Executive* 30 (5): 6–14.

CHAPTER 11

Physician Leadership Development

Bhagwan Satiani and Daniel Eiferman

A leader is one who knows the way, who goes the way,
and who shows the way.
—H. Reginald Buckler, writer and philosopher, 1889

ONE OF THE PERSISTING myths is that leaders are born—that leadership cannot be taught. What may encourage this myth to persist is that some leadership programs may subliminally cause people to think that they were born to lead and hence did not need to learn or earn the privilege to lead (Ryan 2016). Some physicians may fall into this trap, thinking that because they are regarded as leaders of their small team at work, they do not need to learn what it takes to truly lead people. This attitude arises because most physicians work in silos with people who are subservient to them and who are afraid to speak out if their leader is unskilled or ineffectual.

Most physicians are bright, hardworking, altruistic, and comfortable leading within their own scope of activity (Falcone and Satiani 2008). For decades, administrative positions in hospitals were filled with physicians who were wonderful clinicians with demonstrated success in their fields. Or they were on the verge of retirement or perhaps burned-out and forced to look for alternatives to practicing medicine. Hospital administrators have since realized that the best clinicians do not necessarily make the best leaders. As healthcare delivery changed, organizations realized that the attributes needed to be successful physician leaders have also changed and that, for many reasons, including the complexity of demands on modern-day leaders, physicians need to be put on different paths before they can wear different hats.

No doubt some physicians proved to be excellent leaders, but many of the best clinicians who were newly appointed failed. Without any training in managing people, physicians are then asked to govern hundreds if not thousands, plan strategies, act on financial plans, maintain morale, communicate, negotiate, and resolve conflicts. Victor Dzau has labeled these physicians as "accidental leaders" (Stoller, Goodall, and Baker 2016). But the healthcare landscape has entirely changed, and we need better physician leaders. The challenge is echoed in the title of Marshall Goldsmith's popular book: *What Got You Here Won't Get You There* (Goldsmith 2007).

> I suppose leadership at one time meant muscles; but today it means getting along with people.
>
> —Attributed to Mohandas K. Gandhi

The healthcare industry has now settled on the notion that developing physician leaders is in everyone's interest: the interest of health systems, physicians, patients, and the nation. The status quo seemed unacceptable. Rather than waiting for physicians to consider stepping out of their comfort zones and to train themselves to shift into leadership roles, hospitals would have to actively engage and encourage the physicians to partner with them.

One of the best ways to engage physicians is to implement leadership training programs to help them lead and manage the massive change that is rocking the US healthcare system. Having a stake in the system creates a powerful incentive for physicians to truly engage to benefit all stakeholders, not just their own.

PHYSICIAN REPRESENTATION IN LEADERSHIP ROLES

Over a decade ago, between 5 and 10 percent of hospital leadership was made up of physicians (Satiani et al. 2014). In one survey of healthcare executives, 73 percent of hospitals reported that less than 10 percent of physicians were in leadership positions (Satiani 2016). A multitude of factors have propelled physicians to assume leadership roles in hospitals. Among these are an emphasis on clinical excellence and quality in such newer payment models as bundled payments, a shift to value-based reimbursement, and, finally, empiric information pointing to the value of physicians' leading or coleading health systems.

There are a multitude of reasons why physicians are now more than ever interested in leadership roles. Some institutions still follow the traditional model of appointing excellent senior physicians who believe that their time has now come or who have shown loyalty, or even those who have tired of practicing medicine. But newer physicians are attracted by such challenges as population health management and quality and safety of patient care. These physicians are responding to the challenges by acquiring training in the skills needed to succeed.

Part of the problem in the past has been that health systems have not fully invested in training excellent clinicians into successful physician leaders. A survey by the Advisory Board Company demonstrated that when hospitals recruited physician leaders, 59 percent of the institutions did not clearly define their roles, responsibilities, and performance objectives (Falcone and Satiani 2008). In addition, 78 percent failed to evaluate the physicians' performance against existing goals. The best and most comprehensive training may not be adequate to prevent budding physician leaders from failing at their tasks.

A TEAM SPORT

Healthcare is a team sport. Team play becomes more important as the care grows even more complex. No single person, specialty, or role is sufficient to produce the best quality of care for patients.

Physicians are looked on to lead clinical teams. Senior hospital administration is looked at to solve all problems in the hospital.

In turn, administrators need physicians not only to resolve clinical problems but also to push innovative solutions and to convince all other physicians and nurses to embrace quality targets. To accomplish these goals, health systems need physicians who have some background in these skills at the front line to engage with their peers and hospital executives so healthcare can achieve its purpose of affordable, quality care for the population.

Almost all physicians are engaged in some way, but it is purely in clinical terms, taking care of their teams and focusing on quality care and excellent outcomes. Similarly, they may be engaged listening to hospital leadership on a variety of issues. However, physicians appear to be lacking commitment to the institutional mission, vision, and strategic goals.

Press Ganey (2019) describes how engagement efforts could fuel change in culture and therefore in organizational performance. Studying the responses from more than 1.8 million physicians, nurses, and other healthcare workers, the company found that physicians are the least engaged, followed by registered nurses. Senior managers had the highest engagement. Employed physicians exhibited lower engagement than did contract and private practice physicians. The latter finding is disturbing because of the large numbers of physicians now employed. Hospitals need to review their relationship with their employed physicians to address and improve engagement.

Since physician engagement is linked to organizational performance, hospital administrative leadership must work on commonalities to diminish the degree of disconnect in the physician–hospital relationship. Among other things, shared values, being respected, and a sense of accomplishment are excellent indicators of physician engagement and commitment to the organization. Multiple surveys confirm that although compensation is important, it is not the prime driver in this regard. Mutual trust is another factor, which may sometimes be lacking from the physician point of view. When healthcare institutions have objective survey data showing poor engagement scores of physicians, it is futile to hire expensive consulting firms to find answers they may already have.

If as discussed, few physicians are in a leadership role, the lack of engagement may be just one symptom. Gamble (2011) discusses a 2010 online survey of a thousand physicians by PricewaterhouseCoopers. Some 56 percent of respondents pointed to the lack of adequate physician representation and physician leadership as a factor in their absence of trust in hospital relationships.

PHYSICIANS' CHANGING ROLES AS EMPLOYEES

The terminology may have changed, but the yearning for a unified approach to dealing with healthcare is not new. Before health systems used so many employed physicians, engagement had a different meaning. In the traditional medical staff model, organizations worked with independent physicians to make sure credentialing, privileging, and quality of patient care had effective physician leaders. In some cases, the physicians were paid for their medical director roles, but for the most part, their contributions were voluntary and made for a mutually beneficial relationship.

Things changed as employment by health systems made physicians less independent and, often, subservient to hospital administrators. Many senior hospital executives were averse to promoting physicians to leadership roles, because although they may have been great clinicians, they lacked experience in management or leading people as part of a team.

Hospitals ultimately realized that the concept of engagement had changed significantly. They now needed physicians as partners at the highest levels. Partnership is not a luxury anymore.

> Partnership is not a luxury anymore.

Surveys in many hospitals now monitor engagement as a vital metric to report to their board. As governmental regulations increase, it is practically impossible to achieve many quality and other milestones without true physician engagement, where physicians feel they are being listened to and their advice is being acted on.

Among many reasons, some of which have been cited earlier, disengaged physicians feel that the system does not care about them. In addition, they may see no link between their work and the mission or vision of the institution. Physicians may also see loss of control over their surroundings at work as one more reason to prefer detachment and isolation. Reduction in income or research productivity and academic promotion may be another factor making them reluctant to get on this path.

Productivity incentives in compensating physicians puts a premium on their time, especially with the almost 50 percent burnout rate. Leadership training for physicians willing to take it is a major commitment of their time and effort. Hospitals must make allowances for the hours that any training will take away from their clinical productivity.

To try to empower physicians in leadership roles, many hospitals decided to educate selected high-potential physicians in management and leadership principles. Buell (2009) explains that engagement at the meso (organization) level includes active physician involvement by taking on leadership roles, which include strategic planning, decision-making at the highest levels, and execution of these plans. To truly engage physicians—and to improve healthcare in general—health systems must train physicians in the leadership skills they need to succeed.

EVIDENCE TO SUPPORT LEADERSHIP TRAINING FOR PHYSICIANS

The question that remains unanswered is this: Is there enough return on investment to justify the cost of either training physician leaders internally or sending them elsewhere? In terms of dollars and cents, no payback time has been clearly identified. However, many hospital executives and physician leaders agree that training physicians to lead is beneficial for all stakeholders.

Let us look at some empirical evidence to support the idea of training and its impacts on the clinical care and quality component in hospitals. A cross-sectional study by Amanda Goodall (2011) studied the personal histories of 300 CEOs of the top hundred hospitals in 2009. The hospitals were ranked high in cancer, digestive diseases, and cardiovascular disease. She then classified the CEOs as physician or nonphysician executives. The findings indicated a significant positive association between the ranked quality of a hospital and whether the CEO was a physician ($p < 0.001$). The author was careful to say that the study did not suggest that the physician leaders outperformed the professional administrators, but the link between a physician CEO and the ranked quality of the hospital was strong.

Another study, by consulting firm McKinsey in the London School of Economics, interviewed managers and department heads in the UK National Health Service to correlate clinical leadership with performance management (Castro, Dorgan, and Richardson 2008). The authors of the study report that in contrast to hospitals with little clinical leadership, those with the most clinician involvement in management affairs performed 50 percent higher on indicators of performance, such as effectiveness of overall management, performance management, and leadership.

Stoller, Goodall, and Baker (2016) make the case for physician leaders, explaining that clinicians are best suited to lead at the crossroads between quality and cost, technology, and humanity. They admit that physicians in the past were ill suited for these roles because of the lack of appropriate training but point to the recent crop of physicians such as John Noseworthy at the Mayo Clinic and Delos Cosgrove at the Cleveland Clinic. In addition to being superb clinicians, these physicians were also very successful in their leadership roles. The authors also discuss research by Nick Bloom and colleagues, which concludes that the largest positive effect on management and hospital performance was the proportion of managers with a clinical degree. The authors also quote Dr. Cosgrove, who, when asked to explain the advantage in organizational performance when physicians lead, answered, "Credibility . . . peer-to-peer credibility."

Finally, in a systemic review of physician leadership training programs in academic medicine, Straus, Soobiah, and Levinson

(2013) examined ten selected studies suggesting modest positive effects on outcomes important to academic medical centers. Straus and her colleagues concluded that training programs were beneficial to these centers in terms of advancement in academic rank, hospital leadership positions, and success in publishing papers. Although the limited findings did support the positive impact of physicians advancing in leadership positions, the impact of improving engagement at the institution level has not been satisfactorily studied.

SELECTED PHYSICIANS LEADERSHIP TRAINING ORGANIZATIONS

There are several leadership training programs for physicians. Some are led by various professional organizations, and others are developed internally by hospitals and health systems. Here is a partial list of a few programs.

American College of Healthcare Executives

Castellucci (2017) quotes Deborah J. Bowen, FACHE, CAE, president and CEO of the American College of Healthcare Executives (ACHE; www.ache.org): "Educating physicians is not necessarily a new topic. What is different now is the momentum and understanding that if we want to move to a value imperative, physicians have to understand more about the business of health care." She says that of ACHE's 38,000 members in 2017, more than 2,000 were physicians, a 10 percent increase over 2016. ACHE offers multiple in-person educational opportunities as well as e-learning throughout the year. In addition, a fellowship certification (Fellow of the American College of Healthcare Executives, or FACHE) is recognized as a distinctive achievement.

American Association for Physician Leadership

Peter Angood, CEO of the American Association for Physician Leadership (AAPL; www.physicianleaders.org), says that the association's training is "more practical, solutions oriented and reflective of the real world" (Castellucci 2017). Besides its certificate program, Certified Physician Executive (CPE), the association offers many courses, some of which are self-study.

American College of Physicians

The American College of Physicians offers "live meetings, faculty-led online courses, and self-study modules" to assist budding physician leaders (ACP 2021a) and a Certificate in Physician Leadership (ACP 2021b). This is an 18-month course offered in conjunction with AAPL.

Harvard T.H. Chan School of Public Health

Leadership Development for Physicians in Academic Health Centers is a rigorous ten-day on-site program for physicians in administrative capacities to learn from an interdisciplinary faculty (Harvard University 2021b).

Harvard Medical School

Conducted by Harvard faculty for mid- to senior-level surgeons, the program offers a certification for surgical leadership. It culminates with a "Certificate Program for Executive Skills Development and High-Impact Leadership, Inside and Outside the Operating Room" (Harvard University 2021a).

Mayo Clinic

The Mayo Clinic has one of the earliest leadership programs for physicians (Tangalos et al. 1998). The program started as a three-tier approach: one program for department or division chairs, one for all staff, and a third for past participants.

Although the Mayo Clinic runs several programs, a boot camp for leaders is popular with physicians (Mayo Clinic 2019).

Cleveland Clinic

The Samson Global Leadership Academy is a one- or two- week program designed for the clinician and healthcare executive. Participants are paired with an executive coach (Cleveland Clinic 2021a, 2021b).

The Cleveland Clinic–Weatherhead School of Management Executive MBA is an executive degree program for physicians, nurses, and administrators offered in conjunction with the Weatherhead School of Management of Case Western Reserve University (Case Western Reserve University 2020).

American College of Surgeons

The premier organization representing a broad panoply of surgeons offers this annual three-day course for surgeons who practice in academic and private institutions and who wish to enhance their leadership skills across a wide variety of settings, from operating room to boardroom (ACS 2021).

American Academy of Family Physicians

The American Academy of Family Physicians year-long Emerging Leader Institute program for its members focuses on trainees (AAFP 2021).

Examples of Internal Training Programs

Cleveland Clinic

The Cleveland Clinic has probably one of the earliest programs training physicians to lead. James Stoller, MD, has led the annual course, Leading in Health Care, since the early 1990s and has selected high-potential participants for a ten-day off-site program. The program then evolved to include nurses and hospital administrators. The curriculum included emotional intelligence (including 360-degree feedback and coaching), team building, conflict resolution, and situational leadership. The participants then completed a team-based innovation project presented to hospital leadership. Dr. Stoller and his colleagues have determined that 61 percent of the proposed innovation projects have had a positive institutional impact. Moreover, 43 percent of the physician participants have been promoted to leadership positions at Cleveland Clinic over a ten-year follow-up period. The program has changed over the years and is now called the Mandel Global Leadership and Learning Institute (Cleveland Clinic 2021a).

Mayo Clinic

The transition from a command-and-control mindset to a partnership-management mode may be difficult for some physicians who are used to making decisions in silos. Berry and Seltman (2008) describe the "Mayo way" of promoting their clinicians into leadership positions by emphasizing that "physician leadership does not necessarily mean physician management of everything, but physician leadership is an essential element in the direction of everything." Physician accountability is at the heart of the system whose physicians keep the institution's interest above everything else. Most of the administrative work is done at the committee level, where physician leaders are spotted by their ability to work in teams and to build consensus. The clinic emphasizes the fact that there is a constellation rather than a Big Dipper and that every physician is a star. This metaphor emphasizes teamwork and leads to people's alignment with the system. A century after the founding of the clinic, the original dyad, in which the physician is the face of the clinic and the administrator works backstage, prevails. A major difference between the Mayo Clinic and most other health systems is the background of the clinic's executives: Few of the physician CEOs have postgraduate training, and formal training is not a requirement for the CEO position. Not only are CEOs term-limited, but they also usually return to clinical care after their "retirement" from the executive job.

Other Programs

Many other institutions—Yale, University of Kentucky, Virginia Mason, Hartford Healthcare, Wharton, Harvard Business School, and Weatherhead School of Management in Cleveland, to name but a few—have created their own internal programs (Stoller, Goodall, and Baker 2016). Moreover, an increasing number of nonacademic healthcare organizations have created internal physician leadership development programs.

HISTORY AND DEVELOPMENT OF THE WEXNER MEDICAL CENTER FACULTY LEADERSHIP INSTITUTE TRAINING

In 2011, one of us (Bhagwan Satiani) reviewed existing physician leadership training programs and found most to be lacking in several respects. Among other issues, the curriculum was usually haphazardly put together, and admission was nonselective and based often on affordability. The cost for external programs was exorbitant, speakers were not chosen for their own experiences with physicians, the schedule was not friendly to working physicians, and a slide deck was the usual format rather than more direct conversations and open discussions around topics.

Another important deficit was that many programs had an intense focus for a few days, a week at most, after which attendees were sent home with binders full of information to read. After the participants returned home, there was little further contact or dissemination of additional curriculum-based information. In brief, there was little continuity or follow-up. After a short, intense burst of knowledge, the participants were left to figure out the next steps on their own.

With these problems in mind, we then met with several prominent physician leaders outside our medical center, especially those associated with successful internal leadership programs. From these conversations, we developed a list of desired competencies consistent with our local culture. Next, we held a series of meetings with internal stakeholders, chiefly chairpersons of all surgical departments to begin with, since we were contemplating a program for training leaders in the surgical disciplines.

One common theme among the chairs was the lack of succession planning in departments. They wanted to train younger faculty to prepare them for leadership roles. As Athey and Garman (2014) explain so aptly, "The greatest opportunity for improvement in effectiveness was associated with preparing internal leaders for future senior leadership positions."

The main course objective was to strengthen participants' leadership skills to allow them to thrive in the constantly changing arena of healthcare. Many physicians had probably experienced examples of poor leadership practices in their groups, divisions, or departments. Our purpose was to clean the slate and open their minds to starting anew.

> Minds are like parachutes; they work best when open.
>
> —Attributed to Thomas Dewar, Scottish businessman

With these thoughts in mind, we created a list of topics that we would want the program to cover in the initial program (exhibit 11.1). Secondary goals were to improve engagement among faculty members, increase retention of faculty members, and improve quality of care in the institution.

Exhibit 11.1 Brief Description of Initial Leadership Program Topics

Topic	Brief Details
Leadership	Principles of leadership, leadership styles, leadership versus management
Strategy and Vision	Definition of strategy; strategic plan development and implementation; organization mission, vision, objectives; environmental scan; strategic partnerships
Team Building	Teamwork and factors influencing team dynamics; creation of, participation in, and leading teams; using leadership styles to build teams; establishment of holistic diversity in team formation; conflict resolution
Negotiations and Conflict Management	Types of negotiations, conflict resolution, facilitation techniques, principles, processes
Communications	Basic principles and types of communications; influence of culture and background; tools and techniques, including presentation techniques, to communicate effectively
Financial Management, Business Planning	Principles of accounting, financial statements, types of budgeting, financial controls, time value of money, productivity measures, development and implementation of a business plan
Decision-Making and Problem-Solving	Identification of problems, definition of root causes, decision-making processes
Change Management	Definition of change, managing and leading change, identifying stakeholders and mobilization
Healthcare Law	Overview of False Claims Act, Stark Law, antitrust laws, and antikickback law; healthcare reform; comparative view of other healthcare systems; some contractual law for employees; employment models

(continued)

(continued from previous page)

Topic	Brief Details
Human Resources	Recruitment and retention planning and strategies, talent development and management, coaching, employee engagement and satisfaction, dispute resolution, basic federal and state human resource laws
Quality of Care and Patient Satisfaction	National quality initiatives, national quality-monitoring organizations, quality management, developing and maintaining quality assurance programs, customer satisfaction
Burnout in Physicians	Causes of burnout, time management, work–life balance, policies and procedures to address physician behavioral and burnout issues

Although initially intended to be a program for faculty members only in the Department of Surgery at The Ohio State University, the committee decided that the inaugural course would be offered to physicians in all the other surgical specialties. Opening up the program encouraged camaraderie and interaction between faculty members throughout the medical center as well as distributed the costs of the course among multiple departments.

The curriculum for the Talent Management Leader Advancement and Leader Development Academy (TMALDA) was developed by the course directors in conjunction with leaders in the institution as well as from conversations with experts from Ohio State University Fisher College of Business and College of Humanities. With this input, the course directors determined the topics for each session (exhibit 11.2). The TMALDA program started in September 2011 after almost 18 months of planning and consultation.

Exhibit 11.2 Topics and Dates of Sessions for TMALDA

Date	Topic
9/15/2011	Introductory session: leadership competencies, program topics, speaker selection, participant introductions, nuts and bolts of program, including case studies, evaluations, and prizes
10/20/2011	Emotional intelligence and resonant leadership
11/10/2011	Financial management
12/8/2011	Managing change
1/12/2012	Creative thinking in healthcare
2/9/2012	Communications
3/8/2012	Building team trust
4/12/2012	Creative contentions and negotiations
5/10/2012	Quality, operational excellence, and patient satisfaction
6/13/2012	Orchestrating clues of quality: management lessons from the Mayo Clinic
9/13/2012	Diversity in medicine: strategies and leadership competencies
10/12/2012	Ethics for leadership
11/8/2012	Overview of healthcare law: what physicians need to know in the post–Affordable Care Act environment
12/13/2012	Physician's role in creating a premier work environment
1/10/2013	Burnout
2/7/2013	Strategy formulation, implementation, metrics, and adjustment
5/2/2013	Final case study presentations and graduation

Course Format

The program consisted of 17 sessions that usually met monthly for 3.5 hours on a weekday evening. All the sessions were facilitated by experts in their field. The presenters came both from inside The Ohio State University in Columbus and from outside the university (e.g., Mayo Clinic, consulting firms). All sessions were highly interactive, with specific instructions to facilitators that "canned talks" were not an acceptable teaching format. The participants were expected to attend 75 percent of the sessions for course completion. They were required to complete three projects with their assigned team to graduate from the course.

Participant Selection

To select participants for the program, the directors explained the course objectives to the surgical department chairs and gained their buy-in to the program and their commitment to funding the participants. The directors asked the chairs who they believed had the potential to be effective leaders. The chairs then nominated candidates in their department, and 23 candidates were selected to participate from ten surgical departments (exhibit 11.3).

Exhibit 11.3 Number of Participants in the Program, by Department

Surgery	4	Pediatric Surgery	2
Plastic Surgery	2	Urology	3
Ophthalmology	2	OB/GYN	1
Otolaryngology	4	Oral and Maxillofacial Surgery	1
Neurological Surgery	2	Orthopedic Surgery	2

The program was extremely successful. The first class graduated in 2013, with 21 of 23 participants completing the program. Two faculty members dropped out because of their inability to attend 75 percent of the sessions. Nineteen of the participants who completed the course said they were satisfied with the course and felt it was a valuable use of their time. All 21 completing participants responded that they would recommend the course to a peer.

Participants' Evaluation of the Training

The graduates from the program described the benefits they received from the training. For example, a professor of pediatric surgery had this to say:

> The facilitators lined up an impressive faculty that taught us basics of economics, finance, marketing, communication, negotiation, feedback, and organization behavior and development. The sessions were particularly resonant because we were grouped with peers, and our different subspecialty backgrounds brought an interesting diversity in thought and contributions during discussions.

An associate professor of orthopedic surgery offered this feedback:

> It was a tremendous opportunity for all of us who were young faculty to get exposed to an executive business curriculum. It allowed us to develop key relationships with other future leaders in our organization across disciplines that has made OSUWMC [The Ohio State University Wexner Medical Center] stronger. The program broadened our business acumen and helped us develop leadership skills that made us more competitive for local, regional and national leadership opportunities.

Several comments included the following suggestions for improvement:

- Length of sessions (3.5 hours too long)
- Length of program (18 months too long)
- Group projects requiring excess of time to complete

Transition to the Faculty Leadership Institute

Given the success of the program, the CEO of the medical center asked one of us (Bhagwan Satiani) to expand the program to include all faculty members in the College of Medicine. Subsequently, in 2013, the program transitioned and became part of the Faculty Advancement, Mentoring, and Engagement (FAME) center in the College of Medicine and was renamed the Faculty Leadership Institute (FLI). In light of the feedback from the original participants, the program was shortened to 12 sessions, each of which was decreased to three hours' duration. All facilitators were local to Columbus or the OSU Fisher College of Business or were experienced consultants. The participants' total time commitment to participate in the program, including sessions, readings, and project work, was eight to ten hours per month. Participants in FLI were given five books, a twelve-month subscription to *Harvard Business Review*, a 360-dgree evaluation with free coaching sessions, and mentoring with their capstone project at year's end.

By the end of 2018, 167 faculty members had "graduated" from TMALDA and FLI (exhibit 11.4). The biggest challenge has been placing them in the medical center to work with hospital administrative teams to apply their knowledge. Since the programs began, one of us (Bhagwan Satiani) emails a brief ten-minute article related to leadership every 10 to 12 days to all "graduates." The aim is to keep the participants focused on continuing to learn and think about leadership.

Exhibit 11.4 Details of TMALDA and FLI Program Participants

Cohort	Applicants	Accepted	Finished	Moved out of the Medical Center
2011–2013	24	24	22	4
2013–2014	58	29	29	8
2014–2015	44	30	27	7
2015–2016	32	30	30	3
2016–2017	40	31	31	3
2017–2018	40	30	28	2
Total	238	174	167	27

The programs have produced many benefits. Some faculty members have been placed on important committees or medical staff leadership roles because of their experience with FLI. Energized by the FLI program, several physicians have gone on to complete an MBA. Among the consistently positive feedback we have received from participants are comments about the contacts they made during their year with FLI and the many ways they have applied their knowledge at work and in their private lives. About 16 percent of all participants have left the hospital and university, many for leadership roles elsewhere.

Developments After 2019

Although program candidates still need support from their departmental chairs and division chiefs to apply for FLI, the candidates now apply directly to the program rather than having to be nominated. As the program has matured, there are now ten sessions per year, with an expectation of 90 percent attendance. See exhibit 11.5 for the updated 2020–2021 curriculum. Healthcare law and human resources are now being taught through other FAME curricula.

Exhibit 11.5 Curriculum for FLI Program, 2020–2021

Session	Topic
1	Growth mindset
2	BUILD (self-awareness tool) and action planning
3	Coaching
4	Teams
5	Inspirational communication
6	Power and influence
7	Negotiations
8	Decision-making
9	Strategy
10	Change management

Next Steps

The FLI physician leadership course has created demand for more opportunities for physicians to develop their nonclinical skills. The interest has extended to physicians still in their residency and fellowships. In development is an advanced leadership course for program graduates who would like to continue their leadership development. The following steps are in the pipeline:

- LEAD (Lead. Engage. Accelerate. Drive.) was launched in 2019 for surgical residents.
- FUEL (FAME Unites Emerging Leaders) began in January 2021 and serves as a prerequisite for application to FLI. This six-month course is intended for faculty members within the first five years of the completion of their training.
- FLI 2.0 is being developed for graduates of FLI for more in-depth exploration of leadership topics.

INTERNALLY DEVELOPED VERSUS EXTERNAL LEADERSHIP PROGRAMS

There are advantages and disadvantages to both physician leadership programs developed internally and those developed outside the hospital (exhibit 11.6).

With physician incentives increasingly tied to clinical productivity, travel expenses and the lost wRVUs create a disincentive on the part of both the employer and the physician for leadership training away from home. And yet, health systems realize that having no line of succession for leadership is a strategic failure. Because the culture is different and unique at every hospital, the decision to start a program internally or externally rests with leadership.

Exhibit 11.6 Comparison of Internal and External Physician Leadership Training Programs

	Internal Programs	External Programs
Curriculum	Adapted to institutional needs; can be individualized if part of MBA at a university	Fixed, broad based
Cost	Generally less expensive, and many have subsidized applicant fees; usually no revenue for the organization; organizational support needed; internal facilitators are complimentary	Usually more expensive; each facilitator is paid in addition to revenue for the organization; membership may be required to join
Learning Curve	Steeper until program is established	Most are turnkey
Pool of Participants	Depends on size of hospital but generally smaller; ability to combine with nursing or administrative leaders	Larger, depending on size of membership of organization

(continued)

(continued from previous page)

	Internal Programs	External Programs
Facilitators	Usually faculty or hospital employees with a mix of paid consultants; internal facilitators are complimentary	Almost all paid; belong to professional organizations
Certificate or Degree	Variable; degree if part of MBA or a certificate if qualifies for credit course at university	Variable; certificate of competence
After Completion	May be used internally for advancement; if part of MBA, can be valuable anywhere	If recognized nationally, valuable anywhere

CONCLUSION

Clearly one of the more meaningful ways to inspire physicians to engage with hospitals is to partner with them. To operate at the same level as hospital executives, physicians must learn leadership skills. Some physicians may be concerned about committing hours to leadership development. Compensation systems heavy in productivity incentives and concerns about academic promotion and lost research opportunities may discourage physicians from attending leadership programs. Employing hospitals must address these concerns if they are to encourage physicians to train and step into leadership positions. Lack of opportunities to progress after leadership training may also seriously discourage physicians. However, our experience shows significant benefits in a leadership program for physicians. It will probably take a few years as we accumulate longitudinal data, including our biennial engagement survey of our clinicians, to have empiric information to demonstrate a return on investment. One early lesson for us has been to work with hospital administration on a solid plan to provide opportunities for physicians who complete their leadership training.

REFERENCES

American Academy of Family Physicians (AAFP). 2021. "Family Medicine Leads Emerging Leader Institute." Accessed February 15. www.aafpfoundation.org/our-programs/education-initiatives/family-medicine-leads-emerging-leader-application.html.

American College of Physicians (ACP). 2021a. "ACP Leadership Academy." Accessed February 15. www.acponline.org/meetings-courses/acp-courses-recordings/acp-leadership-academy.

———. 2021b. "Certificate in Physician Leadership Program." Accessed February 15. www.acponline.org/meetings-courses/acp-courses-recordings/acp-leadership-academy/certificate-in-physician-leadership-program.

American College of Surgeons (ACS). 2021. "Surgeons as Leaders: From Operating Room to Boardroom." Accessed February 15. www.facs.org/education/division-of-education/courses/surgeons-as-leaders.

Athey, L. A., and A. N. Garman. 2014. "How Senior Leadership Teams Are Changing: A Survey of Freestanding Community Hospital CEOs." Published fall. American College of Healthcare Executives. www.ache.org/-/media/ache/learning-center/research/ceowhitepaper2014.pdf.

Berry, L., and K. D. Seltman. 2008. *Management Lessons from the Mayo Clinic.* New York: McGraw Hill.

Buckler, H. R. 1889. *The Perfection of Man by Charity: A Spiritual Treatise.* New York: Catholic Publication Society Co.

Buell, J. M. 2009. "Achieving Financial Success Through Improved Physician Engagement: Revenue Enhancements Can Be Realized with Stronger Relationships." *Healthcare Executive* 24 (1): 22–24.

Case Western Reserve University. 2020. "Weatherhead's Executive MBA Program Jumps Nationally and Globally in 2020 Rankings." Cleveland Clinic–Weatherhead Executive MBA, Weatherhead School of Management. Published June 29. https://weatherhead.case.edu/degrees/masters/mba/executive/cleveland-clinic.

Castellucci, M. 2017. "Teaching Physicians How to Lead." *Modern Healthcare*. Published March 27. http://modernhealthcare.pressreader.com/modern-healthcare/20170327.

Castro, P. J., S. J. Dorgan, and B. Richardson. 2008. "A Healthier Health Care System for the United Kingdom." *McKinsey Quarterly*. Published February. www.washburn.edu/faculty/rweigand/McKinsey/McKinsey-Healthier-Care-In-UK.pdf.

Cleveland Clinic. 2021a. "Global Leadership and Learning Institute." Accessed February 15. https://my.clevelandclinic.org/departments/global-leadership-learning.

———. 2021b. "Samson Global Leadership Academy." Global Executive Education. Accessed February 15. https://my.clevelandclinic.org/departments/global-executive-education/programs/leadership-academy#curriculum-tab.

Falcone, R. E., and B. Satiani. 2008. "Physician as Hospital Chief Executive Officer." *Vascular and Endovascular Surgery* 42 (1): 88–94.

Gamble, M. 2011. "7 Tips for Physician Representation in Hospital Governance." *Becker's Hospital Review*. Published February 18. www.beckershospitalreview.com/hospital-physician-relationships/7-tips-for-physician-representation-in-hospital-governance.html.

Goldsmith, M. 2007. *What Got You Here Won't Get You There: How Successful People Become Even More Successful*. New York: Hachette.

Goodall, A. H. 2011. "Physician-Leaders and Hospital Performance: Is There an Association?" Published July. http://ftp.iza.org/dp5830.pdf.

Harvard University. 2021a. "Certificate Program: Surgical Leadership." Harvard Medical School. Accessed February 15. https://postgraduateeducation.hms.harvard.edu/certificate-programs/leadership-programs/surgical-leadership.

————. 2021b. "Leadership Development for Physicians." Harvard T. Chan School of Public Health. Accessed February 15. www.hsph.harvard.edu/ecpe/programs/leadership-development-for-physicians.

Mayo Clinic. 2019. "School of Continuous Professional Development. Healthcare Executive Leadership Bootcamp." Accessed February 15, 2021. https://ce.mayo.edu/special-topics-in-health-care/content/healthcare-executive-leadership-bootcamp-2019.

Press Ganey. 2019. *Health Care Workforce Special Report: The State of Engagement.* Published October 22. www.pressganey.com/resources/white-papers/health-care-workforce-special-report-the-state-of-engagement.

Ryan, L. 2016. "Can Leadership Skills Be Taught?" *Forbes.* Published April 1. www.forbes.com/sites/lizryan/2016/04/01/can-leadership-skills-be-taught/.

Satiani, B. 2016. "Preparing Physicians for Leadership Positions in Academic Medicine." *Physician Leadership Journal* 3 (2): 58–61.

Satiani, B., J. Sena, R. Ruberg, and E. C. Ellison. 2014. "Talent Management and Physician Leadership Training Is Essential for Preparing Tomorrow's Physician Leaders." *Journal of Vascular Surgery* 59 (2): 542–46.

Stoller, J. K., A. Goodall, and A. Baker. 2016. "Why the Best Hospitals Are Managed by Doctors." *Harvard Business Review*. Published December 16. https://hbr.org/2016/12/why-the-best-hospitals-are-managed-by-doctors.

Straus, S. E., C. Soobiah, and W. Levinson. 2013. "The Impact of Leadership Training Programs on Physicians in Academic Medical Centers: A Systematic Review." *Academic Medicine* 88 (5): 710–23.

Tangalos, E. G., R. A. Blomberg, S. S. Hicks, and C. E. Bender. 1998. "Mayo Leadership Programs for Physicians." *Mayo Clinic Proceedings* 73 (3): 279–84.

CHAPTER 12

Telehealth

Kevin Post

Telehealth. It's no longer just a nice-to-have, but instead a must-have for patients and healthcare professionals alike during these uncertain times the COVID-19 pandemic has brought about. While we all wish that it hadn't taken a pandemic to propel telehealth forward, for better or for worse, it has. The spotlight is now on telehealth in a big way, and for good reason.
—Joe Harpaz, "5 Reasons Why Telehealth Is Here to Stay," 2020

WHY IS PHYSICIAN engagement critical to the future of telehealth? What are specific strategies for physician engagement?

Telehealth continues to establish its place as a cornerstone of healthcare delivery. The integration of technology into the sacred patient–provider relationship has been, and continues to be, one of the most beneficial yet disruptive challenges that physicians, advanced practice providers (APPs), clinical staff, and health systems have faced. The importance of physician engagement in leading and implementing the strategic use of technology has never been more evident than in the rapidly growing field of telehealth.

The recent COVID-19 pandemic unexpectedly gave the field of telehealth a big boost. Before the pandemic, the adoption of virtual health was slower than anticipated. Now, seemingly overnight, barriers in financial reimbursement and geographical limitations requirements suddenly have been overcome as new and creative techniques appeared. In addition, the adaptability of patients, providers, and health systems greatly increased as all sought ways to provide safe access to healthcare in a manner that maintained acceptable quality standards.

Moving into the future, health systems will continue to move quickly yet strategically further into the world of virtual care and telehealth. There is a sense of urgency that this momentum into virtual care must not be lost, or it will have been a missed opportunity for patients and medical providers alike. As Dacey (2020) explains, "Until late March 2020, the single largest obstacle to widespread adoption of telehealth for office services was the geographic limitations imposed by Medicare's originating site geographic limitation—that the originating site be outside of a major metropolitan area. That was the elephant in the road, effectively blocking the use of the codes for any urban and many suburban areas, regardless of the practicality of it."

THE NEED FOR PHYSICIAN ENGAGEMENT IN THE FUTURE OF TELEHEALTH

Physician engagement in both setting and driving initiatives will be essential in moving telehealth forward. Physicians must lead in creating a climate and culture where patients, providers, clinical staff, and administrative colleagues are motivated to achieve set telehealth objectives. This leadership should include setting and maintaining clear goals that align well with the strategic plan of the health organization and are shared with employees at all levels so that they also feel committed to these goals. A culture of trust, mutual respect, continuous improvement, and transparency with colleagues and patients will be critical in creating the virtual environment that will be most likely to lead to success. Cordero (2020) indicates that involving "clinicians on every level of the telehealth program is key to clinical engagement. If they're connected and engaged, the team is able to accomplish its main goal of positive patient outcomes."

Physicians are uniquely positioned as leaders of both the health systems and their own patient-care teams. While the patient is the most important participant in the individual's own medical treatment plan, the physician serves as the key driver to engaging both the patient and clinical staff in a model of team-based care. A physician's education and practice experience often provide valuable insights and perspectives both inside and outside of direct patient care. Fellow physician colleagues, APPs, nurses, and other ancillary staff often look to the lead of respected and trusted physician leaders. Therefore, physician leaders are key to both engaging the patients and care teams and bringing them along in adapting to the ever-changing roadmap of the telehealth journey.

THE IMPACT OF TELEHEALTH ON MEDICAL PROVIDERS

Medical Provider Mindset

The mindset of medical groups, individual physicians, and other clinical providers contributes greatly to the success of telehealth efforts. Health system and physician leaders must seek to understand their providers and their current status before embracing further efforts with telehealth and virtual care. Health organizations will need to deliberately and clearly educate providers about the benefits and limitations of telehealth and develop a structured, clear process for providers to become proficient in virtual care. Landi (2019) also notes that "as older physicians retire, it is expected that physician willingness will continue to increase, and uncertainty and resistance to decrease."

Using Physician Champions

Most medical groups have physicians and providers who have already served as early adopters of virtual visits and telehealth opportunities. These clinicians were well positioned heading into the COVID-19 pandemic. They already felt comfortable and were functioning efficiently with these new techniques. These providers not only lead the way, by example, in virtual visits and care but also serve as champions of the technology for both health systems and their colleagues. Experienced providers in virtual care have the growth mindset needed to develop system strategies and best-practice approaches to drive widespread provider education, tips, and on-site training. In addition, individual provider training and support can also be achieved via those providers both in arranged education sessions, or in-person or virtual support at the patient's bedside.

Addressing the Fear of Change

Like everyone else, medical providers can have a myriad of opinions. In the same way that they respond to other changes, providers can feel a range of emotions, including fear of the unknown, anxiety, hesitancy, and concern. They may have appropriate questions about maintaining proper levels of quality and safety in patient care. Those leading the change in adapting to telehealth must be willing to listen to others and seek to understand the perceived barriers seen by these providers. Medical staff surveys can be a useful tool to access these areas and guide future training strategy to best target areas of provider needs.

TELEHEALTH EXPECTATIONS FOR MEDICAL PROVIDERS

Health systems and individual providers should be willing to self-assess their future expectations for virtual care. Although these expectations will be heavily influenced by insurance payment policies, other factors should also be considered. There may be opportunities to generate additional revenue or find cost savings aligning with the potential growth strategy of the health organization.

Virtual care may mean that in the future, health systems would need less capital for building structures and space, would need fewer employees, and would have lower overhead costs. Some of these gains may be offset by expenditures for the necessary technologies. Opportunities exist in care approaches such as population health, managed care, and ACOs. Efficiencies may be gained in virtual visit scheduling and in expanded virtual services such as home care. Determining this balance of the percentage of health system patient visits done virtually will evolve, as payment models continue to trend from traditional fee-for-service to population health management.

Individual medical providers will also have to decide their desired level of involvement in virtual care. This decision should not be based on reimbursement alone but should consider the desired patient type, visit type, and style of practice to best fit the patients' needs and the practice. For instance, patient access may look much different in rural than it does in urban settings. Ideally, physicians and other providers should position themselves to adapt quickly to changing consumer demands and reimbursement structure. This flexibility will allow them to move fluidly from traditional face-to-face patient encounters to virtual patient care.

TELEHEALTH TRAINING AND SUPPORT FOR MEDICAL PROVIDERS

Health systems need to develop a strategic, structured, and accessible training program that fits the individual provider's needs. Methods include virtual, recorded video, or in-person training.

Providers may need training in how to access camera options, proper virtual etiquette, documentation, and so forth. Shadowing providers experienced in virtual care as they conduct live virtual visits can also further educate providers new to the technology and can relieve any fears about the process. Additionally, just as there is an art to the traditional practice of medicine, there is an art to virtual care. This new method requires training and a different skill set. Again, engagement by all levels of providers helps them function proficiently and professionally in providing virtual care. Fortunately, medical schools are seeing the need to address telehealth. Warshaw (2018) writes, "To prepare future physicians to use telemedicine effectively, a growing number of medical schools and teaching hospitals are including it in classroom and clinical instruction. According to AAMC data, 84 medical schools (about 58%) included telemedicine as a topic in required or elective courses during the 2016–2017 academic year. In 2013–2014, only 57 schools (about 41%) provided telemedicine training."

PERSONAL IMPACT OF TELEHEALTH ON MEDICAL PROVIDERS

Medical providers may directly see the impact of virtual care on their professional and personal lives. Obviously, reimbursement structures will directly affect not only personal income but also enthusiasm to engage in telehealth. Work–life balance and the desired practice style will also affect providers' level of personal engagement. Additionally, the opportunity to provide and be reimbursed for virtual visits at off-hours (evenings or while available covering emergency department calls, etc.) may provide an additional source of income. To afford the best care for their patients and to best meet their own personal needs, physicians and clinicians should observe how experts at virtual care implement the technology in their practices.

IMPACT OF TELEHEALTH ON CONSUMERS AND THE PATIENT–PROVIDER RELATIONSHIP

The progression of telehealth and virtual care has ongoing influence on healthcare consumers and provider–patient relationships. This progress has been accelerated with the COVID-19 pandemic. Patient expectations and behaviors will continue to evolve; people will seek out health systems and providers that offer enhanced customer service, and people may be beginning a trend of choosing a medical brand rather than an individual provider. Individuals will choose options suited to their unique needs. The transformative forces of digitization and scientific innovation, coupled with the unsustainable cost of healthcare, have led consumers to consider their covered access to care. These financial considerations may affect or override a previous trusting, established relationship with a medical provider.

Before the COVID-19 pandemic, virtual care was most often sought out by younger, healthier, well-off, and tech-savvy patients. However, much of that changed during the pandemic, when it quickly became advantageous for the more vulnerable patients, many of them older adults, to seek care virtually. The virtual visits decreased the risk of infectious exposure while still meeting the need for continued management of chronic health conditions. Vulnerable consumers may experience fear or anxiety about contracting illness by coming to a medical facility, and they are likely to pursue remote options for safe, quality care. For example, at Avera Health in Sioux Falls, South Dakota, a virtual-care nurse assessment detected an obstetric patient who had developed a sudden change in respiratory symptoms—a change that required emergent care. If a virtual visit had not been available, the patient might have hesitated to access direct patient care. Additionally, care platforms quickly became more affordable and user-friendly, thus also accelerating the rate of use. Transparency (in quality and cost) and choice will continue to increasingly drive health consumers.

Another disruptive force for providers and health systems is the increasing connection between individual patient priorities and health insurance plans. Many medical decisions must now consider, among other factors, price, brand, and a medical provider network. Health insurers are striving to develop personal relationships with patients to improve their health and to minimize medical costs, but these relationships blur the boundaries between patients, providers, and insurers. In addition, the increasing vertical integration with health insurers and providers also has an impact on the options for individual care.

TELEHEALTH CARE PLATFORMS AND PORTFOLIOS

The full scope and definition of telehealth is not set in stone. The term *virtual care* is probably the broadest description and definition of the practices. As a rule, there are three primary types of virtual patient care (exhibit 12.1):

- **Telemedicine:** In this classical form of visit, the patient meets with a facilitator at the originating site, with the treating provider at a distant site. Medical monitoring devices and instruments worn by patients are typically connected directly to the provider's computer at the site of the treating provider.
- **Portal visits:** The patients submit their information or request via a secure electronic portal. The care interaction does not occur in real time; instead, the treating provider replies within an accepted time frame.
- **Virtual visits:** Typically, the patient accesses medical care in real time via a webcam, usually through a provider's website. With these virtual visits, the patient does not use a facilitator or go to a care facility. The provider then communicates the diagnosis, treatment plan, e-prescription, and follow-up plan of care directly to the patient during this virtual encounter.

Exhibit 12.1 Virtual Care Components

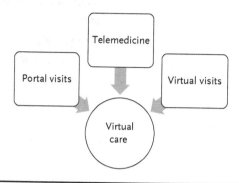

These general virtual care strategies can provide hospital, clinic, long-term, and in-home care. In-home monitoring devices, mobile apps, and other technology-enabled care are becoming increasingly sophisticated yet more user-friendly and affordable. Through these advanced platforms, patient phone calls (free care) can be converted into reimbursed virtual care that improves care quality and patient safety.

Patients will also seek improved access to virtual options for care. In addition to the actual medical visit or appointment, the options should include virtual scheduling and registration. Health systems should offer a virtual front door and develop a goal of meeting patients where they are and in a convenient way. Along that theme, health organizations should take a new look at their current physical employees and facilities and should consider such offerings as virtual greeters and waiting rooms.

COMMON USES OF VIRTUAL CARE

Effective long-term virtual care requires that the right venue and visit types are chosen. Beyond offering some consultative or urgent care visits, physicians and other providers will need to form and maintain a proper relationship with their patients if virtual care is to become a more common practice. They can form these relationships through initial in-person visits or through virtual care as both patients and providers become increasingly comfortable with this venue. Visits must also be in the correct format (e.g., telephone call, in-person visit, virtual visit) for proper evaluation and treatment. The format depends on the patient's condition and the exam, labs, and diagnostics needed.

Common uses of virtual visits include the following (exhibit 12.2):

- Medication refills for stable chronic conditions
- Visits primarily requiring counseling or education (diet counseling, smoking cessation, etc.)
- Minor urgent care conditions (urinary tract infections, minor respiratory illnesses, etc.)

Exhibit 12.2 Some Common Uses of Virtual Care

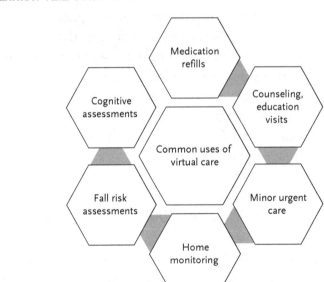

- Home monitoring of both chronic conditions and semi-acute illnesses
- Fall risk assessments
- Cognitive assessments
- Advanced care planning and counseling
- Follow-up visits for appropriate postoperative services

PHYSICIAN ENGAGEMENT STRATEGIES FOR TELEHEALTH

Healthcare organizations must have strategies for how to best engage physicians for both the implementation and the ongoing maintenance of telehealth. Engaging physicians' intellect and the presence of mutual respect between frontline physicians and operational support is vital. Barriers to care and anticipated opportunities must be seen as challenges to be worked through together using the strengths of each other's talents to best strategize and resolve issues. Basic fundamental approaches to boost clinician engagement include early and reinforced education, transparency, shared outcomes, and structured streamlined processes. Perhaps most important, make it fun! A positive culture and friendly competition can improve utilization.

Develop a Common Vision and Purpose

Having a common purpose helps engage both physicians and medical staff. Physicians must see the entire picture. This broader picture or vision often relates to increased quality and safety of patient care, which then aligns with the financial stewardship of the organization. A focus on a shared vision throughout the organization can be a common ground easily understood and supported by medical providers.

Be Transparent with Data

Transparently presenting the data and rewards of telehealth also increases physician support. An open discussion of the data and the benefits to patients, communities, and medical providers reminds physicians why telehealth should be pursued. Discussions like these can help generate ongoing engagement among physicians who, as accepted leaders, can bring along their colleagues and support staff by sharing their understanding of the purpose behind telehealth.

Partner Equally with Physicians

Organizations should treat physicians as partners in any telehealth efforts, making sure these efforts align with the organization's and providers' values and beliefs. A spirit of partnership helps foster engagement by increasing physicians' trust that the organization's telehealth efforts will move forward fairly and with integrity, generating a workplace that physicians feel proud to be a part of.

Develop Effective Education

Providing physician education in an incremental, transparent plan increases the comfort level and, therefore, the support of medical providers. This training should include not only the medical knowledge base but also the practical skills needed to provide virtual care. Kelly Rhone, MD, an Avera Health physician leader in telehealth education, offers this advice: "Unless your career is in performing arts or television, you were not likely to consider your posture, position, and 'telepresence' before starting to use telemedicine to see patients. A good web-side manner is critical to build rapport with your patients on the other side of the camera" (Rhone 2020).

Training in virtual care techniques may include in-person didactic sessions, computer-based practice, and hands-on experience.

Direct-to-consumer training is important to ensure that physicians feel comfortable working through a remote patient encounter. Regular updates on education progression are also highly recommended. By purposely decreasing the unknowns of the telehealth process, organizations can help physicians feel reassured, confident, and more willing to engage in the process.

BARRIERS TO PHYSICIAN ACCEPTANCE OF TELEHEALTH

Organizational leaders must openly acknowledge the existing barriers to physician engagement in this field. In doing so, they help increase trust among the physicians in a medical group. Exhibit 12.3

Exhibit 12.3 Barriers to Implementing Telehealth

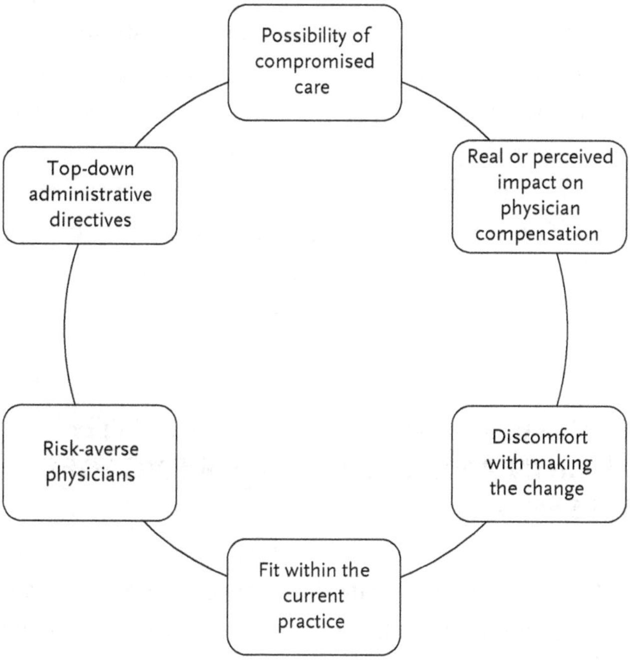

shows some of the primary barriers to physician engagement when an organization is implementing telehealth.

A common concern among physicians and other clinicians is that virtual care may mean compromised care in some situations. This concern is real, and the healthcare organization must allow providers to choose where telehealth fits best in their practices. The organization can help educate its providers about best practices by using real-life examples of other physicians' experiences with telehealth. Additional hesitancy may be due to a real or perceived effect of telehealth on physician compensation; physicians are often risk-averse or may not fully understand the compensation model. Finally, they may feel ill equipped to implement the changes needed for telehealth or worry that it will lead to additional workload. While these barriers are common, by honestly and openly discussing them head-on, health system leaders can work with physicians to resolve these concerns.

Leaders must avoid a few pitfalls when trying to strategically engage physicians. Excessive but unrealistic enthusiasm and inspirational speeches can often turn off physicians and are soon forgotten. Health systems are better served by a transparent presentation of a well-thought-out strategic approach. Additionally, avoid appointing to key leadership positions physicians with inadequate training. Doing so often sets them up for mediocre performance. Finally, overemphasizing financial incentives or oversharing best practices can seem disingenuous and unrealistic to physicians, thus generating disinterest and mistrust.

ALIGNING TELEHEALTH STRATEGIES WITH THE MISSION AND VALUES OF AN ENGAGED HEALTH SYSTEM

As with all initiatives and strategies, health system leaders must be willing to align their telehealth strategies with the mission and values of their organization. One question needs to be answered in detail:

Why are we doing telehealth? As innovative virtual care platforms are being developed and rolled out, a health system's leaders have to know their *why*, hold true to it, and make decisions intentionally from their why. Areas of focus that should be included in this approach are patients, communities, and employees. Organizational discretion, courage, and stewardship are key to the development of transparent virtual care strategies that optimize safety and quality in patient care while driving the overall mission and course of the medical group.

A focus on the needs of the patient must always be at the center in medicine. As we seek to make a positive impact in individual lives, how can virtual systems of care best serve patients? Healthcare means being adaptable in using the multiple modes of digital options to best meet patients when and where they are. Instead of the traditional approach, in which the patient comes to the provider, can providers virtually come to their patients to provide the desired services efficiently and safely while maintaining quality standards? The same care standards, hospitality, and empathy that are so sacred with in-person care must be carried forward into the virtual patient relationship. Additionally, virtual care helps health systems provide care in a more responsive and affordable way, for example, decreasing the patients' travel expenses and time away from work or home responsibilities and increasing the convenience of being treated at home.

Most health organizations have a strategic imperative to serve their communities and populations. Telehealth offers opportunities to provide medical services and access to medical care in groups or areas that may otherwise be difficult to reach. Examples include rural regions and underserved populations and locations. Innovative technologies can also be aligned with telehealth education to help the community better understand the options for access to safe and quality medical care. Finally, telehealth can help bring specialty care to rural regions where the base population would not otherwise provide the volume of patient visits needed to support ongoing on-site services.

Telehealth can improve healthcare employees' satisfaction in another way. Because virtual care innovations often bring care to populations not previously reached, the health system receives more patient visits. The increase in visits, in turn, leads to more patient encounters and subsequent procedures or other treatments and, therefore, employment security for employees. A secondary effect of virtual care can thus be the increased employee satisfaction, engagement, and retention.

Population health initiatives implemented in alignment with telehealth strategies will also take the lead in the health system's efforts to accomplish its mission and values. The core themes of proactively engaging patient populations in healthy living and disease prevention typically coincide with the common overarching goals of serving patients and communities.

At Avera Health in Sioux Falls, South Dakota, for example, Chad Thury, MD, was uniquely positioned during the COVID-19 pandemic as a practicing family medicine physician and a member of the health system's Incident Command Team. Dr. Thury not only engaged his patients and staff in virtual frontline care but also helped influence and drive telehealth efforts at a system level during the pandemic, using system-wide communication channels. As Dr. Thury describes, "Avera has been an industry leader in telehealth for a long time. During the COVID pandemic, our telehealth services quickly expanded to clinic virtual visits. It was gratifying to help lead and champion that endeavor. Being a clinician that was doing virtual visits and not just asking my colleagues to do them provided validity. I learned quickly that many patients are relieved to be able to get quality and efficient care via virtual technology and not risk exposure to COVID" (Thury 2020).

In a broader sense for health systems, telehealth can also drive increased global stewardship because the virtual approach decreases overhead medical costs, the cost per episode of care, and the carbon footprint. The positive effects at a system level can also be seen in increased market share and economic presence.

CONCLUSION

The engagement of physicians and other healthcare professions has been, and will continue to be, essential in the ongoing development and application of telehealth in the United States. The importance of including health professions in the change to virtual is not just a theory; it has been proven to be effective.

Telehealth and virtual care will continue to have a significant impact on patients, communities, and clinical providers as all the stakeholders continue to learn more about how to best implement this tool in the healthcare environment. As new and improved care platforms and portfolios arise, finding methods for affordable and adequately reimbursed virtual care will continue to be of great importance for both patient access and financial stewardship. Health systems and professionals will continue to closely discern how to best use telehealth options to realize their mission and values of patient and community health. And engaged physicians will lead the way.

REFERENCES

Cordero, G. 2020. "5 Ways to Boost Telehealth Engagement Among Clinicians." Health Recovery Solutions. Accessed September 12. www.healthrecoverysolutions.com/blog/5-ways-to-boost-telehealth-engagement-among-clinicians.

Dacey, B. 2020. "Telehealth Is the Future—and the Future Has Arrived." *Medical Economics.* Published April 9. www.medicaleconomics.com/view/telehealth-future-and-future-has-arrived.

Harpaz, J. 2020. "5 Reasons Why Telehealth Is Here to Stay (COVID-19 and Beyond)." *Forbes.* Published May 4. www.forbes.com/sites/joeharpaz/2020/05/04/5-reasons-why-telehealth-here-to-stay-covid19/.

Landi, H. 2019. "1 in 5 Physicians Use Telehealth. Burnout May Drive More Adoption, Survey Says." *Fierce Healthcare*. Published April 15. www.fiercehealthcare.com/tech/22-physicians-use-telehealth-and-burnout-may-drive-more-adoption-survey.

Rhone, K. 2020. Interview with author, September 16.

Thury, C. 2020. Interview with author, September 14.

Warshaw, R. 2018. "From Bedside to Webside: Future Doctors Learn How to Practice Remotely." Association of American Medical Colleges. Published April 24. www.aamc.org/news-insights/bedside-webside-future-doctors-learn-how-practice-remotely.

CHAPTER 13

Engagement Ideas from the Front Lines

Carson F. Dye

SOMETIMES THE BEST IDEAS come from colleagues during a lunch conversation or while sharing a cup of coffee at an ACHE meeting. This is the value of networking—discovering that there are often simple and clear-cut answers to some of the toughest challenges and that these solutions have been tried other places with success.

This chapter includes comments from numerous individuals who have offered their best thoughts and suggestions on how to address physician engagement. To seek out their ideas, I contacted a wide variety of healthcare leaders and asked them a straightforward question: "Can you give me one or two simple suggestions about how you ensure that physician engagement is maximized?" While I did not assign an individual's name to each answer, I have presented the respondents' comments in their own words, with only minor changes for punctuation or formatting. The healthcare leaders who provided comments are listed at the end of the chapter. Comments have been grouped according to general themes.

COMMUNICATION

It is often said that poor communication fuels most problems. People working with physicians will attest to this observation.

Moreover, they would suggest that effective communications may be even more critical with physicians. If engagement is truly based on trust, two-way commitment to purpose and strategy, and a passion for teaming, then communication is the glue that binds all of this. And communication must be two-way; both sides must make the effort to listen sincerely and carefully. This kind of listening happens when there is clarity and transparency. Physicians often believe that management has its own language and that managers are not always open, honest, and authentic. And managers often believe that physicians are just not interested in processes, procedures, and strategy. Thus each party often misunderstands the other's messages.

Here are a variety of thoughts and suggestions that the healthcare leaders I contacted offered on communication:

- "Communicate often and in varying ways (e.g., personal visits, monthly newsletter, periodic 'alerts') with physicians."
- "Actively listen during conversations: Don't interrupt. Don't finish the other person's sentences. Don't use the words 'no,' 'but' and 'however.'"
- "Our medical staff holds quarterly meetings. We require in all of our physician employment contracts that each employed physician attend no less than two per year. As a result, we get high attendance. It builds a sense of team within the medical staff and allows us more opportunities administratively to speak in front of a large percentage of the med staff in one sitting."
- "It may seem simple, but different types of physicians require different types of communication. Obviously, you do not talk with surgeons the same way that you do with family practice docs. I think you should tailor your styles and techniques based upon specialty but also based upon age and length of time with your organization. This all goes to say—you really have to know your docs to

communicate with them. And I think that is the real key to engagement. I might even go further and say, 'Every doc is different, so you better have a personalized style for each one.'"

- "Focus groups at a restaurant with 10–12 doctors and their spouses. I find I get more candid information from the spouses than the physicians sometimes."
- "Transparency—open, clear and frequent dialogue . . . I find providers are OK with 'no' as long as they understand the 'why.'"
- "Create a CEO–physician newsletter."
- "We hold an annual physician-led retreat with board and senior leadership a part of their sessions."
- "It is good to have lunches with new and young physicians who have been on staff for 3 years or less."
- "We hold monthly dinners with hospital-based physician leadership."
- "Expansion of medical directors program where they communicate with other physicians on important issues and programs, admin."
- "No doubt, though, my 40+ years of experience has taught me that the *key* ingredient, or the secret sauce of engagement, if you will, is to make certain people understand the 'why' and make sure that 'why' speaks to their heart. Once you get that well communicated, involving them in the development of processes to achieve the 'why,' good things happen."
- "Sit down with a couple of trusted medical staff leaders to identify your 'A' players in terms of respect by medical staff, positive attitude, and engagement. Use that informal core of providers to spearhead patient safety efforts."
- "I listen to the physicians' ideas on how we can make their experience be efficient."

- "During COVID—we decided to hold our medical staff meetings via Zoom, instead of canceling. The attendance was extraordinary! Providers were more engaged than ever—we believe some of this was the flexibility that Zoom offered the providers who are in many locations, working many shifts!"
- "Listen!"
- "Close the loop, don't leave issues/questions hanging."
- "If answer is 'no' then say it. Along with the 'why' behind the decision."
- "Our physicians indicated they wanted a relaxing space to get away and also to see the executive leadership more to have conversations. As a response to this we remodeled a beautiful area with lounge chairs, a television, places to congregate or relax, etc. We also provide a chef-cooked meal once a week for them to enjoy in their own area."
- "While it might seem obvious [I recommend] spending time in the medical staff lounge and rounding to have spontaneous conversations as well as visiting offices (or having calls during COVID) support engagement. Communication, communication, communication."

CULTURE

Although the term *organizational culture* is used frequently, it is difficult to define. Most definitions ultimately suggest that it is a description of the values, beliefs, and typical behaviors of an organization. Basically, organizational culture is the personality of the organization. Culture consists of the values, expectations, standards, norms, and tangible signs of the various players inside an organization. Mostly, it is about their behaviors. It manifests itself in multiple ways, including how people behave, communicate with one another, view policies and processes, and show (or not show) emotions. Some characteristics of culture are tangible, while others are intangible. Organizational culture can also be thought of in terms of formal, informal, quality-driven, or financially driven environments.

Clearly, though, it is a key driver of physician engagement. Consider these viewpoints:

- "Show up every day as an authentic servant leader and follow the 10 principles outlined years ago by Robert K. Greenleaf, and you will go far. His profound wisdom has served me well. I share this as a recent example of how I see people when dealing with difficult situations such as a restructure we just announced today. I shared this thought with someone when they reached out to me to thank me for being open, meeting with the team, and allowing for dialogue at a time of significant organizational transition."

- "It is never easy—I think you have heard me talk about leadership as stewardship for the hearts, souls, and minds of people. I take that extremely seriously, and it is a heavy burden to carry. It is never easy to make these types of decisions, knowing you impact people's sense of identity, security, image to their family, ability to provide for their family, etc. Behind every job/title is a person created in the image of God who deserves human dignity. That said, I always remember a comment my father said, and it was good advice but hard to live by at times. 'There will come a time when business and friendship cross; don't confuse the two.' With these transitions, I still want to show respect and dignity to the individuals—I have seen this done poorly in the past, and that pains me. It is not good leadership to take the heart and soul out of the human being. Time is a healer for all involved, and there is a process of grief that occurs in these transitions."

- "I believe it is essential to create and sustain a culture wherein physician leadership is highly valued and has significant input into the institution's strategy."

- "In working with them on reducing medical supplies expenses, I found them competitive and argumentative (can't lose). And I allow them some slack here."

- "I am putting into place many of these initiatives because the health system has not had close working relationships with the medical staffs at the hospitals in the past."

- "Personally, I don't find doctors different than anyone else when it comes to engagement. I would argue that treating doctors differently is both unproductive and tactically flawed."

- "The National Transportation Safety Board (NTSB) has taught the world how to create highly reliable and safe work processes. The formula is relatively simple to articulate and essential toward achieving engagement with any group. Same with doctors. The first step is the most important . . . [D]eeply involve the people using the process in its development. So, in simple terms, once the 'why' is clear, the 'what' and 'how' become the work of those using the system. Doctors are the same as everyone else; they want to do a good job. When they understand 'why' and are actively involved with determining the 'what/how,' magic can happen."

- "We need to make it easy for physicians to practice at our facility while providing excellent care to their patients."

- "[It is a] [t]ough transitional time for our physicians and healthcare leaders. Our physicians are clinicians trained to treat—and not all are ops and/or business-savvy—and don't want to be."

- "Those in for the haul are on a learning curve that I'm confident will move the needle for healthcare!"

- "Put patients at the center of every discussion/issue/opportunity."
- "To enhance their connection to the executive leadership team there is a monthly 'Wine and Cheese' evening session. During these events, there is a small array of heavy hors d'oeuvres, wine, and an informal come-and-go setting where the physician and executive leadership group have informal conversations and get any questions answered they have."

FINDING COMMONALITY

As simple as it may sound, a powerful component of engagement is commonality. As human beings, we all hope to find commonality in others—similarity, connection, and fellowship. We find it by interacting with those who have like backgrounds but also by sharing common goals. Some physicians prefer to practice in smaller settings, whereas others enjoy the larger and more complex tertiary centers. And some physicians prefer to focus exclusively on clinical matters, while some enjoy getting involved in the operations, business, and strategy of their organizations. Much has been written about the vast differences between physicians and administrators. A question might be posed, however: Are the differences really that considerable? Although the contributors suggested fewer ideas under this theme, their recommendations are helpful:

- "I'm sorry, but I really think there is one big key to physician engagement. It is to engage with them—and engage a lot. What I mean is that if you want your physicians to be engaged, you need to go to them and go to them frequently. You need to be in a clinical area literally every day of your work life. They need to see you where they practice and do their work. Too many of us expect them to come to the C-suite or the boardroom or the meeting rooms. That is not the way to engage them. And when you are frequently—and again, I repeat, frequently—out and about where they are, they will eventually realize that you are interested in what they are interested in. That is my secret, and I think it is pretty simple."

- "Even though I am not a clinical person, I try to read as many clinical journals and articles as I can. My examples would include the *New England Journal of Medicine* and *Medscape* and *Health Economics.* I will sometimes print an article that is clinical in nature and take it to a physician and ask him what it means. I recall doing this years ago, and the doctor said to me, "Are you crazy? You really want me to explain this? Why?" I said I felt I needed to understand some of what physicians did and that [this] would help. We grew to be great friends after that, and I even shadowed him in his office a few times. It really paid great dividends."

- "'Finding commonality and a genuine relationship'—A common concern among physicians is having a CEO who uses authority as though it was given like a birthright. . . . [T]his has to be garnered through your efforts in creating a genuine relationship. Finding 'common' issues, challenges, concerns and showing yourself behind the attempts to involve and correct, or make effort to resolve these challenges."

- "'Removing barriers and building bridges'—it's tough; the human factor always will make it tough to navigate the organization's inevitable politics and struggles. . . . Helping people see the commonality of goals, rather than differences, lightens the struggle by developing a team mindset and in building the team. Being the person to build the bridges . . . not the obstacle!"

- "I think a lot of C-suite leaders miss the boat because they do not really understand physicians and their nature. It is not that they are an alien species, but they do have differences with most C-suite people. They deal with the 'now' and not the 'later.' They are not as strategic; they do not think long term. And they have been taught to be skeptical and cautious about issues that are not known to them."

BUILDING TRUST

Trust, much like culture, is difficult to define. But talk to any physician about administrators, and more often than not, the word *trust* will surface. And to have physicians highly engaged requires that they have great trust in the culture and its leadership. A physician quality expert said long ago that trust with administration was somewhat like reducing variance in clinical settings. This physician felt that if you could always count on the integrity of what the administration told you, then there was no variance. Consider the following thoughts on how to build trust:

- "Provide accurate data and actionable reports physicians can believe and act on."
- "Being honest and genuine are my best defense. Make sure my data is right the first time I show it to them."
- "We do an annual physician engagement survey to take the temperature as to where they are at. We make a big deal of this and make sure that we try to get great participation."
- "Relationship is built upon trust, and trust must be earned."
- "I also ensure that we are providing the highest levels of care/service to the patients they refer to our facility."

- "Engage physician stakeholders early and often. There is nothing more frustrating to both the administrative leader and the physician stakeholder than trying to 'sell' what might be a great idea that has gotten out ahead of any meaningful discussions with the docs."
- "Be prepared to show quantitative evidence of how physician engagement can benefit not only the hospital but the docs and their patients. Most will sign on and be highly engaged once they see this data."
- "Trust. You must create an environment where it is clear that you want physicians to be key players in the decision-making process."
- "Again, trust development with physicians is essential for administration to maximize the potential of the health system."
- "Engage them where they are."
- "Work to address issues and opportunities as partners. This means shared investment and risk."
- "Tell the truth!"
- "Developing an integrated leadership forum with administrative and clinical leadership to discuss strategy and growth periodically. Physician partners appreciate a relaxed conversation about the direction of healthcare in general as well as specifics to the operation."
- "I think a lot of mistrust between physicians and administration is tied to often having faulty data. Whether it is quality data or finance data or other types of data, often we seem to have mistakes in how it is calculated or the sources of the data. All you need to do is have one or two slips in the data category, and you lose all trust. That makes it really tough to gain back. So I would suggest for great physician engagement, be certain that the data you share with your docs is solid and reliable."

PARTICIPATION IN DECISION-MAKING

Highly effective organizations have active physician involvement in decision-making. They rarely make any major assumptions or reach any significant conclusions without input from physicians. And as has often been mentioned, this input needs to be ongoing rather than sporadic. Participation can come in many ways. It can be as formal as ensuring that physicians sit as active and full-fledged members of committees, task forces, and boards. It can also be as simple as stopping by a physician's office to ask for thoughts and suggestions on a particular issue or problem. Successful healthcare leaders actively make sure their physicians have the chance to provide input and to give counsel on strategy, operational changes, and other organizational matters. Consider these suggestions for participation in decision-making.

- "We have a physician advisory committee for our employed medical group that participates in decision-making. They meet quarterly and help vet important decisions."
- "You may have to share some decision-making. If administration doesn't want to—don't pretend! Don't even try!"
- "We have also ensured we are including many different physicians on a multitude of committees to get their feedback and/or ideas to assist in propelling initiatives forward."
- "Be transparent when you have physicians work with you on task forces or board committees. One of the things I do as a CEO is at least once yearly, I seek out each physician who is a member of any of our board committees or organization's task forces and ask them, 'Are you OK with what you are doing on this group? Do you feel comfortable with the information you are receiving? Do

you feel your voice is heard? Do you feel that you are truly playing a part in helping our system improve?'"

- "We are such a large system that I often worry that we are not really hearing from the primary care people out in the hinterlands. We started a focused primary care strategy where we did two things. First, we created a primary care guidance council. They meet quarterly. Our key board members and I attend, and our system CMO runs the meetings. We make sure they are significant meetings and we share a lot of information, but we also spend a lot of time listening. The second thing we did was assign several senior leaders to make at least 2 monthly visits to primary care practices to sit and listen to issues and concerns. So far these have really helped. We are getting good feedback."

- "Don't rely on just your CMO to be the representative of the entire medical staff. The CMO is viewed by many physicians as just another administrator, and the CMO also may not be fully trusted by all specialties. Get other physicians to provide their input and thoughts, especially if it is a key decision."

SHOW APPRECIATION AND RECOGNITION

Studies have consistently shown that recognition and appreciation pay dividends. The acknowledgment can range from a simple thank-you said in person to more formal recognition programs that may involve gifts. Showing appreciation to physicians is fundamental to interacting with them. Moreover, recognition and appreciation are a basic human need. People respond to appreciation because it confirms that their effort is valued. Studies have shown that the best recognition is both timely and personal and that it serves as an acknowledgment of a person's behavior, effort, or business results that have helped the organization's successes. While some have suggested that physicians get their own recognition from their patients, these professionals are part of a larger organization, whose appreciation the physicians would also value. The following thoughts provide suggestions for recognizing and commending your physicians:

- "Thank them often, and celebrate the heck out of team-based, measurable results you are striving for."
- "While a lot of the industry seems to think that recognition programs are silly for physicians, we go all out. We have big celebrations during Doctor's Week, and we also have an annual holiday reception that is stretched out timewise from 2:00 p.m. to 10:00 p.m. on a Saturday to give everyone the chance to just show up and mix."
- "We send Amazon coupons to each physician who celebrates an anniversary on our medical staff. This is sent with a personal note."
- "We do an annual holiday get-together for all of our retired physicians. It is amazing to see how many come to the event and would not want to miss it. Even though they are no longer practicing in our system hospitals, they still talk to people, and I feel it continues to fire the spirit of engagement."
- "As basic as it might sound, we do a lot of social get-togethers. Frankly, I hear more from physicians at these meetings than I do at formal settings."
- "I keep a box of thank you notes in my top right desk drawer. I usually go through a box of 50 every month. It really does not take that long, and I think it means a lot more than an e-mail. And I have always felt that this really helps our physicians in their engagement. They know the guy in the C-suite recognizes what they do."
- "Years ago, we did away with the physician recognition program. We started it up again two years ago, and the response has been amazing. We give years of service awards

and we have special awards for leadership service, and we also recognize the retired physicians. When we restarted it, we decided not to have a long, drawn-out program with speakers and just shortened it greatly. The focus is on social mixing before and during dinner. And the best idea of all came from our CMO, who suggested that everyone was to go home with extra pieces of cake!"

LEADERSHIP DEVELOPMENT

Physician leadership development programs have boomed in health-care. And many organizations have found that the best results come from programs that are mostly internal and customized for their physicians. The better customized internal on-site programs are tailored to the needs that the physicians themselves identify and are not simply a group of canned educational programs. They also provide ample opportunity for personal interaction among the participants, because this builds esprit de corps. In-house programs are also less expensive and can include more physicians, making the program more cost-effective. Furthermore, they provide additional opportunities for building camaraderie among physician leaders. Project assignments used in leadership academies make the learning experience more applicable to real-world matters. Because the projects also give the physician participants the chance to focus on issues that are outside the purview of their practice, the work tends to enlarge their view of the healthcare system. The following ideas are consistent with these precepts:

- "Physician Leadership Academy: We have a ten-month cohort of 15–20 potential physician leaders, with primarily in-house speakers (trust development with our own experts). Cohort members select a *real* health system challenge to evaluate and develop options. They give year-ends with a report on an actionable solution. Collegiality, true leadership growth, and confidence in their real leadership engagement potential has been the outcome year after year."

- "Get your more promising doctors involved in leadership development. Set up a formal program, and bring in some outside speakers. Find ways to get them involved in projects. This should be done for more than just your elected medical staff officers. Some of our younger up-and-comer physicians have gotten involved. They love to learn more about the policies and legal aspects and finances of healthcare. This will prepare them to lead one day, but it also gets them very engaged."

- "You know that all physicians are really well suited to be leaders. But you need to give them some help. They are eager learners and if you give them training and information, they will get much more engaged."

- "At the midpoint of our physician leadership development program (6 months), we offer our physicians the chance to have individualized one-on-one coaching. We initially thought this would further build them as individual leaders, but we also found that it increased their feelings of engagement."

- "After we put three cohorts through a physician leadership development academy, we asked the graduates of the three programs if they wanted more. On top of additional educational presentations, we also arranged site visits to some other health systems. I was amazed at the camaraderie that developed out of this. I am convinced it has really built much greater engagement."

- "After a couple of months into our first leadership development program, we realized how important the mealtime during those programs was for our physicians. Many of these physicians, most fairly young in their careers, had not really known each other, and the meal kickoff gave them the chance to get to know each other more and, I think, raised engagement levels. Frankly, everyone talks about engagement being an individual thing, but I see it as also being part of feeling connected to a group with common goals. We later tacked on a summer picnic for the physicians and their families, and that has gone really well also."

ORGANIZATIONAL STRUCTURE

- "We have Shared Governance Councils."
- "Remove the barriers so [the physicians] can practice medicine. Hence my next pearl of wisdom . . . [H]ardwire for an effective physician engagement structure."
- "Coordination of a medical executive committee composed of 'section chiefs.' Include COO to engage physicians in respective macro-level ops decision-making—Physician Recruitment, Finance, EMR [electronic medical record] integration, etc. This structure concurrently minimizes the us/them mentality and culture."
- "Create a CEO ad hoc advisory group to provide input monthly on strategic and operational issues."
- "Develop a physician manpower advisory group to clarify and guide the development of practices and clinical needs."
- "Establish a board executive / physician leadership breakfast group to discuss important issues."
- "Develop a nurse/physician rounding program to share what is going on with respective nursing units."
- "We hold past chiefs meetings with the CEO and COO on a regular basis."

- "We are establishing a medical director for perioperative services and other key services."
- "We have service lines with true dyad leadership— lead physician and a key administrative leader. Equal/ shared responsibility for success of the entire service line. Responsible to CEO/COO level. Key decisions mutually made here. Again C-suite trust is essential."
- "Also all service-line leaders meet together monthly with CEO, COO to insure that direction and support for individual service lines is in concert with overall system strategy and plans for other service lines so 'all boats rise' together."
- "I have had great success with developing an integrated leadership forum with administrative and clinical leadership to discuss strategy and growth periodically. Physician partners appreciate a relaxed conversation about the direction of healthcare in general as well as specifics to the operation."
- "Dyads can really work well in a variety of ways. There is no one best approach. We have some dyads that may not look like dyads, but the physician and the executive working together know they are a team. We also have some dyads that are more formal and developed around our service lines, and they are set up differently, but each one works well. The more dyads you can have, I think, the greater your physician engagement will be."

THE EHR

- "Enhance physician participation in EHR ongoing education: Provide an $XX discount to the annual medical staff dues for those who attend the full session(s)."

- "Our EHR project was a key test for us in physician engagement. We got a large group of physicians together early on and tried to get them to see the EHR as a way to actually improve care. We were straight from the start with them and told them the move would involve a lot of new learning and changes in how they did their work. It was interesting one day in one of our early meetings to hear our head of surgery say that he finally figured out that he would not have to carry paper charts around all day and he thought that would be great. Then others started chiming in saying much the same thing. Then our COO asked the group how they could help the entire medical staff see it this way. That became a key turning point. But we did not force it; we let them come to the conclusions themselves."
- "Some specialties are more comfortable with computers. So to get higher levels of engagement, we tailored our training based upon specialty. One of the primary care docs told me how much he appreciated this."
- "Our conversion was a great chance to enhance physician engagement. We started out by telling all the physicians that we wanted this to be their project and we wanted them to lead it. We got three physicians to colead the system-wide steering committee, and we have physicians at all levels, probably almost 100 of them, involved from the start to finish."
- "Physician engagement flourished during a lot of the physician training programs. We made them fun events, and we were cautious to make sure there was no time wasted. And we always created different ways for them to learn from each other."
- "Our EHR vendor had physicians who came to lead the process. This helped our engagement."

UNDERSTANDING WHAT THEY DO

While the next two areas may relate in part to the earlier-discussed idea of commonality, the concepts are slightly different. The ability for C-suite leaders to have a better feel for what physicians actually do on a day-to-day basis and for physicians to have a greater understanding of administrative work can increase each group's appreciation for one another and reduce misunderstandings that can impede engagement. The following suggestions, while simply common sense, can produce profound results:

- "Real simple—anyone who has done any Lean training knows the saying 'Go see, ask why, show respect.' Go to the gemba, it is called. The word *gemba* means 'real place.' Do this and do it a lot, and you will definitely increase engagement."
- "Round together, and show interest in their work."
- "Make regular C-suite rounds—expect the medical group CMO, COO, CFO, and CEO to be in the clinics on a regular basis so they are not just 'suits on a screen.'"
- "Rounding with top 100 admitters, etc."
- "I also routinely attend the board meetings of several of the larger physician groups that utilize the health system and those that we have professional service arrangements with."
- "Intentionally involve doctors with 'teammates.' Gently force them to meet, get to know [each other], and learn process design techniques with nonphysician colleagues. More magic."
- "As a leader, be 'omnipresent.' One of the things I regularly do, which has paid enormous dividends over the years, is connect with doctors when they don't expect to see me. I round on weekends, early mornings, and evenings often. I know I have made an impact when they say, 'What are you doing here?' My answer is *always* the same: 'What are *you*

doing here?' That invariably leads to good chitchat about what's going on in their lives, their practice, whatever."

- "I always go to their grand rounds. While I rarely understand half of what is presented, I feel it is worth my time."
- "OK, want to raise physician engagement? Think about it—our admin suite represents about 0.8% of our total square footage, and the areas where patients are receiving care or housed represents about 60% of our total square footage. This should clearly tell us as administrators we should spend a lot more time out there! And this would help with engagement of all of our healthcare workers."

HELPING THEM TO UNDERSTAND WHAT YOU DO

- "We invite all elected medical staff officers to each board night. They don't have a vote in anything, but they participate in discussion and know that we are being transparent at the board level."
- "There must be an enthusiasm engendered to have physicians seek further education with internal development programs and support for advanced degrees, such as MBAs, MMMs, and 'boutique' degrees such as patient safety and quality as well as predictive analytics."
- "Invite as guest(s) ops leaders for information and data share as appropriate for decision support."
- "Financially, I have tried to help them to understand accrual-basis accounting before. They can understand if you are skillful enough to explain, but they cannot internalize their understanding as they do not need to use the concept every day. Focus on cash method; they can be better than any accountants."
- "Starting a physician leadership institute has been one of the best things we have done."

- "Make sure the person(s) know why the organization is doing whatever it's doing. The 'why' part is fundamental and *critical*."

ECONOMICS

While many people believe that money (or economics of some sort) is the real key to engagement, ample studies show that it is not the sole driver. Yet some aspects of economics can work against organizations when leaders are trying to drive higher levels of engagement. Here are a few suggestions:

- "Move toward and take pride in value-based (not volume-based) incentives."
- "Pay physicians for leadership. Simple as that. Their time is worth something. You don't have to go overboard with it, but you do have to recognize them this way. And frankly, it is far less about the money than it is the respect you are showing them for their time."
- "We have had a lot of participation and success in our ACO. But I would have to say that the payments made were viewed more as a nice recognition factor rather than being financially real meaningful."

SETTING CLEAR EXPECTATIONS

- "Do periodic performance reviews with physicians. That keeps them engaged with the bigger picture."
- "All physicians should have some kind of annual review. And it should not be punitive. It should be a great chance to recognize them for their work and contributions."

ADDITIONAL THOUGHTS FROM HEALTHCARE LEADERS

- "[Maximizing physician engagement is] so individual, based on the physician and issue, that I cannot say there is a specific tool or tactic."
- "Last, for those physicians that turned CMO, they transform so quickly to the administrative side, and understand what health system administrators do. I wonder why!"
- "I have actually found doctors generally easier to engage than others in the health delivery system, but maybe that is just a function of my experiences."

PARTICIPANTS IN THE SURVEY

I am deeply indebted to the following healthcare leaders for their litany of ideas and suggestions:

Michael A. Anaya Sr., FACHE

Larry Anstine, LACHE

Bob Baxter, FACHE

Mark H. Belfer, DO, FAAFP

Denise Brooks-Williams, FACHE

Thomas T. Chan

Michael H. Covert, FACHE

Olas (Chip) Hubbs III, FACHE

Jeff Jarreau, SHRM-SCP, SPHR

David Kapaska, DO

William Kenley, FACHE

Janelle Lee, RN

Ronda K. Lehman, PharmD, FACHE

Glenn Loomis, MD, FAAFP

Scott A. Malaney, FACHE

G. Daniel Martich, MD

Scott Nygaard, MD

Tim Putnam, DHA, FACHE

Michelle Taylor-Smith, RN, FACHE

Tom Whalen, MD, FACHE, CPE, CPHQ

John Woodrich

CHAPTER 14

Measuring Physician Engagement

Katherine A. Meese and Carson F. Dye

*Engaging doctors, even the old guard, is a management
challenge that can be tackled, measured, and improved.*
—Thomas H. Lee and Toby Cosgrove, "Engaging Doctors
in the Health Care Revolution," 2014

HOW DO HEALTHCARE leaders know if their physicians are
engaged? We must measure their engagement, of course, and we
must be certain that we know exactly what we are measuring. Healthcare organizations are filled with examples of constant measurement.
Patients' vitals are measured, as are their outcomes and their satisfaction. Every dollar is counted, and supplies are carefully stocked.
In an era of quality-focused, value-based care, a hospital's staffing,
budgets, volumes, and errors are all carefully measured, tracked,
and managed. Leaders are held accountable for deviations from
goals and targets, and merit incentives and bonuses are based on
hitting the target.

But what about the people in the organization? What of our
physicians?

WHY MEASURE ENGAGEMENT?

If physician engagement is paramount for delivering high-quality
care to patients, creating healthy teams, and promoting flourishing,

then it must be both measured and managed. Perhaps more than any other industry, healthcare depends on humans to create and deliver it. Unlike other capital-intensive industries, with heavy machinery and expensive equipment that must be carefully maintained, healthcare primarily uses people to achieve its aims. The end product hinges on how well these people are *properly maintained*, meaning how healthy and engaged they are and how well they function individually and in teams.

Yet despite this critical role, organizations often relegate the measurement of engagement to some back burner or an annual to-do with little accountability for the outcome. Like other things on the back burner, they sometimes escape our attention until they are on fire. Healthcare organizations need not wait until they lose their employees or notice poor outcomes and degradation of team dynamics to address the issues born of disengagement. Just as the organization measures other important outcomes, it must do thoughtful measurement of engagement and other related constructs.

The other critical reason to measure these constructs is that the organization needs good baseline information to understand the impact of major changes or events. Consider the COVID-19 pandemic as an example. Organizations without pre-pandemic measurements of engagement cannot know how the pandemic affected their physicians. How do they address the effects of the COVID-19 crisis and separate what needs urgent attention from more durable matters?

Physicians are people. In general, certain conditions must be present for people to be engaged in their work. Everyone wants autonomy. Everyone wants a sense of purpose and meaning in their work. Everyone wants to feel that their skills, efforts, and contributions are valued. That said, how these conditions are optimally created may vary according to the physician's specialty, age, life stage, and other interests. No single solution will improve engagement for all. That is why measuring engagement and soliciting feedback for improvement are inseparable. The most important element of measuring, managing, and improving engagement is developing routine listening mechanisms to learn how and what your physicians need to be engaged and supported.

HOW TO MEASURE?

Annual Versus Frequent

There are several potential approaches to measuring engagement. Many organizations that already systematically measure physician engagement and satisfaction often do so annually. This approach aims not to burden physicians with frequent surveys and often serves as the basis for leadership incentives. While there are benefits to this approach, it also has some downsides.

First, this approach may not account for seasonality. For example, if the measurement is taken at the same time each year, there may be months or seasons when engagement typically ebbs or flows. The pattern could be affected by a variety of factors, including flu season, elections, holidays, timing of professional conferences, or a fresh influx of new residents or students.

Second, an annual measure provides no interim information to inform leaders' improvement efforts. For example, consider a clinic manager who discovers during an annual review that the clinic's physician engagement scores were worse than those of other similar clinics in the organization. The receipt of this news starts the clock until next year's measurement is taken. If this manager seeks to boost employee engagement scores through a variety of activities (such as compensation redesign, team-building activities, offering more autonomy in scheduling), the person has no feedback on whether these efforts are measurably working until the next year. The result could be many months and dollars wasted on efforts that may not substantially move the needle.

Finally, consider the burden felt by physicians in completing surveys. Lengthy annual surveys are often viewed unfavorably by physicians, who already feel they are being asked to do so many duties related to the care of patients and document such care in EHR systems.

Many organizations are moving more in the direction of shorter but more frequent surveys of employees; some observers have deemed these *pulse* surveys. The idea is that the short survey allows leaders to take a quick pulse on employees and to gain more frequent feedback on changes being made. These surveys may range from one to ten questions and may be offered as frequently as daily. For example, some organizations use a designated space on the company's intranet or home page of the EHR to ask one multiple-choice question each day. The end users do not need to click on a link or visit a separate survey but can answer the question by simply selecting their answer and then move on about their day. Others may answer a short monthly survey via e-mail.

The benefit of this more frequent approach is that it allows organizations to gather timely feedback without overburdening employees with long surveys. The drawback is that capturing single items periodically can make some of the more robust types of statistical analysis challenging. For example, one might first ask a single question about engagement and, later, a single question about opinions of a new compensation plan that was adopted. It would be difficult to determine whether there was a relationship between the two items without being able to statistically control for other related factors.

External Vendor Versus Internal Administration

When considering how to measure and track physician engagement over time, the organization must decide whether to conduct the measurement and analysis itself or use an external vendor. Each approach has pros and cons, which will be discussed in more detail in the paragraphs that follow.

External
Many large healthcare systems use external vendors to conduct their physician engagement assessments. This approach has several benefits. First, external companies often offer benchmarking against other similar institutions. Such comparisons help the organization understand how it is doing relative to its peers, and this information

may be especially helpful when an organization is assessing its desirability as a workplace for top talent. That said, leaders must also consider whether the benchmark organizations are truly accurate comparisons. For example, comparing one academic medical center to another may provide skewed insights if other dynamics such as city-, state-, and patient-level characteristics are not included in the choice of a benchmark. Though the vendor could choose a benchmark center with a similar number of beds and metropolitan characteristics, it might fail to account for the competitive dynamics that would yield significant differences in expected turnover rates. Consider also the impact of recent EHR conversions on physician engagement. This alone could make comparisons between different organizations quite illogical.

Another benefit of using an external vendor is its ability to manage and analyze the data into usable reports for managers. These reports make the information accessible and easy to digest. For smaller organizations without robust in-house data analytics, this benefit may make outside vendors an especially appealing option.

There are also downsides to external vendors. First, many vendors will not allow the organization to obtain its own raw data, even in a de-identified and confidential format. This restriction is typically imposed under the auspices of ensuring respondent confidentiality. However, it also precludes the organization from doing more in-depth and sophisticated analysis, and the vendor's data is almost entirely unusable for research purposes. Some vendors offer more of a hybrid approach: the organization collects its own data, but the vendor guides the organization in choosing metrics and creating user-friendly dashboards and reports. Another major downside is cost. Large national engagement vendors can be expensive. Smaller organizations or those that are financially constrained may find this cost prohibitively high.

Internal

Some organizations may find it advantageous to conduct periodic measurements of their physicians in-house, rather than outsourcing them to an external vendor. This approach may be appealing for organizations with robust internal data analytics capabilities or limited financial resources to hire external vendors or for those interested in their raw data for advanced analytics and research purposes.

For organizations that lack these capabilities, it may be helpful to consider working with a local or regional university partner that can design, implement, and analyze the survey. That said, this approach comes with a few caveats. There may be some tension between measurement tools that concisely provide information for management and those that are long enough to provide value for academic research. The other consideration is whether the organization would be comfortable with any of the results being published. This possibility should be discussed and negotiated in advance. Confidentiality can often be maintained by only generally describing the organization in the academic manuscript, such as "a critical-access hospital in the Midwestern United States."

Another downside to the internal approach is that physicians may be leery of an in-house survey and may have concerns over how confidential the results truly are. Their wariness may contribute to the already-low response rates that surveys often garner among physicians.

Non-Survey-Based Measurements

There are other important ways to gauge physician engagement in an organization. Although surveys can provide objective measures to track over time, it is sometimes also hard to capture the nuance of physician engagement. Nothing beats having trusting relationships with physicians and a precedent of open and honest communication that is acted on. If these conditions exist, then asking physicians what would improve their jobs, engagement, and well-being will be likely to generate a host of workable solutions.

Leaders may also find value in scheduling individual interviews and focus groups to gauge the state of physician engagement and garner ideas for improvement. Nevertheless, if there is a culture of distrust of administration, or retaliation for delivering uncomfortable feedback, then this approach is unlikely to help identify the true root cause of the challenges. Leaders must be sure to systematically code and organize the results of these types of meetings to allow progress to be measured over time and to ensure that the items discussed are acted on or addressed. Failure to do so can result in the old refrain "We keep telling management the same thing, and nothing gets done."

Physician Involvement in Measurement and Improvement Efforts

Studies of human behavior in the workplace have found that people want to be involved in decisions that affect their work and that they want autonomy. Physicians are no different. Organizations should be proactive in asking their physicians to help lead efforts to improve engagement. What does an ideal workplace look like to them? What kinds of things in the workplace make their work more difficult? How should feedback be captured from their colleagues? How can they be involved in leading the changes? While it may not be easily feasible for every organization, some might want to consider having a physician steering committee develop and administer the engagement survey. Think about it: A group of physicians (1) defines engagement, (2) develops the questions to measure it, (3) manages the survey process, (4) reports the results, and (5) manages the plans to address the issues and concerns. After all, who is better qualified to do all these tasks than the very people involved with the concern?

WHOM TO MEASURE?

Physicians. Obviously. This is a book on *physician* engagement, right? But . . .

One cannot understand physician engagement without understanding the *ecosystem in which a physician operates*. For example, consider burnout. Leaders and their colleagues who are burned out themselves experience depersonalization, which may make it difficult to empathize with those around them (de Paiva et al. 2017). This situation can perpetuate conditions that increase burnout among those they are responsible for managing, supporting, or working alongside (Maslach, Schaufeli, and Leiter 2001). Imagine an angry and belligerent passenger on an airplane in the seat next to you. Doesn't this person ruin your flight, too? Your flight experience is not solely based on the level of customer service and cleanliness on the plane—the other passengers have a role.

Additionally, even the best-intentioned actions may have unintended consequences that cannot be detected with siloed measurement. Consider the rapid implementation of inpatient telemedicine during the COVID-19 pandemic. Many large health systems implemented some form of inpatient telemedicine, which may have involved the use of tablets or webcams in the patient room. The physician would "visit" the patient remotely in an effort to conserve PPE and to limit exposure to COVID-19. The nurses, however, often found themselves being asked to enter the patient room more frequently to assist the patient with accessing and using the technology. Such an approach offered a benefit to the physician at the expense of the nurse. Measuring the entire care team helps managers understand how programs, initiatives, and changes affect all members of the team and how these results may in turn affect physician engagement.

WHAT TO MEASURE?

First, we must distinguish what researchers mean by engagement and what leaders often mean by it. This distinction is important in decisions about what to measure organizationally. Some researchers have defined engagement as a positive motivational state that is measured as vigor, dedication, and absorption in one's work (Schaufeli et al. 2019). When healthcare leaders often refer to engagement, they may mean several research concepts that, taken together, create an almost-mystical sense of devotedness to an organization and its ideals. To healthcare leaders, engagement may encompass things like belonging, volunteering for extra tasks, going above and beyond, organizational commitment, a sense of loyalty to and camaraderie with each other, and other harder-to-define elements.

If an organization uses a commercial vendor, the company is likely to offer a suite of questions with varying degrees of psychometric validation. These questions may also have varying degrees of flexibility, as the vendor is probably interested in consistency across organizations for benchmarking purposes.

Nevertheless, organizations considering in-house measurement should include a variety of constructs to give a complete picture of how the physician is doing. Engagement is an important aspect of the physician's well-being, but it is not the only one. There is some debate in the scholarly literature about whether burnout is the opposite of engagement. Can burned-out people also be engaged? Can engaged people also be planning to leave the organization? Are engaged people automatically satisfied with their jobs? The best answer is to measure them all to get a full and nuanced picture.

At minimum, an organization should consider a formal measure of engagement, measuring people's satisfaction with their work, their team, and their organization. Given the epidemic of clinician burnout, measures of burnout and distress should also be captured. Organizations must also understand whether physicians feel valued and supported and have the resources necessary to do their work well. These more subjective measurements should be paired with objective measures of engagement such as turnover, reduced clinical hours, and reports of disruptive behaviors.

Most vendors will have questions that address these different but related concepts. But what should the organization ask if it is trying to measure on its own? Fortunately, decades of academic research have yielded a host of concise and psychometrically validated measures. Current trends in employee surveys recommend using the most concise validated measures possible to avoid survey fatigue and for a better chance of completion.

There are several employee engagement surveys that are publicly available and nonlicensed (free to use). The US Department of Veterans Affairs (VA) publishes its annual employee survey instrument, which has been developed by a team of psychometricians (VA 2018). This typically concise survey (30 questions or fewer) touches a wide range of important topics, including climate of civility, job satisfaction, burnout, supervisor support, and moral distress. The Copenhagen Psychosocial Questionnaire, now in its third version, contains a number of helpful measures and conveniently comes in a long, medium, and short version (Burr et al. 2019).

In addition to multiple-choice or short-response questions, good surveys include open-ended questions inviting physicians to share their concerns and what is working well. Exhibit 14.1 suggests a few open-ended questions.

Exhibit 14.1 Some Open-Ended Questions for Engagement Surveys

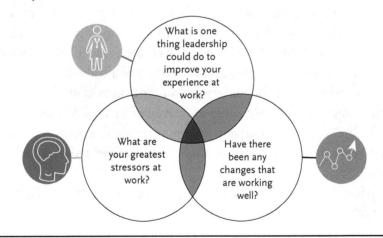

What is one thing leadership could do to improve your experience at work?

What are your greatest stressors at work?

Have there been any changes that are working well?

WHAT TO DO WITH THIS INFORMATION?

Physicians have to know that they are being heard and taken seriously and that changes they have suggested are being made. Often worse than negative feedback is no feedback at all. Silence sends a message. For example, one person in a newly romantic relationship texts the other to say "I love you" for the first time. No response *is* a response. Similarly, anyone who takes the time to complete a survey, honestly answer questions, and provide input may prefer to hear "We appreciate your suggestions and input, but we are struggling with how to find resources to implement this change," rather than no response. No response leaves the individual wondering if their voice was heard and, even worse, if it was heard but nobody actually cares. Remaining silent is one of the worst things to do when you are working with physicians.

Any request for feedback or information should have a communication plan for how results will be shared and how the organization will respond to areas that need attention or improvement. Failure to do so can almost guarantee that fewer people will see the value of participating in the next round of surveys, and may worsen disengagement.

CONCLUSION

What makes physicians tick? What do they like and dislike? How much do healthcare leaders know what motivates their physicians? Physicians are a critical part of healthcare organizations, and their level of engagement can mean success or failure. Healthcare leaders must determine what physician engagement means for their organizations. They need to develop excellent measuring tools, measure engagement frequently, and take action with the findings. Tomlinson (2020) says it well: "Today's healthcare leaders can't afford to ignore physician engagement. Engaged physicians are the lifeblood of healthcare organizations and our most direct link to patients. When their morale suffers, care quality and safety can suffer as well."

REFERENCES

Burr, H., H. Berthelsen, S. Moncada, M. Nübling, E. Dupret, Y. Demiral, J. Oudyk, T. S. Kristensen, C. Llorens, A. Navarro, H.-J. Lincke, C. Bocéréan, C. Sahan, P. Smith, and A. Pohrt. 2019. "The Third Version of the Copenhagen Psychosocial Questionnaire." *Safety and Health at Work* 10 (4): 482–503.

de Paiva, L. C., A. C. Gomes Canário, E. L. Corsino de Paiva China, and A. K. Gonçalves. 2017. "Burnout Syndrome in Health-Care Professionals in a University Hospital." *Clinics* 72 (5): 305–9.

Lee, T. H., and T. Cosgrove. 2014. "Engaging Doctors in the Health Care Revolution." *Harvard Business Review* 92 (6): 104–38.

Maslach, C., W. B. Schaufeli, and M. P. Leiter. 2001. "Job Burnout." *Annual Review of Psychology* 52: 397–422.

Schaufeli, W. B., A. Shimazu, J. Hakanen, M. Salanova, and H. De Witte. 2019. "An Ultra-Short Measure for Work Engagement: The UWES-3 Validation Across Five Countries." *European Journal of Psychological Assessment* 35 (4): 577–91.

Tomlinson, I. 2020. "Why Hospitals Can't Afford to Ignore Physician Engagement." *Vituity.* Published March 6. www. vituity.com/blog/why-hospitals-cant-afford-to-ignore-physician-engagement.

US Department of Veterans Affairs (VA). 2018. "National Center for Organizational Development. VA All Employee Survey." Accessed September 30, 2020. www.va.gov/NCOD/VAworkforcesurveys.asp.

Conclusion: Summing Up the Book's Lessons

Carson F. Dye

We describe a new concept of physician engagement. Such engagement requires more than mere cooperation—an agreement not to sabotage—and strives instead for full collaboration in relentless improvement. To be sure, we still need physicians to work hard as individuals and keep care within the family of the local hospital and physician community. But physician engagement can no longer be about short-term maximization of fee-for-service revenue; it must further the long-term strategy of improving outcomes and lowering costs—increasing value for patients.
—Thomas H. Lee and Toby Cosgrove, "Engaging Doctors in the Health Care Revolution," 2014

THIS BOOK HAS BEEN intended to be somewhat of a how-to guide. Healthcare leaders have many ways to engage physicians. Moreover, because of the great differences among physicians in age, specialty, work location, and so forth, organizations need to take multiple approaches to help enhance engagement.

The contributors to this book examined these multiple approaches, describing their upsides and downsides and recommending how the readers could apply them to their best advantage. The following paragraphs summarize what we hope most readers will have learned about enhancing physician engagement.

READY PHYSICIANS TO BE ENGAGED

Dr. Savoy opens our book with an expansive and dynamic look at some of the prerequisites to getting physicians more involved. She broadly defines physician engagement and sets the tone for the tactics provided in the rest of the book. Her suggestions on accountability, teams, and interpersonal relationships are foundational to success in any tactic attempted to enhance engagement.

REDUCE BURNOUT FIRST, THEN ENGAGE

Dr. Casey sees burnout as the opposite of engagement. He believes that burnout must be addressed before a leader tries any type of strategy to increase engagement. His insight on leading and lagging indicators of burnout is useful for any healthcare leader. And his description of how to apply Arthur Pink's motivational factors to causes of burnout are outstanding insights on how to organizationally minimize burnout so engagement can be increased.

THE ELECTRONIC HEALTH RECORD

Anyone who has been even near healthcare the past decade knows that the adoption of electronic health records (EHRs) has been a great challenge when it comes to keeping physicians engaged. As the former Cerner senior physician, Dr. Kerschl has overseen hundreds of organizational implementations and offers several helpful suggestions on how to ensure that the EHR does not add to the problem of physician disengagement. He shows readers how to guarantee that the soft factors of an EHR adoption are not missed and gives several tips based on the IKEA effect.

HAVING A CHIEF MEDICAL OFFICER IS NOT A GUARANTEE ENGAGEMENT WILL OCCUR

Dr. McWilliams confronts a critical issue head-on—the fact that many organizations leave total responsibility for physician engagement with their chief medical officers (CMOs). He addresses some of the tougher questions such as who the CMO does represent, and he defines the CMO role in detail. He explores what makes a physician qualified for the CMO position and the characteristics that help this executive the most in driving physician engagement. Dr. McWilliams also discusses the dilemma caused when a CMO's administrative duties conflict with clinical ones.

DYADS, TRIADS, AND QUAD DYADS

The dyad concept has a long and successful history, and while readers may feel familiar with them, there is often more to them than meets the eye. Dr. McWilliams provides a comprehensive discussion of dyads and other variations of the structural model. He sets forth clear recommendations for ensuring that dyads are successful and relates how they can enhance physician engagement.

ASSESSING PHYSICIANS FOR LEADERSHIP

Many organizations have realized that one of the best ways to grow physician engagement is to involve more physicians in leadership and to provide them with leadership development programs. Dr. Casey gives tactics on how to identify potential physician leaders early on. He shows how health organizations can give them opportunities to grow into better leaders, and he describes key attributes for physician leaders as they work to enhance physician engagement.

SUPPLY CHAIN

While the topic of supply chains may not excite many healthcare leaders, Dr. Ransom shows clearly how involving physicians in this matter can greatly enhance physician engagement and can help institutions better manage their costs and improve quality.

GETTING PHYSICIANS ENGAGED ON BOARDS

Dr. Satiani and Dr. Dillhoff discuss the importance of physician engagement at the highest level of the organization—the board. They provide insight into the legal aspects and then give suggestions on various ways to get physicians involved at this level.

USING QUALITY TO DRIVE ENGAGEMENT

In this chapter, Dr. Byrnes shows unequivocally how patient quality and physician engagement are correlated. In fact, he provides several suggestions that organizations can use to drive higher physician engagement and enjoy the side benefits of improved quality and patient safety. He shows ways to use data and dashboards to drive not only high quality but also engagement. Finally, Dr. Byrnes presents several great ideas for celebrating physicians' and other clinical staff's accomplishments.

DISRUPTIVE PHYSICIAN BEHAVIOR

There is no quicker way to diminish physician engagement than to experience disruptive physician behavior and not manage it correctly. Although the topic is often hidden behind closed doors in many organizations, Dr. Henson delves into both the causes and the consequences of this type of behavior. She lays out effective ways to build accountability in the organization and describes the excellent Vanderbilt University model of monitoring and handling disruptive behavior.

PHYSICIAN LEADERSHIP DEVELOPMENT PROGRAMS

While Dr. Casey gave insight into assessing physicians for leadership in chapter 6, Dr. Satiani and Dr. Eiferman give concrete examples of physician leadership development programs. They specify the types and content of the curriculum and show how physicians can develop through these programs. They also show how this education ultimately drives higher levels of engagement.

TELEHEALTH

Since COVID-19 hit the United States, telehealth and virtual health have seen astonishing growth. Dr. Post discussed several issues that have an impact on physician engagement. He provides specific insight into Avera Health's telehealth programs, which are among the largest and most advanced in the country.

THOUGHTS FROM THE TRENCHES

Clearly some of the best suggestions to deal with problems and issues come from informal networking. As editor, I offer brief anecdotal suggestions that I sought out from various healthcare leaders around the United States. This chapter, with its cogent and logical suggestions, may prove to be the one most dog-eared and frequently read.

THE IMPORTANCE OF MEASUREMENT

In the final chapter, Dr. Meese and I assert that if physician engagement is indeed necessary for high-quality patient care and the flourishing of healthcare systems, then healthcare leaders need to measure this essential factor. We answer three fundamental questions about measurement: why measure, how to do it, and who and what to measure. The chapter compares various measurement approaches, such as external versus internal analyses, and annual versus more frequent assessment. Finally, we recommend actions to take with the information obtained through measurement.

FOR MORE THEORY BEHIND THIS BOOK

Readers are also encouraged to read (or revisit) the companion volume of this book: *Enhanced Physician Engagement*, Volume 1, *What It is, Why You Need It, and Where to Begin*. There they will find more insights on building enhanced physician engagement in their organization.

REFERENCE

Lee, T. H., and T. Cosgrove. 2014. "Engaging Doctors in the Health Care Revolution." *Harvard Business Review* 92 (6): 104–38.

Index

Note: Italicized page locators refer to exhibits.

Burnout, framework for mitigating: appreciation and, 55, 59–60; compacts and, 59; growth and development and, 55, 61; input and, 55, 57–58; rounds with physicians and, 58–59; social connection and, 55, 60–61; work structures and processes and, 55–57

"Burnout's Mounting Price Tag" (Henry), 47

Business stories: types of, *36*

Buy-in: adoption of orthopedic implant approach and, 146; electronic health records and dynamics behind, 74; management dyads and, 113, 114; physician engagement plans and, 2; physician-led dashboard design and, 198

Bylaws: defining disruptive behavior in, 222

Byrnes, John, 7, 200, 316

Camaraderie: building, 292, 293

Camera options: virtual care and, 266

Capacity: response examples, *133*; in three Cs of leadership, 128, 132–34, 142; time and, 132

Captain-of-the-ship mentality: physicians and, 57

Career development, 39, *41*

Carter, T. J., 74

Case Western Reserve University: Weatherhead School of Management, 242, 244

Casey, Kevin M., 6, 7, 314, 315, 317

Castellucci, M., 240

Certified physician executive, 95

Change: adaptive, soft factors and, 71–73; organizational culture and, 73; telehealth and addressing fear of, 264

Change agency: favorable, management dyads and, 114

Change management: physician leaders and, 93

"Changing Roles and Skill Sets for Chief Medical Officers" (Sonnenberg), 87

Character: response examples for, *130*; in three Cs of leadership, 128, 129, 142

Chart quality and accuracy: scribes and, 57

Chemistry: response examples for, *131–32*; in three Cs of leadership, 128, 129, 131, 142

Chen, P. W., 214

Chief clinical officers, 91

Chief executive officers, 92, 294, 295, 297; medical executive committee and, 104; personalized thank you letter from, 205; physician, and ranked quality of hospitals, 239; responsibility of engagement and, 167; selection of board members and, 177

Chief financial officers, 90, 92, 297; management quad (or dual dyads) and, 121; management triads and, 120

Chief medical officers, 2, 5, 28, 181, 182, 290, 297, 300, 315; adoption of orthopedic implant approach and, 145, 146; burgeoning presence of, 87; characteristics of, that support physician engagement, 98–99; clinical expertise of, 97–98; clinical *vs.* administrative career identities of, 102; credentials and additional degrees for, 94–95; business suit or white lab coat? dilemma of, 101–2; dilemmas faced by, 6; disillusionment with (scenario), 125; experience of, 96; external candidates for, 100–101; internal candidates for, 99–100; internal *vs.* external validation for, 102; knowing what to look for in, 91–92; leadership style of, 97; making the most of, 87–105; management quad (or dual dyads) and, 121; management triads and, 119, 120; managing disruptive physician behavior and, 220; old battles between administration and physicians and, 88–89; organizations and question of need for, 88; organization size and position of, 91; other C-suite leaders *vs.,* 90; of the past: the coast into retirement, 90; personal characteristics of, 96–97; personalized thank-you letter from, 205; physician leadership councils and, 103–4; qualifications for, 94; representation and advocacy roles of, 89; role of the job for, 92–94; supported by multiple levels of physician leaders, 103; where candidates come from, 99–101

Chief nursing officers, 90, 92, 104; management quad (or dual dyads) and, 121; management triads and, 119, 120

Chief of orthopedic surgery: adoption of orthopedic implant approach and, 145

Chief of supply chain: adoption of orthopedic implant approach and, 145, 146

Chief operating officers, 92, 294, 295, 296, 297; management quad (or dual dyads) and, 121; management triads and, 119

Chief physician executives, 91, 92

Chokshi, D. A., 2

Christensen, Clayton, 145

Christ Hospital: board member composition at, *172*

Circadian rhythm disruption: disruptive physician disorder and, 214

Cleveland Clinic, 171, *172*, 239; internal leadership training programs for physicians, 243; leadership training programs for physicians, 242

Cleveland Clinic–Weatherhead School of Management Executive MBA, 242

Clinical care: evidence to support physician leadership training and impact on, 238–40

Clinical decisions: technical *vs.* adaptive change and, 71–72

Clinical directors, 110

Clinical expertise: of chief medical officers, 97–98

Clinical journals, 286

Clinical perspectives: administrative perspectives *vs., 135–36*

Clinical productivity: physician incentives tied to, 254

Clinical quality: physician engagement and, 192, 193

Clinical support staff: celebrating successes with, 202

Clinical teams: physician leaders needed for, 235–36

Clinician training: for best practices, 160

Cloud technologies: electronic health records and, 82

CMO Academy (American Association for Physician Leadership), 95

CMO Leadership Academy (Association of American Medical Colleges), 95

Coaching: administrative members of dyads, 116; physician, supply-chain issues and, 157–59; physician leadership development and, 293; physicians, in optimizing supply utilization, 149; physicians selected for leadership roles in dyads, 116; physicians with behavioral issues, 224–25. *See also* Mentors and mentoring

Cochrane, 151

Codes of conduct: disruptive physician behavior and, 218

Cognitive assessments: virtual care and, *270,* 271

Cognitive impairment: disruptive physician behavior and (case study), 215–16

Colla, C., 176

Command-and-control leadership approach, 127

Commitment: compliance *vs.,* 76

Commonality: finding, physician engagement and, 285–87

Common-cause variation, 200

Communication, 1; critical importance of, 31; as key input driver of physician engagement, *14*; lack of, from information technology or leadership around electronic health records, 78; maximizing physician engagement through, 279–82; power of storytelling, 35–37; standardizing through SBAR (situation, background, assessment, and recommendation), 37; styles, adapting to, 34–35; in team huddles, 39

Communication technology modalities, considerations for, *32–34*; e-mail, *32*; in-person meetings, *34*; memos, *32*; podcasts, *33*; social media, *32–33*; texting, *32*; video messages, *33*; virtual meetings, *34*

Communication types: four basic, *35*

Community hospitals, 167

Compacts: mitigation of physician burnout and, 59

Compassion about patient care, 196–97, 207

Compensation, 39, 59, 236; burnout not about, 52; hospital boards and issues related to, 175; physician board members and wRVU (work relative value unit) basis of, 182; for physician leadership, 299; for serving on a for-profit board, 178. *See also* Bonuses; Incentives

Compensation committees, 176

Competencies: Joint Commission standards and, 219; in selecting board members, 177

Compliance: commitment *vs.*, 76

Condescending language, 212

Confidence, 126

Confidentiality: of board proceedings, 184; physician engagement assessments and, 306

Conflicts of interest: board trustees and, 179; direct or indirect, board members and restriction on, 174; reducing, optimizing supply

utilization and, 149; reducing, supply-chain issues and, 160–61

Connors, R., 76

Consensus building: chief medical officers and, 93

Consumers: telehealth and impact on, 267–68

Coordination of care: electronic health records and, 68, 81

Copenhagen Psychosocial Questionnaire, 310

Cordero, G., 262

Corrective action plans: disruptive physician behaviors and, 223, *223*, 224

Cosgrove, Delos (Toby), 239, 301, 313

Cost containment: high physician engagement and, 168

Cost-efficiency: as healthcare priority, 147

Cost(s): balancing efficiency, access, quality, and, 149, 150–51; lower, electronic health records and, 68; product reviews and, 152; transparent information on, 154

Counseling and education visits: virtual care and, 270, *270*

Courage: development of transparent virtual care strategies and, 275

COVID-19 pandemic, 133, 264; critical significance of physician engagement and, 3; measurement of engagement and, 302; physician leader's role during, 162–63; telehealth and, 7, 261, 267, 308, 317; virtual visits and, 276; Zoom meetings during, 282

Creativity: physician leaders and, 99; stimulating, *140*, 140–41

Credentialing, 200; board actions related to physicians and, 178; for chief medical officers, 94–95; chief medical officers and, 92; Joint Commission standards and, 219; medical executive committee and, 104; in traditional medical staff model, 237

expectations for, 264–65; telehealth training and support for, 265–66. *See also* Advanced practice providers; Nurses; Physicians; Primary care physicians

Medical schools: "education by humiliation" in, 213; faculty, financial incentives, and, 162; perpetuating abuse phenomenon and, 214, 225; telehealth and, 266

Medical staff leaders: managing disruptive physician behavior and, 220

Medical staff model: traditional, engagement and, 237

Medical staff surveys: addressing fear of change in, 264

Medicare, 3; originating site geographic limitation, 262

Medication refills: virtual care and, 270, *270*

Medscape: National Physician Burnout & Suicide Report, 52, 53; physician burnout survey, 215

Medscape, 286

Meese, Katherine A., 8, 318

Memos: communication pros and cons of, *32*

Mentors and mentoring, 178; administrative members of dyads, 116; continued growth of leaders and, 142; the dyad in their relationship, 116; mutual respect and, 141; physicians selected for leadership roles in dyads, 116. *See also* Coaching

Meso (organization) level: engagement at, 238

Micro-level engagement activities, 169

Miller, D. W., 104

Miller, V. D., 71

Misaligned intentions: differing points of view about, 14

Mishra, P., 57

Mission: clear expectations and, 19; disengaged physicians and, 238; telehealth strategies aligned with, 274–76, 277. *See also* Vision

Mobile apps, 269

Mochon, D., 74

Monitoring and tracking system: for physician misbehaviors, 221

Montgomery, A., 48

Morale: disruptive physician behavior and, 217

Moral injury: burnout *vs.*, 61–63; definition of, 61–62

Morgan, J. W., 134

Motivation: intrinsic, for the work of leadership, 127–28; physicians considering a seat on hospital board and, *183*; relating burnout to, 52–53, *53*

Mount Carmel System, 171, *172*

Muhelstein, D., 176

Name calling, 212

Narcissistic disorders: disruptive physician behavior and, 214

National Health Service (United Kingdom), 239

National Physician Burnout & Suicide Report (Medscape), 52, 53

National Transportation Safety Board, 284

Negotiations: pricing, reducing number of products and, 153, *153*; reduction of supply-chain costs and, 147–48

NEJM Catalyst Insights Council, 26, 28

Nelson, Bob, 203

Networking: value of, 279

New England Journal of Medicine, 286

Newsletters, 280

"New Way to Engage Physicians" (Peden), 1

New York Times, 214

"No margin, no mission" mantra, 75

Nonpunitive awareness interventions: for apparent pattern of unprofessional behaviors, 223, *223*

Non-survey-based measurements, 306–7

Norton, M. I., 74

Noseworthy, John H., 47, 81, 83, 193, 239

Not-for-profit boards: time commitment issues and, 178

Not-for-profit hospitals, 167, 176; current state of physician representation on boards of, 171

169–70; poor engagement scores of, 236; recruiting and engaging for board participation, 180–82, 316; retired, holiday get-togethers for, 291; roadmap for those wanting to sit on hospital boards, 177–78; supply consumption for, *156,* 156–57; typical characteristics of, *15*; viewing as organizational partners and collaborators, 5; wanting to sit on hospital boards, road map for, 177. *See also* Assessing physicians for leadership; Disruptive physician behavior; Physician leadership development

Physician shortages: burnout and, 48

Physicians leadership training organizations, selected: American Academy of Family Physicians, 242; American Association for Physician Leadership, 241; American College of Healthcare Executives, 240; American College of Physicians, 241; American College of Surgeons, 242; Cleveland Clinic, 242, 243; Harvard Medical School, 241; Harvard T.H. Chan School of Public Health, 241; internal training programs, examples of, 243–44; Mayo Clinic, 242, 243–44

Physician well-being: electronic health records and, 81–83

Physician wellness programs, 54

Pink, Arthur, 314

Pink, D. H., 61; motivational factors applied to burnout causes, 52, *53*, 314

Pister, K., 224

Planners, *35*

Podcasts: communication pros and cons of, *33*

Poor performance: providing feedback about, 20

Population health, 7; management, 179; virtual care and, 265, 276

Portal visits, 268, *269*

Porto, G., 212

Positive working environments, 39, *40*

Post, Kevin, 7, 317

"Practical Points on Private Nursing" (Dewitt), 211

Prakash, S., 171

Predictive analytics, 298

Press Ganey, 16; on engagement efforts and change in culture, 236; white paper on engagement, 192

Price transparency, 167

PricewaterhouseCoopers: online physician survey, 179, 182, 237

Pricing negotiations: reducing number of products and, 153, *153*

Primary care physicians, 62, 182; electronic health records and, 70; hospitalist model and, 60

Primary care strategy: creating, 290

Prior experience: leadership roles and, 128

Privileging, 200; board actions related to physicians and, 178; in traditional medical staff model, 237

Problem-solver attitude: of physicians, *195,* 196, 207

Product assessments: engaging physicians on supply choice and, 151–53; golden rule of one-page summary for, 152

Productivity: chief medical officers and, 93; disruptive physician behavior and, 216, 217

Productivity incentives: as disincentivizing to physicians attending leadership programs, 254, 255; physician burnout rate and, 238

Profane language, 212

Professional codes of conduct, 19

Professional development, 39, *41,* 41–42, 44

Profitability: physician engagement and, 12

Progress: feedback about, 20

Project assignments: in leadership academies, 292

Promedica Toledo: board member composition at, *172*

Promoting professionalism pyramid, *223,* 223–24

Soft factors, 74, 314; adaptive change and, 71–73; success of initiatives and, 70
Sokolov, J. J., 5, 59, 104
Sonnenberg, Martha, 87, 88
Soobiah, C., 239
Special-cause variation, 200
Specialties: associated with physician burnout, 215
Specialty society reviews, 151
Specialty task forces: giving physicians a voice and, 221
Splitters, 88
Stakeholders: building trust with, 288; charting and ordering of tests and, 62; supply variance tool used with, *156*, 156–57
Standards of care: disruptive physician behavior and violations of, 218
Stanford Medicine: Value-Based Selection Committee, 157
Stanford method: technique and example, *22*
Stark laws, 119
Stark violations: avoiding, 161
STAR (situation/task, action, result) model: technique and example, *25–26*
Start with Why (Sinek), 67
Statistical process control charts, 199, 200
Statutory requirements: chief medical officers and, 94
Stereotypes: about physicians, 88
Stewardship: development of transparent virtual care strategies and, 275; leadership as, 283
Stoller, James K., 239, 243
Stories: business, types of, *36*; memorable, tips for creating, *36*; most effective, 36–37; team huddles and, 39
Stories That Stick (Hall), 36
Storytelling: power of, 35–37
Strategic plan: importance of both physician engagement plan and, 2
Straus, S. E., 239, 240
Stress management, 220

Substance abuse: disruptive physician behavior and, 214
Successes: celebrating, 202–3, 316
Succession planning, 141–42; lack of, in departments, 245; physician leadership development programs and, 99
Suicidal ideation: burnout and, 51
Sunday newspaper: full-page tributes placed in, 204–5
Supply-chain issues, 7, 145–64, 316; balancing quality, efficiency, access, and cost, 150–51; clinician training for best practices, 160; conducting comprehensive review, 151–53; engaging physicians in optimizing supply utilization, 149; financial incentives and, 161–62; group meetings and, 159–60; implant preference program, 145–47; improving, traditional efforts for, 147–49; physician coaching and, 157–59; physician leader's role and, 162–63; presenting physician-specific data to stakeholders, 157–59, *158*; reducing conflicts of interest around, 160–61; reducing number of products in support of better pricing negotiations, 153, *153*; reducing supply-chain costs, 147–48; role in physician engagement in optimizing product choice to drive quality and cost benefit, 163–64, *164*; supply consumption for health system physicians, *156*, 156–57; transparency of data and, 153–57
Supply-chain leaders, 150
Surgical implants: supply-chain issues and, 148
Survey fatigue: avoiding, 310
Surveys, 237, 306; annual, 303; board, 171, 173; change management, 70; disruptive physician behavior, 212; electronic health record use, 79; employee engagement, 310; engagement, 16–17; engagement, open-ended questions for, 310,

310; engagement ideas from the front lines, 279, 300; giving physicians a voice in, 221; medical staff, 264; physician, 179, 182, 237; physician burnout, 215; physician engagement, 4; physician leader, 235; pulse, 304

Swensen, Steven, 2, 191

Talent Management Leader Advancement and Leader Development Academy: benefits and positive feedback, 252; curriculum development for, 247; details of program participants, *252*; faculty member "graduates" of, 251; number of participants in program, by department, *249*; participant selection, 249–50; participants' evaluation of the training, 250–51; program course format, 249; success of program, 250; topics and dates of sessions for, *248*; transition to the Faculty Leadership Institute, 251

Teaching hospitals: telehealth and, 266

Team charters, 19

Team huddles: effective, 39; leadership rounds and, 29

"Teamlet" huddles, 39

Teams, 314; administrative, 55; dyad, 28, 44; high-performing, trust and, 17; leadership, 26, 27–29; triad, 28, 44

Technical problems: adaptive challenges *vs.*, 71, *72*

Technology-enabled care: user-friendly and affordable nature of, 269. *See also* Electronic health records

Telehealth, 7, 261–77; aligning strategies of, with mission and values of an engaged health system, 274–76; barriers to physician acceptance of, *273*, 273–74; care platforms and portfolios, 268–69, *269*; common uses of virtual care, 269–71, *270*; consumers, patient–provider relationship and impact of, 267–68; COVID-19 pandemic and, 7,

261, 308, 317; fear of change and, 264; future of, need for physician engagement in, 262–63; medical provider mindset and, 263; medical providers and expectations for, 264–65; ongoing significant impact of, 277; personal impact of, on medical providers, 266; physician champions and, 264; physician engagement critical to, 261; physician engagement strategies for, 271–73; training and support for medical providers, 265–66. *See also* Virtual care

Telemedicine, 7, 268, *269*; courses in medical schools, 266; COVID-19 pandemic and use of, 308

"Telepresence": considerations for, 272

Termination of privileges: disruptive physician behaviors and, 224

Tests: stakeholders and charting and ordering of, 62

Texting: communication pros and cons of, *32*

Thank-you: notes, 60, 291; recognizing individuals with, 206–7, 290

Them-versus-us attitude: minimizing or eliminating, 5

Thinkers, *35*

Thomas, R. J., 96

Three Cs of leadership, 128–34, 142; capacity, 128, 132–34, *133*, 142; character, 128, 129, *130*, 142; chemistry, 128, 129, 131, *131–32*, 142

Three Es. *See* Physician executive skills

Throwing equipment, 212

Thury, Chad, 276

Time: physicians considering a seat on hospital board and, *183*

Titles for physician executives: distinction between, 91–92

To Err Is Human (Institute of Medicine), 3

Tomlinson, I., 311

Town halls: giving physicians a voice and, 221

Traditional management structures: operational nature of, 112

Training: administrative members of dyads, 116; diversity, 173; the dyad in their relationship, 116; in effective communication, 31; in electronic health record systems, 80, 82, 296; experience and, 96; leadership, 127; medical, causes of physician disruptive behavior and, 213–14, 225; physicians in optimizing supply utilization, 149; physicians selected for leadership roles in dyads, 116; telehealth, 264, 265–66; in virtual care techniques, 272–73. *See also* Physicians leadership training organizations, selected

Trandel, E., 114

Transparency, 281; clinical dashboards and, 201; in culture of accountability, 18; data, supply-chain issues and, 153–57; data, telehealth and, 272; in decision-making, 289–90; in gainsharing distribution, 146; group meetings on supply-chain issues and, 159; physician board members and, 181; price, 167; supply utilization and, 149; telehealth and, 267; virtual environment and, 262. *See also* Accountability; Trust

Triad leadership model, 28, 44, 108. *See also* Management triads

Triads, 315

Triple aim: physician leaders' roles and, 93

Trust, 236, 295; absence of, in hospital relationships, 179, 237; building, 287–88; character and, 129; culture of, telehealth and, 262; defining, difficulty in, 287; in dyad relationships, 108, 109, 110; effective communication and, 280; high-performing teams and, 17; management dyads and, 113, 114, 122; physician engagement surveys and, 17; physician-led dashboard design and, 198; relationship building and, 26. *See also* Accountability; Integrity; Transparency

Trustees. *See* Boards of trustees

Tu, T., 176

Turnover, 56; disruptive physician behavior and, 213. *See also* Retention

Twitter, *33*

Underserved populations: virtual care and, 275

United States: hospital board demographics in, *173*; number of hospitals in, 167

University Hospitals Cleveland Medical Center: board member composition at, *172*

University of Cincinnati: board member composition at, *172*

University of Kentucky: internal physician leadership development programs, 244

Urgent care, minor: virtual care and, 270, *270*

US Department of Health and Human Services (HHS): database on not-for-profit hospitals in California, 170

US Department of Veterans Affairs: annual employee survey instrument, 310; disruptive behavior study, 213

US Navy, 37

Value-based care, 93, 107, 148, 179, 301

Value-based incentives, 299

Values: physicians considering a seat on hospital board and, *183*; telehealth strategies aligned with, 274–76, 277

Value story, *36*

Vanderbilt University School of Medicine: interventions for unprofessional events, *223*, 223–24, 317

Vendors, 309; consolidating, leveraging pricing negotiations and, 152–53, *153*; electronic health record, 77, 78, 82, 296; optimizing supply utilization and, 149; unknown, COVID-19 crisis and, 163

Ventilators: supply-chain issues and, 148

Vertical integration: with health insurers and providers, 268

Vice president of medical affairs, 91, 92

About the Editor

Carson F. Dye, FACHE, president and CEO of Exceptional Leadership LLC, is a seasoned consultant with more than 40 years of leadership and management experience. Over the past 20 years, he has conducted hundreds of leadership searches for healthcare organizations, helping to fill CEO, chief operating officer, chief financial officer, and physician executive roles in health systems, academic medical centers, universities, and freestanding hospitals.

Mr. Dye has provided clients with extensive counsel in succession planning, leadership assessment, CEO evaluation, coaching, and retreat facilitation. He is certified to use the Hogan Leadership Assessment tests for evaluation, coaching, and leadership development. He also has extensive experience working with physician leaders and has helped organizations establish physician leadership development programs.

Mr. Dye has served as an executive search consultant and partner with Witt/Kieffer, TMP Worldwide, and LAI/Lamalie Associates. Prior to these roles, he was partner and director of Findley Davies's healthcare consulting division in Toledo, Ohio. He has 20 years of experience in healthcare administration, serving in executive-level positions at St. Vincent Mercy Medical Center in Toledo, the Ohio

State University Wexner Medical Center in Columbus, Clermont Mercy Hospital in Cincinnati, and Cincinnati Children's Hospital Medical Center.

A regular faculty member for the American College of Healthcare Executives (ACHE) since 1987, Mr. Dye has presented workshops for 40 state and local hospital associations. He also teaches in the ACHE Board of Governors Examination preparation course. In addition, Mr. Dye is a faculty member of the Governance Institute and has held faculty appointments at the University of Alabama at Birmingham in its executive MHA program and at The Ohio State University in its Health Services Management program.

Mr. Dye has written ten previous books, all with Health Administration Press, including three James A. Hamilton Book of the Year Award winners: *The Healthcare Leader's Guide to Actions, Awareness, and Perception*; *Developing Physician Leaders for Successful Clinical Integration*; and *Leadership in Healthcare: Values at the Top*. Other notable titles include *Exceptional Leadership: 16 Critical Competencies for Healthcare Executives* and *Winning the Talent War: Ensuring Effective Leadership in Healthcare*. The Dye–Garman Leadership Competency Model, found in *Exceptional Leadership*, has been used by many healthcare organizations as a competency model for assessment, executive selection, development, and succession planning. Mr. Dye received his BA from Marietta College and his MBA from Xavier University.

About the Contributors

John Byrnes, MD, currently serves as senior vice president and system chief medical officer for Adventist Health, a multistate health system with 21 hospitals. Dr. Byrnes is nationally recognized for his expertise in quality and patient safety. He has contributed to ten books on quality and outcomes reporting. He has written two books, *The Quality Playbook* (Second River Healthcare, 2015) and *The Safety Playbook* (Health Administration Press, 2018). He is a frequent keynote speaker at healthcare events around the country.

Kevin M. Casey, DO, MBA, FACEP, FAAEM, CPE, is chief clinical officer at Mercy Health–Toledo. Dr. Casey has served as a chief medical officer, vice president of medical affairs, emergency department director, and emergency medicine residency director. Dr. Casey completed his medical degree at Ohio University College of Osteopathic Medicine and completed his internship and residency at what is now Mercy Health–St. Vincent Medical Center in Toledo. He holds an MBA from the University of Tennessee at Knoxville and has served in healthcare leadership positions since 2006.

Mary Dillhoff, MD, MS, FACS, is a board-certified surgical oncologist with The Ohio State University Wexner Medical Center at OSUCCC–James Cancer Hospital. Dr. Dillhoff completed general surgery residency at Ohio State University and did two years of research while earning a master's degree in medical science from Ohio State. After completing her residency, she completed a fellowship at Memorial Sloan Kettering in New York City. She has authored and coauthored more than 140 peer-reviewed publications and ten book chapters. Her clinical interest is treating hepatobiliary and upper gastrointestinal cancers.

Daniel Eiferman, MD, MBA, FACS, is an associate professor of surgery and director of special operations for the quality department and director of nutrition services at The Ohio State University Wexner Medical Center. A graduate of Northwestern University, he went on to study medicine at the University of Kentucky, completed his surgical residency at Rush University/Cook County Hospital, surgical critical care fellowship at Ohio State University, and MBA at the Fisher College of Business. Dr. Eiferman has developed a leadership elective for surgery residents that focuses on performance improvement, team building, and physician resilience.

Lily Jung Henson, MD, MMM, FAAN, FACHE, is the CEO of Piedmont Henry Hospital in Stockbridge, Georgia, where she previously served as the chief medical officer. Dr. Henson is a former Thomas C. Dolan Executive Diversity Program scholar of the American College of Healthcare Executives (ACHE) and formerly served as a Regent at Large in ACHE's District 2. She practiced neurology for 25 years in Seattle, focusing on multiple sclerosis.

Dr. Henson received her medical degree from Northwestern University Medical School and her master's degree in medical management from Tulane University School of Public Health and Tropical Medicine.

Walter C. Kerschl, MD, CMD, FACP, MMM, is currently the chief medical officer of West Virginia University Medicine at Camden Clark Medical Center in Parkersburg. For six years prior to his current position, Dr. Kerschl worked as a chief medical officer for the Cerner Corporation, helping to improve EHR adoption and satisfaction levels by leveraging his leadership experience and expertise in informatics. Dr. Kerschl practiced internal medicine in Virginia for more than 25 years across multiple venues, including outpatient, inpatient, home care, and long-term care. During those years, he held multiple leadership positions; owned his own practice; focused his efforts on quality of care, innovation, and informatics; and has given back to his community through his not-for-profit foundation, providing medical care in Haiti. Dr. Kerschl started his education at the University of Rochester after winning a Bausch and Lomb Science Medal, continued at Geisel School of Medicine at Dartmouth College for his medical degree, completed an internal medicine residency at the University of Virginia, and expanded his leadership knowledge with a master's degree in medical management at Carnegie Mellon University.

Terry R. McWilliams, MD, MSJ, FAAFP, has been director and chief clinical consultant with HSG Advisors in Louisville, Kentucky, since 2013. Dr. McWilliams focuses primarily on physician leadership and governance, shared vision development, compensation planning, and clinical transformation. On retirement from the US Navy, after more than 20 years as a family physician and clinical administrator in a variety of roles and practice environments, Dr. McWilliams served for a decade as the vice president of medical affairs and chief medical officer at Newport Hospital, an acute-care community hospital in an academic health system. Dr. McWilliams received his medical degree from the University of Pittsburgh School of Medicine and a master of science in jurisprudence degree in hospital and health law from Seton Hall University School of Law.

Katherine A. Meese, PhD, is an assistant professor in the Department of Health Services Administration at the University of Alabama at Birmingham (UAB) and serves as the director of wellness research at UAB Medicine. Dr. Meese has more than six years of industry experience, which encompasses work in ten countries, on four continents, and includes management for a large academic medical center. Her work has been published in *Anesthesia & Analgesia*, *Health Services Management Research*, *Journal of Health Administration Education*, and other journals. Dr. Meese's research interests include physician and healthcare providers' well-being and burnout, team performance, quality and safety, and delivery models that enhance organizational learning.

Kevin Post, DO, is chief medical officer with Avera Medical Group in Sioux Falls, South Dakota. He is a board-certified family medicine physician with 15 years of clinical experience. Dr. Post has served in family medicine, in emergency medicine, and as a physician adviser before starting his current role in the Avera Health system. Dr. Post began his medical career as a primary care physician providing care in clinic, long-term care, and inpatient settings, including emergency and obstetrical care. After 12 years at Hegg Health Center Avera in Rock Valley, Iowa, he transitioned to work in emergency medicine for Avera Sacred Heart in Yankton, South Dakota, and for a hospital in Sioux City, Iowa.

Scott B. Ransom, DO, MBA, MPH, FACHE, is a partner in the health and life sciences advisory at Oliver Wyman. He serves as a consultant to hospitals, health systems, academic medical centers, physician groups, insurance companies, private equity firms, and universities on issues related to strategy-enabled transformation, organizational redesign, restructuring and turnaround management, medical education, physician and faculty integration and engagement, clinical and research operations, and mergers and acquisitions. Dr. Ransom is a Distinguished Fellow and a past president of the American College of Physician Executives. He is a Fellow in several other professional organizations, including the American College of Obstetrics and Gynecology, American College of Surgeons, and American College of Healthcare Executives.

Bhagwan Satiani, MD, MBA, FACHE(R), is professor of clinical surgery in the Department of Surgery at The Ohio State University. He is the former director of the Faculty Leadership Institute. The author of six books, 190 peer-reviewed papers, and 13 book chapters, Dr. Satiani focuses on physician leadership, surgeon workforce and attrition, vascular ultrasound, and the business aspects of healthcare.

Margot Savoy, MD, MPH, FAAFP, FABC, CPE, CMQ, FAAPL, is chair and associate professor in the Department of Family and Community Medicine at the Lewis Katz School of Medicine at Temple University and Temple University Hospital and chief quality officer for the Temple Faculty Practice Plan. She graduated from the University of Maryland School of Medicine in 2002; completed the Crozer-Keystone Family Medicine Residency Program in Springfield, Pennsylvania, in 2005; and graduated from the University of North Carolina at Chapel Hill Gillings School of Global Public Health in 2008 with an MPH in public health leadership with a focus on public health practice. She is certified by the American Board of Family Medicine and the Certifying Commission in Medical Management and is a Fellow of the Advisory Board Company.